FEDOR PETROVICH LITKE

The Rasmuson Library
Historical Translation Series
Volume X
Marvin W. Falk, Editor

FEDOR PETROVICH LITKE

A. I. ALEKSEEV

edited by Katherine L. Arndt
translated by Serge LeComte

University of Alaska Press
Fairbanks

Library of Congress Cataloging-in-Publication Data

Alekseev, A. I. (Aleksandr Ivanovich)
 [Fedor Petrovich Litke. English]
 Fedor Petrovich Litke / A.I. Alekseev ; edited by Kathy Arndt ;
translated by Serge LeComte.
     p. cm. -- (Rasmuson Library historical translation series ;
v. 10)
 Includes bibliographical references and index.
 ISBN 0-912006-86-2 (pbk. : alk. paper)
 1. Litke, F. P. (Fedor Petrovich), graf. 1797-1882. 2. Explorers-
-Russia--Biography. I. Title. II. Series.
G296.L53A7513 1996
947'.07'092--dc20   96-21674
 [B]   CIP

Originally published in Russian in 1970 (Moscow: Nauka).

International Standard Series Number: 0890-7935
International Standard Book Number: 0-912006-86-2
Library of Congress Catalog Card Number: 96-21674
English Translation © 1996 by The University of Alaska Press.
All rights reserved. Published 1996.
Printed in the United States of America
by BookCrafters, Inc.
on recycled and acid-free paper.

This publication was printed on acid-free paper that meets the minimum
requirements of American National Standard for Information Sciences-
Permanence for Paper for Printed Library Materials, ANSI Z39.48-1984.

Publication coordination and production by Deborah Van Stone
with assistance from Kate Sander.

Cover: Portrait of F. P. Litke, made in Arkhangel'sk on 4 December 1823.

CONTENTS

LIST OF ILLUSTRATIONS

IN LIEU OF A PREFACE

In the first quarter of the nineteenth century Russia made considerable progress in the naval sciences, including the expansive development of hydrography of the seas. This era is characterized by the voyages of Russian mariners to all corners of the earth, including round-the-world trips. Each naval officer dreamed of going "into the blue yonder," that is, of going on a voyage around the world, or at least of visiting Russian America.

After I. F. Kruzenshtern and Iu. F. Lisianskii, the first circumnavigators, completed their voyages on the *Neva* and *Nadezhda* in 1803–1806, a great number of Russian mariners followed their lead by bringing glory to the Russian Navy, surprising the world with their geographical discoveries, and enriching science with their research on the high seas. These men sailed completely around the world, or at least went halfway around it: L. A. Hagemeister, V. M. Golovnin, M. P. Lazarev, O. E. Kotzebue, Z. I. Panafidin, F. F. Bellinsgauzen, M. N. Vasil'ev, G. S. Shishmarev, P. A. Dokhturov, I. M. Kislakovskii, E. A. Klochkov, I. S. Tulub'ev, S. P. Khrushchov, A. P. Lazarev, P. E. Chistiakov, M. I. Murav'ev, and F. P. Wrangell. Some of them made the trip two or three times. Take, for example, M. P. Lazarev, one of the first to discover Antarctica, who commanded the *Suvorov* in 1813–1816, the sloop *Mirnyi* in 1819–1821, and the *Kreiser* in 1822–1825. Or take the remarkable Russian navigator L. A. Hagemeister, who took the *Neva* out again immediately following the return of Kruzenshtern and Lisianskii and sailed it to Novo-Arkhangel'sk [Sitka]. There he managed the affairs of the Russian-American Company for several years.[a] After that, he sailed on the *Kutuzov* in 1816–1819 and on the *Krotkii* in 1828–1830, thus going twice around the world.

These Russian navigations around and halfway around the world made considerable corrections on the map of the world's oceans. Especially valuable were the geographical discoveries made by F. F. Bellinsgauzen and M. P. Lazarev in the Antarctic Ocean, particularly their discovery of our sixth continent, Antarctica, and the discoveries made by many other navigators in the basin of the Pacific Ocean. The activities of O. E. Kotzebue, who sailed around the world on the *Riurik* in 1815–1818 and the *Predpriiatie* in 1823–1826, were imbued with an entirely new quality. On the initiative of this remarkable commander and the outstanding academician E. Kh. Lents, the first oceanographic experiments were made—measurement of ocean depths, sampling of the ocean floor, measurement of deep-sea water temperature, observations of water transparency and currents, and also research on the atmosphere. Without a doubt, O. E. Kotzebue's expeditions laid the foundation for precise, systematic meteorological and oceanographic observations.

The activities of Russia's naval officers on their voyages to Far Eastern seas and to the shores of Russian America were extremely useful. It was during these expeditions that the Aleutians, the Kurils, and Sakhalin Island and the shores of Kamchatka, Alaska, etc., were fundamentally described and put on the map, and also investigated with respect to physical geography.

The development of Russian circumnavigation furthered the comprehensive study of the Baltic, Okhotsk, and Bering seas and part of the Sea of Japan. This does not mean, however, that the seas mentioned above were being studied only during ocean voyages. During the first quarter of the nineteenth century, rather important and specialized hydrographic work was already taking place on all of Russia's seas, perhaps with the exception of the seas of the Northern Sea Route.

For example, *An Atlas of the Baltic Sea and the Gulf of Finland and the Kattegat,* compiled by G. A. Sarychev, was published in 1809. *An Atlas of the Gulf of Finland,* compiled by L. V. Spafar'ev, appeared in 1814. In 1828 the continuous hydrographic expedition called the Baltic Sea Survey was created. It was headed by the famous geodesist F. F. Shubert.

Extensive hydrographic work was also taking place in the White and Barents seas. A chart of the White Sea was made in 1806 under the leadership of L. I. Golenishchev-Kutuzov. It was here in the early 1820s that the activities of F. P. Litke began. He was leader of the first hydrographic expedition to the northern seas.

An atlas of the Caspian Sea, prepared by A. E. Kolodkin, appeared in 1826, and an atlas of the Black Sea compiled by I. M. Budishchev came out in 1807. It was in 1825 that E. P. Manganari, one of the most experienced Russian hydrographers, began his outstanding research on the Black Sea.

Until 1805 all questions on hydrography and other scientific oceano-graphic research were governed by the "Committee for the Dissemination of Nautical Knowledge and the Improvement of Nautical Arts" which had been created by the Admiralty College on 25 November 1799. In April of 1805 a Ministry of the Navy, consisting of the Admiralty College and Admiralty Department, was established. The former governed military questions and the latter dealt with scientific problems. On 24 August 1827, the Admiralty Department was reorga-nized into two independent sections under the Main Naval Headquar-ters: the Office of the Hydrographer General, directed by Gavriil Andreevich Sarychev,[1] the outstanding scientist and founder of Russian hydrography, and the Naval Scientific Committee.

The first specialized handbooks on hydrographic work and hand-books summarizing scientific works on marine hydrography to appear in Russia were due exclusively to the fruitful activities of G. A. Sarychev. It is true that other such works appeared in Russia before Sarychev (see the works of F. I. Soimonov and S. I. Mordvinov), but they were based on foreign sources. Their writings were based on the hydrographic methods of foreign navies. Sarychev succeeded in creat-ing an original work called *Laws Governing Ocean Geodesy*, published in 1804 and reprinted in 1825 under the title *Geodesic and Hydro-graphic Laws*. This second edition can be considered a new work because it summed up the methods for hydrographic research in Russia and introduced new means of researching and compiling oceanographic data.

It is with Sarychev's name that F. P. Litke's voyages are linked. His ocean travels took place during the best period of his life and were filled with tireless scientific activity. In the history of Russian geographical science and in the history of Russian marine hydrography, Litke achieved a prominent place. His name will live on eternally among geographers and navigators.

How did Litke earn such high honors? Well, that is what this book is about—the personality of a remarkable Russian scientist, navigator, and organizer of science in Russia, and his contribution to Russian and world science.

Fedor Petrovich Litke

Even during his lifetime, Litke's personality drew the attention of the scientific community, scientists, geographers, seamen, and historiographers. Several works on his life and activities were published after his death. A few popular books were also published. The birthday of this illustrious scholar, outstanding traveler, organizer of science, and prominent statesman is still celebrated.

Despite the vicissitudes of fate, Litke's long and fruitful life is connected by a single thread and not once was it interrupted. This connecting thread is characterized by his love and dedication to science. His life can be divided into two unequal periods. The first embraces Litke's travels on the sloop *Kamchatka*, the brig *Novaia Zemlia,* and finally on the sloop *Seniavin.* These were the years when the inquisitive mind of young Litke greedily drank in everything he saw and heard, when the young, but already well-known traveler expounded on and gave meaning to all that he observed. This was the time when Fedor Petrovich Litke became a scientist recognized in Russia, as well as abroad. The second and major period of his life was when he was taken away from his immediate scientific occupations. At this time Litke was given charge of educating the tsar's son so that he might one day become head of the Russian Navy in fact, and not just in title.

Even though court life weighed heavily upon Litke, it was not without its advantages. Having been admitted into the royal family and possessing all the necessary qualities of an intelligent and farsighted courtier, he could use his position to request favors much more easily than others. It was from this privileged position that he gradually gained influence with Grand Duke Constantine, who called Litke his third father (God the Father, Sovereign Father, and Father-educator Litke). This association between C. N. Romanov and Litke lasted all their lives.

One must also mention the great service Litke performed in taking charge at the proper time of organizing the Russian Geographical Society, which was so long in preparation. When one looks at archival materials and especially at the private correspondence of Litke dealing with court life, one is surprised how a man who literally did not move a step away from his pupil (it was only a few years later that Litke was allowed to leave the grand duke's side during the night) could correspond widely with many scholars, find time to meet with them, and organize the most important scientific organization of that time—the Russian Geographical Society.

xiii

As soon as Litke found himself free from his court duties, he immediately gave himself to science and became the most active figure of the Geographical Society. He established contacts with scientific and geographical organizations of other countries and drew closer to the Academy of Sciences. Through all these associations with science, it was only right and logical that he should be named president of the Academy of Sciences.

Litke remained at this post until the end of his life. He never made rash decisions, but at the same time he was not afraid to defend his own opinions and those of the Academy of Sciences. During the 1860s and 1870s, when Litke headed the Academy of Sciences and the Geographical Society, many remarkable geographic expeditions were organized. Perhaps the most outstanding were the hydrographic expedition of the Caspian Sea under the leadership of N. A. Ivashintsov and P. P. Semenov's travels in Tien Shan.

Litke accomplished much during his long life. His works and rough drafts, his diaries, his scientific notes, his social and governmental correspondence, his personal letters (especially those addressed to Wrangell), all are of great interest to science. Many researchers have studied these archives, but there is so much information that up to now it has not yet been fully assessed. Most of the work on Litke had been based on his published works and his autobiography (published by V. P. Bezobrazov). Bezobrazov, Litke's first and only biographer, managed to come out with only the first volume.[2] In it one can find a brief, general sketch of his life and activities, a summary of the book's contents and the meaning of Litke's biography, and an account of Litke's archives. In his book Bezobrazov underscores what he thinks are Litke's characteristic features as a navigator. Undoubtedly Litke's autobiography is the most important part of the book. The publisher included speeches by O. V. Struve and F. F. Veselago which deal with Litke's scientific merits, along with some secondary documents.

Despite the clearly expressed loyal nature of Bezobrazov's article, in which Litke's luck and prosperity are explained by the tsar's support, it has many merits. In the first place, it is a factual account based on archival sources (unfortunately without footnotes). It is a truthful and argumentative characterization of Litke as a man and scholar, and finally it contains detailed observations of important moments in Litke's life and activities which Litke did not bother to describe in his autobiography. Throughout his book, Bezobrazov talks about Litke's honesty and modesty whenever he has the opportunity. Undoubtedly, Litke possessed these remarkable qualities in full measure. However, one must remember that he was a man of his time—an experienced courtier, not devoid of self-interest and careerism, though he regretted that his best productive years passed not as he had wanted (in the pursuit of science), but at the royal court.

The first volume on Litke, written by Bezobrazov, cannot, under any circumstances, purport to show all details dealing with the circumstances and activities of Litke's life. It does not give a scientific analysis of Litke's voyages or his contributions to hydrography, geography, and the organization of science in his country. It is only material toward a biography of an outstanding Russian navigator and organizer of science. It cannot be anything else, since Bezobrazov published his book only six years after Litke's death, when there was insufficient material gathered. And it was not yet time for a comprehensive and objective evaluation of Litke's life and scholarly activities.

In the years that followed, no fundamental research on Litke was done in Russia, even though his name had entered the annals of geographic literature, dictionaries, guide books, encyclopedias and calendars. After O. V. Struve's and F. F. Wrangell's accounts of Litke's merits, which appeared immediately after his death, P. P. Semenov-Tian-Shanskii, whom Litke had recommended as his successor to the post of vice chairman of the Geographical Society, began to review Litke's life and activities and assess his work during his long years of participation in the society.[3]

Interest in the life and activities of this navigator has noticeably increased in our Soviet era. Many articles have come out in periodicals. Several books and brochures and even a story about Litke have been written.[4]

The literature on Litke can be divided into two genres: one that is based on archives and one that deals with the life and activities of Litke, or only his voyages, based on Litke's writings and documents gathered in the sole volume of the biography by Bezobrazov. Undoubtedly, enlistment of new archival materials is of utmost value when working on Litke's biography.

Of much interest is the monograph of Litke's great-grandson, N. F. Litke (a manuscript of a dissertation, containing valuable material which shows Litke's role in the development of Russian geographical science). Unfortunately, this work has yet to be published. Most researchers can only assess it from a synopsis of the dissertation. L. S. Berg has brought to light previously unknown facts about Litke's voyage in 1846 in the Mediterranean Sea. B. N. Komissarov brought out several curious episodes dealing with young Litke while he served on the sloop *Kamchatka*, under the command of V. M. Golovnin. These facts were based on one of Litke's unpublished diaries.

We will have occasion to refer to all these works repeatedly below. It must be said, however, that none of them can claim to be a scientific biography of F. P. Litke. Such a deduction can be made because, except for N. F. Litke, none of the authors referred to the large archival legacy left by the navigator or made use of the diverse materials on his life and activities that have been scattered to various Russian archives.

We have attempted to research all archival documents concerning this question that are preserved in the Central State Archive of Ancient Documents (TsGADA); the Central State Archive of the Navy (TsGAVMF); the Central State Military History Archive (TsGVIA); the Central State Archive of the October Revolution (TsGAOR); the Central State Historical Archive (TsGIA and TsGIAL); Archive of the Academy of Sciences SSSR (AAN); Archive of the All-Union Geographical Society (AVGO); the Central State Archive of Literature and Art (TsGALI); the Manuscript Division of the M. E. Saltykov-Shchedrin Public Library; the Manuscript Division of the Institute of Russian Literature (Pushkin House) AN SSSR; and in the State Historical Archive of the Estonian SSR (GIAE). It is quite possible that even with all these sources, Litke's archival legacy has yet to be exhausted. But as we see it, we were successful in collecting all primary, and in many cases secondary, information on this legacy. We also used some materials, primarily illustrations, which Litke's descendants kept and which were presented to us by his great-great-grandson F. N. Litke and N. V. Dmitrieva.

We offer our sincere gratitude to all associated with the above-mentioned archives and to the navigator's great-great-grandson, Fedor Nikolaevich Litke, and also to N. V. Dmitrieva for all her help, to Dr. L. A. Demin, Engineer Rear Admiral, and to E. V. Iastrebov, doctoral candidate of geography, for proofing this manuscript and for their invaluable suggestions.

CITATIONS AND NOTES

1. A. I. Alekseev, *G. A. Sarychev* (Moscow: Nauka, 1966).

2. V. P. Bezobrazov, *Graf Fedor Petrovich Litke*, vol. 1, 1797 to 1832. Supplement to *Zapiski imp. Akademii Nauk*, vol. 57, no. 2 (St. Petersburg, 1888). (Hereafter V. P. Bezobrazov, *Litke. Autobiography ...*)

3. P. P. Semenov-Tian-Shanskii, *Istoriia poluvekovoi deiatel'nosti Russkogo geograficheskogo obshchestva (1845–1895)* [History of a half century of activity by the Russian Geographical Society (1845–1895)], vols. 1–3, (St. Petersburg, 1896).

4. See the lists of works on and by Litke at the end of this volume.

* * *

a. In the period 1806–1810 Hagemeister was merely in the Russian-American Company's employ as commander of the *Neva*. It was during his subsequent voyage as commander of the *Kutuzov* that he briefly managed the company's colonial affairs, January through October 1818 (Richard A. Pierce, *Builders of Alaska: The Russian Governors, 1818–1867* [Kingston, Ontario: Limestone Press, 1986], pp. 3–4).—Ed.

THE SEA CALLS

Fedor Petrovich Litke's father came from a family of Russianized Germans. Litke, who carefully researched his genealogy, left us detailed information on this in his autobiography. Litke's great-grandson, Nikolai Fedorovich Litke, compiled the Litke family tree using this autobiography.[1]

The first information about Litke's grandfather, Johann-Filipp Lütke [I. F. Litke],[2] goes back to 1735 when, as Master of Theology, he concluded a contract with Gentleman [*Kamerger*] Korf, head of the Academy, for the position of co-rector at the Academy secondary school [*gimnaziia*] for a duration of three years with an annual salary of 350 rubles. "Master Litke," according to his grandson, "was a man of many talents, a writer on physical sciences and a theologian."[3] Several of his works and translations dating between 1755 and 1757 are well known. He knew French quite well and had a good command of Russian. He did not remain a co-rector for long, because as early as 1736 he occupied the position of rector at a church school, but he did not remain long there either because of his quarrelsome and restless character. On 26 January 1737 he received his pension and a year later went to Sweden, and from there to Poland. The date of his return to Russia has not been established. The only date known for sure is that in 1745 I. F. Litke was the pastor of a small Lutheran parish in Moscow. It is also known that in Moscow he ran a boarding school which the future Prince Potemkin-Tavricheskii often attended in his youth. When an epidemic of plague broke out in Moscow, the Litke family moved to Kaluga, where I. F. Litke died in 1771.

After his death, his wife (about whom nothing is documented) moved to St. Petersburg with her daughter Elizaveta and younger sons Karl and Aleksandr. There they lived with the court silver- and goldsmith Konstantin Kuz'mich Kulichkin, whose daughter Anna subsequently became Aleksandr Ivanovich Litke's wife. The mother died soon after. Besides the three children already mentioned, I. F. Litke had two older

1

sons: Ivan, who came to a very bad end (he got drunk one night, disappeared, and was never heard from again) and Petr-Avgust, who was born in March of 1750.

The younger sons, F. P. Litke's uncles, were educated in the Naval Corps and on 4 May 1782, both were promoted from naval cadet [*gardemarin*] to midshipman [*michman*].[a] They were in school with future hydrographer L. V. Spafar'ev; future hero of the Battle of Athos, T. M. Bychenskii; future Minister of the Navy A. V. Moller, and others. In 1785 Aleksandr retired from the navy due to illness and went to work at the customs house. Toward the end of his life he held the post of Inspector of the Radzivillov Customs District. Karl Ivanovich Litke served in the navy until he died. In 1787, he especially accompanied Catherine II and Potemkin during their trip along the Dnepr on their way to Ekaterinoslav, while commander of the vessel *Orel*. In 1789, Captain Lieutenant Karl Litke became the commander of a rowing flotilla on the Black Sea. In 1790 he was honored by Admiral I. M. de Ribas for his military actions on the Danube. All those who served with him had nothing but praise for him. Even Potemkin was pleased with him. Karl Litke died at the Battle of Izmail, holding the rank of captain second rank. In his autobiography, F. P. Litke wrote that his father loved his own brother and because of his memory of him, he wanted to make a sailor out of Fedor. Fate favored that wish.

Litke's father, Petr Ivanovich Litke, probably studied at the university secondary school. However, there is no doubt that it was under his learned father's tutelage that the son developed a passion for the sciences, specifically chemistry. Nevertheless, Petr left home early and in 1768 (at the age of sixteen) joined the Narvskii Carabineer Regiment at the rank of sergeant. From 1775 to 1776 Petr Litke served as adjutant to Prince N. V. Repnin and was a member of his entourage on his trip to Constantinople. From 1781 to 1782 he managed Prince Repnin's Vetluga estate. In July 1784 he retired and rented out Prince Repnin's estate in Voronezh, called Rep'evka. That same year he moved in and on 15 December he married Anna Ivanovna, the daughter of a Moscow doctor named Engel. His sister Elizaveta, who in 1787 married Repnin's secretary, Petr Pankrat'evich Pankrat'ev, also moved to the estate.

The older children of Petr and Anna Litke were born at Rep'evka: Evgenii in 1785, Natal'ia in 1789, and Anna in 1793. The children, especially Evgenii, were taught by a tutor hired from St. Petersburg, K.

Ia. Reshet. During this time the Litke family became acquainted with the priest E. A. Bolkhovitinov, the future Metropolitan Evgenii, whom Fedor Petrovich Litke later visited often.

The Litke family lived at Rep'evka until 1794, when P. I. Litke was promoted to the rank of major first class and became a member of the Lithuanian government, stationed in the town of Grodno. This came about thanks to the help of old comrades-in-arms who were now government officials, State Secretary D. P. Troshchinskii and Senator P. I. Alekseev. But in June 1795 he was given a new position—that of Councilor of Customs in St. Petersburg.

Petr Litke moved his family to St. Petersburg. That year his daughter Elizaveta was born. Life was then going smoothly, as was his service. Litke received awards and promotions. In 1796 he was promoted to collegiate councilor. In February 1797 he became a member of the College of Commerce and inspector of the St. Petersburg and Kronstadt customs houses. Still preserved is the original patent, signed by Paul I on 12 April 1797, awarding Collegiate Councilor Litke the Order of St. Anna Second Class for zealous service and his "effort to increase customs revenues."

The happiness and well-being of Petr Litke's family ended with the birth of Fedor, or, as he was registered, Friedrich-Benjamin, and the death of Petr's wife Anna Ivanovna. She died two hours after giving birth on 17/28 September 1797.[b] Petr was deeply depressed and even contemplated suicide, but common sense prevailed. He wrote a letter to his wife's mother, Elizaveta Kasperovna Engel, who was then living in Kiev with her second daughter, Elizaveta Ivanovna (married name Furman).[4] He asked his mother-in-law to move to St. Petersburg. At that time Fedor Ivanovich Engel visited Kiev and secured his mother's consent to go to Petr Litke "if it will please you and if you find it necessary." The grandmother soon arrived in St. Petersburg and moved into the Litke home, along with her granddaughter Anna Furman, who became Fedor Litke's childhood companion and with whom he remained close until her death in 1850.

While his father and grandmother had been corresponding, little Fedor became the charge of Mariia Ivanovna Pal'm, a widow with three pleasant-looking daughters, Mariia, Roza, and Ekaterina. The daughters took turns in taking care of Fedor. Petr Litke's frequent visits to this house brought him closer to the Pal'm sisters. Their care for his son reassured him of their honesty and decency. Apparently, he decided to get his younger children settled as soon as possible, and for this reason he married Ekaterina Andreevna Pal'm one year after his wife's death. His new wife was around seventeen years old at the time. "She was quite beautiful," Fedor Petrovich wrote later, "but aside from that she did not have any other quality which would have given her the right to be friends with a man such as my father. Her mind was very limited. She had no education whatsoever. Even her outward, social character was ponderous and two-faced. She did not even possess that simple kindness of heart which often makes up for all other shortcomings."[5]

Soon after this marriage, Elizaveta Kasperovna moved in with her son Fedor Ivanovich Engel, taking little Fedor with her. By that time, Fedor Engel had already become a prominent statesman. He carried the rank of state councilor and served in the College of Foreign Affairs. Later he was promoted to state secretary and had access to Tsar Paul I. During the reign of Nicholas I, he became State Secretary of the Department of the Economy, and 1828 become a member of the State Committee and chairman of the Petition Commission. From 1829 to 1830 he was in charge of the Ministry of the Interior, and from 1832 until his death in 1837, he served in the State Council's Department on Polish Affairs. He was an intelligent and well-educated man, but at the same time he was weak and spineless.

Fedor Litke lived under his grandmother's care until 1804, when he was sent to school. In his memoirs he wrote that he remembered little about this period. When he was naughty, they would frighten him with his uncle, who could give him "pinches." He recalled meeting Emperor Paul on the street one day, as well as his funeral procession, which he watched from the window of his grandmother's house near Tuchkov Bridge. No one pampered the boy except his grandmother. But he was soon taken away from her, too. Little Fedor was taught to read and write at an early age so that when he went to boarding school he could already decipher quite a bit.

The master of the boarding school was Efim Khristoforovich Meier, a man who had earlier taught the Second Cadet Corps. He was tall and gaunt with a hooked nose, powdered head, and a long queue. He was not a vicious or vengeful man but "according to the pedagogical system of the times he considered the 'cane' the alpha and omega of education. It was literally a cane because he carried out his 'executions' with thin canes, not rods."[6] The boarding school was located near Tuchkov Bridge. Fedor remained at this school only six days. On the seventh, he showed up at the house of his father, who was then living on Vasil'evskii Island, on Bol'shoi Prospekt.

Fedor Litke recalled these years with sadness. He remembered his father as a serious, uncaring man, always busy and never paying attention to him. "I never remember him having caressed me. If only he had pinched my cheek, but I got only thrashings, for the most part at my stepmother's instigation."[7] Litke could not say that his father did not love him. He simply did not show his emotions in public, so as not to spoil the boy, and little Fedor understood that.

He remained in boarding school until 1808. These years were taken up by boredom and cramming. As a result the boy was badly developed physically, he was fearful, shy, and unresourceful. In addition, he was very quick to take offense and hot tempered. For the four years he spent at the school, he could "mutter some things in German, French, and English; knew four rules of arithmetic, and fractions, and in geography knew the names of the main countries and their cities."[8]

Petr I. Litke died on 8 March 1808. A pension was not awarded after his death. Another misfortune occurred in May of that year—grandmother Elizaveta Kasperovna died. She died at sixty-three, unable to bear the burdens that had fallen to her—the death of her daughter and her beloved son-in-law. At a family gathering it was decided to relegate the Litke children to different families. P. P. Pankrat'ev took the older sister, Natal'ia, to Kiev. Anna and Elizaveta went to live with Aleksandr Ivanovich Litke. Roza and Vladimir (from the second marriage) went to live with a friend of their father, Senator Alekseev. Fedor again went to live in Fedor Ivanovich Engel's house where he had spent his childhood with his grandmother. Fedor Litke's stepmother, Ekaterina Andreevna, married the director of the Currency Bank, a certain Zavalishin, a couple of years after Petr Litke's death.

Eleven-year-old Fedor had come to live in the house of his uncle Engel at a time when the coarse Anna Karlovna began to take charge of the household. Under such conditions, there was no way that the boy could get an education. "My uncle had taken me to his house as he would have taken a boy off the streets so that he would not starve. He paid no attention to me unless he wanted to scold me or pull me by the ears. I remained without supervision, without guidance, without a single teacher, from the ages of eleven to fifteen! There was no way I could ever make up for the loss of those four years, no matter what the efforts."[9]

Young Litke's education was so neglected that F. I. Engel did not even find time to enlist him in the Naval Corps, even though his father had often talked about it and the necessary papers had already been prepared. The boy was left to himself. Using his uncle's large library, he read anything he could get his hands on. An elderly nurse took care of him, his uncle, and a certain Petr Petrovich Peterson who was in charge of the Engel household.

Fedor spent the summer of 1808 in a small dacha [summer home] on Kamennoostrovskii Prospekt, next to the bridge across Karpovka. By fall his uncle had moved into a house at the corner of Nevskii and Vladimirskaia. In this house Fedor lived with the sons of one of Engel's university friends, the retired actor Rakhmanov. The room where the boys were housed was one that gave access to another. They slept side by side on a large Turkish divan. Few days went by without fighting, with Litke most often the loser. He recalled that "all the days were so senselessly monotonous, that nothing remained in my memory except the foolishness, coarseness, and moral corruption along with a hard slap in the face received from my uncle for calling him Fedor Ivanovich [a respectful form of address]; he demanded that I call him 'uncle dear.'"[10]

In the summer of 1809 Litke became closely acquainted with the artistic family of his roommates with whom he had spent the winter. His uncle went to his dacha, while Fedor went to live with the Rakhmanovs. The boys were left to their own devices. They roamed the countryside and often played on the islands. On Sundays they usually strolled in Stroganov Garden. Here people walked sedately and music reigned. Fedor Litke often met the then famous General Bagration during these strolls.

In the fall of 1809 Litke moved with his uncle to One Ismailovskaia, where his uncle had purchased a two-storied house with a mezzanine. In the winter he charged Fedor with recopying various papers in French and German. Usually Litke occupied himself at the office where his uncle's vast library was located. The boy spent endless hours reading books. Mondays, when dinner parties were organized, were real holidays for Fedor. On those days interesting people gathered at the Engel house. Among those who came here often were A. N. Olenin, president of the Academy for the Arts; the fabulist I. A. Krylov; lyceum director

E. A. Engelhart; princes I. S. Meshcherskii and V. M. Volkonskii, and many others. With mouth agape, an enraptured Fedor listened to the adult conversations until they sent him to bed. The library and these meetings remained imbedded in his memory all his life. They took the place of school, and helped his intellectual development.

Litke's aunt Elizaveta Ivanovna Pankrat'ev died in 1809. In the spring of 1810, P. P. Pankrat'ev followed her. Litke's sister, Natasha, who was being raised by them, moved in with uncle Aleksandr Ivanovich Litke in Radzivillov.

In the summer of that year the crews of the warships of the Mediterranean squadron, who had earned a series of outstanding naval victories under the command of Admiral D. N. Seniavin, returned to Russia. Several of the ships had been sold in Trieste. Their crews were returning to their homeland on the march. One of the columns was headed by retired commander Timofei Mikhailovich Bychenskii, a hero of the Battle of Athos, with whom Aleksandr Ivanovich Litke had studied in the Naval Cadet Corps. The route taken by this column passed through Radzivillov. Bychenskii and his officers found themselves welcomed at the home of his old friend.

What happened next was as if it were in a fairy tale. One of the officers, Ivan Savvich Sul'menev, a participant in Seniavin's campaigns and battles and commander of the captured Turkish ship *Sed-el-Bakhr*, saw Natasha and fell head over heels in love with her. Soon after, he asked for her hand in marriage. His offer was accepted, and they were married on 29 June. On the same day Fedor's second sister, Anna, also got married. She became the wife of postmaster Karl Karlovich Girs. On 8 October 1810, the Sul'menevs moved to St. Petersburg and took residence in Kronstadt where Ivan Sul'menev was stationed.

After the death of the Pankrat'evs their children Vladimir (sixteen years old) and Teofil (fourteen years old) were also taken as charges of F. I. Engel. Fedor Litke found himself in the company of his cousins. Vladimir and Teofil were preparing to enter a military school. Teachers were sent to them to get them ready. It is not surprising, then, that young Litke learned something along with his cousins. In addition, he recopied their homework for them and traced their drawings. According to Litke, with French books on mathematics, history, literature, and philosophy "[I] fell upon everything with greed, I read everything, deciphered, translated. What didn't I translate! Whole courses in geometry (I almost began studying Euclid), various excerpts from history, comedies by Molière; I wrote out whole sections from a historical dictionary."[11] At that time Fedor had already memorized much of Derzhavin's and Krylov's poetry.

Such a concentrated self-education went on for two years. Only his uncle's carelessness prevented Litke from entering the lyceum in Tsarskoe Selo, the director of which was none other than Engelhart, his uncle's friend. For the same reason, he was unable to enter the Naval Corps. His uncle simply waved his hand, having decided that no good would ever come of his nephew.

An event essentially changing the boy's life occurred at this time. He was in a navy environment. The main "culprit" was Ivan Sul'menev, who had taken the place of father for young Litke. "From the first minute we met, he loved me as a son and I loved him as a father," Litke remembered later. "This feeling and relationship did not change for a single instant in our forty-year acquaintance. In his old age, he showed these same feelings toward my wife and children."[12]

At first the boy seldom saw his sister and brother-in-law, but he began to visit them more often as of the summer of 1811. He would ride alone to Kronstadt on sailing launches that departed from the quay near the Senate. Usually they were run by old retired boatswains. Litke loved to listen to these old sailors' stories about their campaigns and sea battles under the leadership of Admiral Seniavin. Fedor liked to feel the wind blowing in his face. He would watch the motion of the little sailing vessel with eager eyes and ask to stand at the helm. When he was permitted to do so, he was the happiest in all the world.

He felt free in Kronstadt. He explored all the corners of the Admiralty, roamed all the docks and even began to compile a description of the Kronstadt Port. He loved to sit on the wall of Kupecheskaia Harbor and look at the sea for hours as ships arrived and left, as he listened to the many sounds of the Kronstadt Roads. Fedor even ventured onto military ships. On one of them, the brig *Merkurii,* a distant relative by the name of E. E. Kulichkin served as a senior officer. He allowed the boy to go with the sailors in skiffs under sail, to participate in the lessons on sailing, to climb on the brig and even to clean cannons.

Little by little, all of these things were preparing Fedor Litke for the harsh and respected profession of sailor, about which his father had dreamed. In the Sul'menev house, the boy often heard conversation about the navy, about its history, about current events, about war, and about the destiny of the Russian Navy. Gradually he became so intimately linked with the sea that he thought of nothing else.

He made up for lost time as he greedily absorbed all the knowledge around him. At this time Litke was reading books on sailing and even managed to take several lessons in arithmetic and geography from D. M. Golovnin, the brother of the well-known navigator and a distant cousin of Sul'menev.

And how much he drew that was useful and amazing from the stories told by Ivan Sul'menev himself, who had lived a hard and heroic life! He was born in 1773, and in 1786 entered the Naval Corps, which he completed in 1789 with the rank of midshipman. From that time on he sailed on all manner of ships of the Baltic fleet, in the Atlantic, and in the White and Barents seas. Naval service took him to the Black Sea, where he served with the squadron of Admiral D. N. Seniavin.

In the winter of 1811–1812 the Sul'menevs moved to St. Petersburg. Now Litke could visit them and the harbor more often. In the spring of 1812, I. S. Sul'menev was appointed commander of the second detachment of three-cannon gunboats. At that time the commander of the whole flotilla (of 100 boats) was Rear Admiral A. V. Moller, who would eventually become Minister of the Navy. In May Sul'menev's detachment, equipped in Kronstadt, crossed to Sveaborg in skerries [small, flat-bottomed boats] and on 19 July left from there for Riga, which the detachment was assigned to defend.

Sul'menev's absence gave Fedor an excuse to visit his sister more often without telling his uncle Engel every time he did. Now he spent most of his time at the harbor and came home only to sleep. He sailed on skiffs, listened to tales told by sailors who had served with Sul'menev and Golovnin, visited S. I. Minitskoi, captain of the oar-powered fleet, and continued to read everything, especially travel accounts. He remembered the day news of the Battle of Borodino reached St. Petersburg for the rest of his life. Fedor ran as fast as his legs would carry him from Kazan' Cathedral, where he had heard the news, all the way to Galernaia Harbor in order to tell this news to his friends.

The events of 1812 shook Russian society. Both the young and the old were literally infatuated with military exploits. And the passionate boy of fifteen could not remain on the sidelines, especially since his cousin, Nikita Pankrat'ev, served as adjutant to Kutuzov himself. Several times

Litke beseeched his intractable cousin to use the little pull he had to get him into the service, but his attempts were futile. It was yet too early for Litke.

In the fall of 1812 Natal'ia Petrovna [Sul'menev] received a letter from her husband who told of his military life in the flotilla. At first the ships were in the Daugava River, then from 14 to 22 September they took part in military operations against the French on the Aa River. During these battles the Russians captured enemy batteries and freed the town of Mitava. The letter ended with an invitation for the family to come to Sveaborg where the flotilla would be in port for the winter.

When Fedor found that out, he easily convinced his sister to take him with her. Besides, his uncle was not opposed to his trip.

Meanwhile, the government had decided to evacuate all valuables and to move the Baltic fleet to England should Napoleon invade the capital. The Navy school began evacuation to Sveaborg. Natal'ia Petrovna took advantage of this event. She decided to sail to Sveaborg on the frigate *Pollux* which was commanded by Ivan Nikolaevich Butakov, the founder of the Butakov naval dynasty and a colleague of Ivan Sul'menev.

At the end of October, the frigate weighed anchor in Kronstadt and went to sea. Litke remembered this first trip to sea aboard a real military ship for the rest of his life. Everything seemed so familiar to the boy, yet he was impressed by the new experience. It was one thing to observe a ship from shore or at anchor and another to take part in a voyage. Only a sailor can appreciate the beauty of the wind blowing into the sails and the sound of the waves at the helm. The frigate seemed alive; it quivered on a steep wave, it slowly heeled as it tacked. For Litke everything was of great interest as he followed Lieutenant Aleksei Ivanovich Selivanov around the ship, asking questions which the officer always answered patiently.

A day after the frigate arrived in Sveaborg, the oar-powered flotilla came into port. A large number of people crowded the fort. With great difficulty Sul'menev succeeded in renting a tiny apartment. There was no room in it for Litke. It was decided that he would live with E. E. Kulichkin, a distant relative.

Fedor Litke was going on sixteen, The question as to whether he would become a sailor had already been decided. The time came for him to enter the service. In those days it was too late for him to enter the Naval Corps. He had to prepare for the Naval Corps examination on his own. Litke dreamed of distant voyages and tried to study the naval sciences as carefully as he could, mathematics, geometry, trigonometry, algebra, and physics, above all. Without these one could not become a naval officer. Sul'menev contacted Fedor Vasil'evich Gruzdov, an instructor at the School for Navigators, and got him to prepare Fedor Litke for his mathematics examination. Every day Litke, wearing a light coat, would run clear across Sveaborg to his teacher's house. Since his unsystematic readings at his Uncle Engel's had been of some use, his lessons at Gruzdov's went smoothly. The student proved intelligent. He understood everything and he already knew something in advance. He quickly reached the next level. After that he was assigned to another teacher who taught him the basics of spherical trigonometry and navigation.

Litke spent all his free time among sailors, exploring the fine details of a ship's structure. One time, such curiosity almost cost him his life. In the fall the *Saratov* (one of Admiral Kraun's ships on its way to England) was aground near Grokhara. In the winter they decided to remove its masts. Fedor went along with the crew assigned to the task. At one point in the work several masts came crashing down, killing one sailor and almost hitting Litke, too.

That same winter Litke began to hang around with officers. They all knew that he was preparing for the examination for officer's rank. The young officers readily accepted this cheerful and well-read young man into their circle. Fedor Litke threw himself into this new life with a youthful zeal. His studies came easily and did not take up much of his time. He did not miss a single ball or a single evening out. He danced with diligence and began to court women, even managing to fall in love.

But winter came and it was time to take his exams. Litke applied and a commission was set up to receive the examinations. They asked many questions but all were favorably disposed toward him. "To tell the truth," Litke wrote several years later, "the examination was simply a necessary formality. They all knew me and even loved me. They all respected my brother-in-law and so everything was done privately, in part with jokes and facetious sayings."[13]

The process was finalized. And so, on 23 April 1813, Naval Minister I. I. Traverse presented to the tsar: "Nobleman Litke, seventeen years old,[14] educated at his own expense in the sciences pertaining to navigation. He asks permission to be accepted into service in the fleet; and since he was in the top percentile of those taking the Commission's examination in the sciences and also has a good knowledge of elementary algebra and can draw well, I respectfully request that he be accepted into service with the rank of midshipman [*michman*] if your Majesty kindly agrees." The tsar's resolution to this request was brief: "Naval cadet [*gardemarin*] for one sea voyage."

And thus began his career as an officer. Even though he held the rank of naval cadet, he performed the duties of midshipman. Meanwhile a naval campaign to Riga similar to that of the previous year was hurriedly being readied. The flotilla consisted of three detachments, twenty-one vessels in each. The first detachment was commanded by Sul'menev. The entire flotilla was commanded by the future hero of the Battle of Navarino, L. P. Geiden. The gunboats handled well even under sails raised on two masts. Each boat had three cannon, two at the bow and one at the stern. Litke was stationed aboard the galiot *Aglaia* which bore the broad pennant of Sul'menev, the detachment's commander.

On 9 May the flotilla set sail. The new naval cadet had no specific duties. He stood watch under the officers' supervision. And Ivan Sul'menev himself observed him daily. The crossing was successful. The flotilla arrived in Riga where, in expectation of orders and because of an armistice, it remained until July. Thereafter they were ordered to sail for Danzig in order to aid the Russian army which was besieging the fort there.[15]

Again Litke saw new places. Just as he was forming impressions of Revel, Moonzund [Muhu], and Riga, his eyes opened up to Irbe Strait, Cape Kolka [Kolkasrags], the Venta River, Libava [Liepaja], Memel' [Klaipeda], Kurish-gaf [Kurisches-Haff, now Kurskii Bay], Pillau [Baltiisk], and finally Danzig. The flotilla sailed near the shore and the view was wonderful. Work and the watch did not hinder Naval Cadet Litke. In his free time, he loved to stand by the side and look intently at unknown shores and think of how many new shores he would yet see and perhaps even new countries.

The oar-powered flotilla was stationed in Putziger-wik Bay. Those participating in this campaign, especially the young officers, thought that they would go into battle immediately, but it seemed that they had been forgotten. Several days passed, and then several more. "I was bored. My brother-in-law was living ashore, where I could go only rarely because of the distance. I had no duties on board the vessel. I had no company, or worse than none. As usual, I studied as much as I could with the help of the few books I had with me, but without much zeal."[16]

Finally, in the second half of August the oar-powered flotilla moved directly toward Danzig by order of Admiral S. K. Greig. On 21 August the Russian ships approached the batteries on Vester-Platte, at the mouth of the Wisla River, and opened fire on them. The cannonade lasted several hours while the enemy batteries returned shot for shot. Toward evening the flotilla moved out of the reach of enemy fire.

On the following day the bombardier vessels shot up the main fort, but the main battle took place on 23 August. Land troops attacked the city outside the fort, while the flotilla again bombarded the batteries on Vester-Platte. The heavy fire lasted all day. Toward evening, the flotilla again returned to Putziger-wik. The wounded were taken to the hospital, and the dead were buried. Damage to the vessels was quickly repaired. The flotilla rearmed itself and prepared to land.

The decisive battle took place on 4 September. The gunboats and bombardier vessels shot up the fort and Vester-Platte. The landed troops attempted to entrench themselves at the mouth of the Wisla while the land forces attacked the fort. The boats fired one after the other until dark. Sul'menev's detachment performed its duties well. Its cannons knocked out two battery guns with accurate shooting, as the boats led by the *Aglaia* got within closer than a cannon shot to the batteries.

Captain Second Rank Sul'menev led the battle with intelligence and bravery. He gave Litke the opportunity to prove himself, having entrusted him with a serious and important task. A launch was given to Litke to transmit Sul'menev's orders to each of the boat commanders all day long. Until late evening Litke's launch found itself in constant danger of attack. A boat flew into the air before his very eyes, with only four rowers and the commander unhurt. Shots whistled above the heads of the launch's sailors, whose spirits were kept up by the young naval cadet. At times the shots fell very near with a hiss, and frothing spray flew for several sazhens around. Litke forgot to eat, to rest. Inspired and happy, he hurried to fulfill the orders given by his favorite commander, Ivan Savvich Sul'menev. The battle ended late that evening. The flotilla received orders to return to Putziger-wik.

Fedor Litke was recommended for a medal. "For outstanding bravery, shown during the naval siege of Danzig," he was awarded the Order of St. Anna Fourth Class. On 23 September, for distinction in battle,

Fedor Litke was promoted to the rank of midshipman ahead of schedule. Within a few days the young man turned sixteen. His battle companions warmly congratulated him on his awards and on his birthday. The one most happy and proud of Litke was Sul'menev, who had not been mistaken about his ward. For his own actions at Danzig, Sul'menev was awarded a golden sword with the inscription "for bravery."

At the end of September, the flotilla moved to Königsberg for the winter. As before, Litke spent time at his books and in perfecting his nautical knowledge. "As customary, I studied and worked," he wrote, "but without much purpose. A navigator came to my quarters and taught me astronomy by Gamalei,[17] but I read more by myself."[18] Litke lived in a hotel with Sul'menev. In December he went to St. Petersburg with Sul'menev, who was ordered to take a large sum of money there.

Litke lived in St. Petersburg until May of 1814. During this time he studied much, as usual, and practiced practical astronomical calculations. He translated, read a lot, and even became a habitúe of book stalls.

Despite his studies, he found time for entertainment. He did not miss an evening at the Olenins, where he was not very sure of himself in the company of the hosts or charming women. Every Monday Fedor Litke and Ivan Sul'menev dined at F. I. Engel's house. His uncle received him warmly. An interesting and varied crowd always gathered at Engel's house for dinner. An impressionable Fedor avidly took in the interesting and intelligent conversations that usually occurred among the guests.

Four months flew by unnoticed. In May Sul'menev and Litke returned to Königsberg. Work was bustling aboard the ships of the flotilla as sailors were getting ready to sail to Sveaborg. The war had ended and the flotilla was returning to its base. But these preparations were interrupted by sudden orders to sail for Danzig. There was talk of saving the transport ship *Sv. Feodor*, which had been damaged on its way to supply the flotilla. The rescue operation was led by Sul'menev. They succeeded in saving part of the cargo.

On 11 June the flotilla sailed out of Königsberg and, after a safe passage in clear summer weather, it arrived in Sveaborg. There were meetings, dinners, picnics, balls, and dances, which Midshipman Litke attended as an active participant. The port commander of Sveaborg, Admiral N. A. Bodisko, who had been a friend of Litke's father, was very hospitable to Fedor. At Bodisko's, Litke felt at home. This is evidenced by the fact that, when his brother-in-law Sul'menev was again given orders to go to St. Petersburg on a mission, Litke was not particularly pleased at first when he was asked to go along.

From August 1814 to February 1815 Litke lived with the Sul'menevs in St. Petersburg. Again he studied astronomy, navigation, and mathematics and read numerous books. Now, however, his reading was more directed. He chose mainly literature dealing with the nautical sciences. He also visited Engel, who was more and more kindly disposed toward his nephew. During this period he often met with his cousins Vladimir and Teofil Pankrat'ev. They served in the Guards and had just returned from an army which had seen combat. They had much to talk about.

Soon the time came for Fedor Litke to return to service alone. In February of 1815, seen off with good advice, the tears and sobs of his sister, and the strong manly embraces of Sul'menev, Litke departed for Sveaborg.

From the time he arrived in Sveaborg until going out to sea, the young midshipman stayed with Admiral Bodisko and served as his personal junior officer. His duties consisted "in being officer of the day all morning in front of the admiral's office and dining at his house all the time." After that he was assigned to the galiot *Aglaia*, on which he had already sailed with Sul'menev. The commander of the vessel was a relative of the admiral, a certain Egor Ivanovich Vistingaus.

The galiot received orders to stand guard in one of the channels leading to Helsingfors [Helsinki]. Litke's duties were light. From summer to late autumn they remained in the same spot. But Litke was not idle. "Again, I carefully reread books on navigation by Gamalei, including the supplements. I read the sailing directions for the Gulf of Finland, carefully following along on the chart. At night, I studied the constellations according to Gamalei's books. With the simple octant of our navigator, I tried to measure their distances, etc. All of these things came in handy later on,"[19] he recalled many years later. In addition, Fedor read a lot. He took books out of the club library when he went ashore. Trying to get a deeper understanding of what he read, he wrote out comments and reviews on the books and made notes in his diary.

Litke's monotonous stay was interrupted only once. The high command decided to give a practical lesson in sailing to a group of young officers. Around fifteen young people were gathered on the brig *Molniia*. They spent several days sailing to Revel and back. During this exercise Litke earned high recommendations from the brig's captain.

The winter of 1815–1816 was Litke's last in Sveaborg. It brought about many changes in his life. Admiral Bodisko died unexpectedly. His death made an indelible impression on Litke. He went to St. Petersburg on leave. At the beginning of February Sul'menev was promoted to Senior Major of the Naval Cadet Corps (that is, assistant director) and Litke helped his relatives move into their new apartment near the Corps.

After returning to Sveaborg, Litke found out that he had been assigned as adjutant to the new port commander, L. P. Geiden. He soon felt very much at home in the house of Geiden, who kindly allowed him the use of his large private library. At this time in his life, Litke studied the log of the ship *Tverdyi* and wrote a sketch of Seniavin's campaign. Unfortunately, time did not preserve this sketch for his descendants. Soon after there came into his life an opportunity dreamed of by every sailor, and especially a young officer. He was leaving on a round-the-world voyage.

CITATIONS AND NOTES

1. AVGO, r. 100, op.1, d. 187.

2. In German his family name was pronounced "Lütke," but Fedor Petrovich always wrote it "Litke" in Russian.

3. V. P. Bezobrazov, *Litke. Autobiography ...*, p. 7.

4. It is interesting that Litke's cousin, Elizaveta Fedorovna Furman (daughter of Fedor Furman and Elizaveta Ivanovna Engel) was the mother of two scholars: the well-known traveler Aleksandr Andreevich Bunge and lawyer Fedor Andreevich Bunge. After the death of Elizaveta Ivanovna, F. Furman remarried and had the children Andrei, a Decembrist, and Natalia, who married F. P. Litke's brother, Aleksandr.

5. V. P. Bezobrazov, *Litke. Autobiography ...*, p. 26.

6. Ibid., p. 34.

7. Ibid., p. 35.

8. Ibid., p. 36.

9. Ibid., p. 40.

10. Ibid., p. 44.

11. Ibid., p. 57.

12. Ibid., p. 54.

13. Ibid., p. 70.

14. Actually Litke was not yet even sixteen—A. A.

15. Gdansk (Danzig) belonged to Poland for several centuries (1458 to 1783); it was captured in 1783 by Prussia, from which it passed to the French in 1807.

16. V. P. Bezobrazov, *Litke. Autobiography ...*, p. 72.

17. P. Ia. Gamalei's textbooks on navigational astronomy were quite popular among the sailors of that time—A. A.

18. V. P. Bezobrazov, *Litke. Autobiography ...*, p. 72.

19. Ibid., p. 82.

***

a. Michman, midshipman, was the lowest officer's rank in the Russian navy (V. Dal' *Tolkovyi slovar' zhivago velikoruskago iazyka,* 2nd edition, vol. 2 [St. Petersburg and Moscow: M. O. Vol'f, 1881], p. 330).—Ed.

b. That is, 17 September by the Old Style (Julian) calender followed in Russia at the time, and 28 September by the New Style (Gregorian or modern) calendar. The Julian calendar was eleven days behind the Gregorian in the eighteenth century and twelve days behind in the nineteenth.—Ed.

VOYAGE AROUND THE WORLD

"I sold you out; an expedition to Kamchatka is being organized for next year under the command of V. M. Golovnin, and he, at my request, agreed to take you along,"[1] Ivan Sul'menev wrote to Litke in the early spring of 1816. This news made the young midshipman ecstatic, but at the same time, it forced him to take a closer look at his chosen profession.

In those years the name of Vasilii Mikhailovich Golovnin was on the tip of every young naval officer's tongue. His recent adventures "as a captive of the Japanese," his voyage aboard the *Diana,* his unquestionable authority, and his strictness with his subordinates gave his name the aura of a brave, highly educated seafarer with an unbending will. Fedor Litke understood that a voyage around the world with such an experienced commander would be excellent schooling for him, and at the same time would be a difficult test of his nautical knowledge. He wanted to emerge from this difficult but alluring trial with honors. Again he took up his books. He read and reread Kruzenshtern, Lisianskii, Cook, Sarychev, in an attempt to learn as much as possible about the distant countries he was soon to visit. He did not forget his practical applications of astronomy, either. He reread textbooks on navigation and Sarychev's book on hydrographic work.

The immediate purpose of the *Kamchatka*'s round-the-world voyage was the following: "(1) To deliver to Kamchatka various naval and military supplies and other necessities for this region. Also, to supply the port of Okhotsk with goods which, due to the remoteness of these places, are impossible or extremely difficult to transport there overland. (2) To review the colonies of the Russian-American Company and investigate the actions of its employees in respect to the native inhabitants of the regions it occupies. (3) To determine the geographic position of those islands and places under Russian dominion which have not yet been determined by astronomical means, and also, using small vessels, to examine and describe the northwest coast of America from latitude

60° to latitude 63°."[2] The instructions noted that the third and last point was to be carried out only if it were not done by the expedition of O. E. Kotzebue aboard the *Riurik*.

Fedor Litke was senior among the midshipmen who were sailing. The other midshipmen were: Fedor (Ferdinand) Petrovich Wrangell, who later became an outstanding navigator and scientist, and Fedor Fedorovich Matiushkin, a friend of Pushkin back at the Tsarskoe Selo Lyceum. From the outset Litke clashed with the senior lieutenant, Nikandr Filatov, who had served under Golovnin on the *Diana*. The lieutenant had his commander's trust, but according to Litke, there were times when he abused that trust. There were frequent quarrels between Litke and Filatov that finally reached the point that the midshipman decided to sign off the sloop in Kamchatka and return to St. Petersburg via Siberia. The reasonable Ferdinand Wrangell, who became Litke's bosom friend for life, dissuaded him from such an act. It is not surprising that twenty-five years later, in answer to Wrangell's letter of 20 May 1842, Litke wrote, "Life aboard the *Kamchatka*. What a moment! And how lucky I was to have met you at such a time and in such circumstances. What unpleasantness and bitter minutes readied my flightiness, my thoughtlessness, my insolence, my selfishness, all due to my inexperience! What a different and, perhaps, wrong and even destructive direction my life might have taken had the good in me not found succor, support, encouragement, in your friendship, in your conversations, and especially in your example. In the wardroom of the *Kamchatka*, the very location of which served, it seems, as a part of its character, everything conspired to turn a young, inexperienced man from the path of truth and embitter him forever. I am indebted to you alone for the good that overcame a bad beginning."[3] This memory of the wardroom of the *Kamchatka* remained with Litke due to his almost daily arguments with Filatov. There were times when Fedor was admonished by Golovnin himself based on Filatov's calumnies.

The senior officer on the *Kamchatka* was Captain Lieutenant Matvei Murav'ev, with whom Litke had become good friends in Sveaborg, even though there was a great difference in their ages. It was thanks to Litke that Murav'ev came on that trip. He had mentioned to Litke in passing that he would like to sail with Golovnin. Litke wrote to Sul'menev about it and he in turn asked Golovnin. Thus the question was decided. The third lieutenant on the sloop was Fedor Kutygin. The crew also included

*Ferdinand
Petrovich Wrangell*

four naval cadets: Ardalion and Feopempt Lutkovskii (brothers of Golovnin's fiancee), Stepan Artiukhov, and Vikentii Tobulevich. The navigators were Grigorii Nikiforov, Prokopii Koz'min and Ivan Afanas'ev. Petr Il'in was apprentice navigator, Anton Novitskii was the ship's doctor, Vladimir Skorodumov and Ivan Rozhnov were the doctor's assistants [*fel'dsher*], and Mikhail Tikhonov [Tikhanov] was the expedition's artist. In all, the crew of the *Kamchatka* numbered 130.

The Naval Ministry occupied itself in outfitting the sloop for its round-the-world voyage. The crew was given the best provisions. The sloop was equipped with the newest navigation instruments. The library was filled with the best Russian and foreign books on seafaring. "Besides the usual munitions and provisions issued to ships, we had many reserve supplies. We also had orders to buy in England a sufficient quantity of various things and of the newly invented preparations to prevent scurvy,"[4] wrote Golovnin.

The sloop *Kamchatka* set sail on Sunday, 26 August 1817. Litke remembered Ivan Sul'menev's exhortation and that very evening wrote the following in his diary: "Well! Honorable and sensitive man! You

*Vasilii
Mikhailovich Golovnin*

will not be deceived in your hopes; your ward will be worthy of you. Good behavior, diligence in service, and keenness of observation— these are the means which will pave my way."[5] These words became a vow which Litke kept not only during this voyage, but throughout his remarkable life.

Passage through the Baltic and North seas lasted two weeks. On the night of 10 September , the *Kamchatka* arrived safely in Portsmouth. On the way it had stopped briefly in the Copenhagen Roads, during which time Wrangell went ashore to purchase fresh provisions and to look for a pilot.

In his autobiography Litke affirms that from the outset of the voyage Golovnin took a dislike to him "mainly because of my own fault, but partly because of certain unpleasant circumstances over which I had no direct control. My overactive personality, rashness and lack of knowledge of how things worked in the service (where was I supposed to have learned this?), the fact that I had been spoiled by my former commanders—all of these things must have made me look like a good-for-nothing in the eyes of the captain."[6]

Golovnin was strict, but just. He did not pursue the ostentatious side of a matter. He demanded that everyone on the sloop know his business and that everyone should be healthy. It was not by chance that the majority of the sailors were skilled in two specialties. It was also not through mere luck that his sailors returned from a voyage healthier than when they had set off. It is highly improbable that Golovnin was overly strict with Midshipman Litke. It only seemed to the impressionable young man at the beginning of the voyage that he was being unjustly offended. At the end of the trip Litke understood that Golovnin had only wanted what was good for him. Not to get ahead of the story, let us only say that until his death, Golovnin took an interest in Fedor Litke's destiny. He was often protective of him and corresponded with him. Litke himself wrote that at the start of his voyage he "had no understanding of the service, but returned a real sailor, a sailor of the school of Golovnin who in this, as in everything, was unique. His system was to think only about the essence of a matter without paying attention to its outward appearance. I especially remember his answer to Murav'ev, who was outfitting the *Kamchatka* and probably asked something about masts and spars: 'Remember, that we will not be judged by the pulleys on our ship or any other such nonsense, but by what we do well or poorly in another part of the world.'"[7]

They remained in Portsmouth ten days. During that time, the whole crew went ashore and many went to London. Litke liked Portsmouth very much. Several pages of his diary are filled with descriptions of this port. From 12 to 17 September, Litke went to London with Filatov, Matiushkin, and Lutkovskii. During that time he studied the English capital. The young midshipman liked London so much that he wrote an entire chapter on it in his diary. When he returned to the sloop Litke celebrated his twentieth birthday with his friends.

It is necessary to mention that despite his youth and his seemingly carefree outlook on life, Litke was very serious in carrying out his duties, although he scarcely wrote about it anywhere because he was too modest. From the outset of the voyage, he kept a detailed diary which his first biographer, V. P. Bezobrazov, mentions only in passing. More substantive reference to Litke's diary kept during his voyage on the *Kamchatka* was made by the Soviet researcher B. N. Komissarov.[8] Unfortunately, however, he made far from full use of this document; he used the diary primarily to illustrate the activities of Grigorii Ivanovich

Langsdorf [Georg Heinrich von Langsdorff][9] in Brazil and to characterize the Indian population in Brazil. The diary testifies to Litke's
exceptional industriousness and persistence in attaining knowledge.
Later in this book we shall try fully to use Litke's diary writings, and in
describing the voyage of the *Kamchatka* we will try to adhere to it along
with Golovnin's book on that topic.

After loading everything that had been purchased in Portsmouth
(charts, books, instruments, rum, vodka), the *Kamchatka* weighed
anchor on 21 September. Accompanied by a strong tailwind, the sloop
quickly sailed into the Atlantic Ocean. Golovnin held a course for the
Canary Islands in order to stop at Tenerife and replenish the supplies of
water, fresh provisions, and wine. The weather amended the captain's
plans. An exclusively favorable wind brought the sloop to the Canary
Islands in fourteen days, and continued to blow with the same strength
and in the same direction. After assessing his supplies and weighing his
chances, Golovnin decided not to stop at Tenerife. The sloop passed by
the island La Palma, the westernmost of the Canary Islands. The
officers, especially the young ones, could only curse the weather and
their captain for not allowing them to enjoy the beauty of the Canary
Islands.

On 22 October, at a longitude of 29° 28' 50", the *Kamchatka* crossed
the equator. "At the moment when we considered ourselves to be on the
equator," Litke wrote in his diary, "we raised the flag and gave a nine-
gun salute."[10] Nor did they do without the traditional celebration of
Neptune, who was played by passenger Schmidt, a native of Finland on
his way to work as a navigator for the Russian-American Company. "He
made himself a costume out of rags," wrote Litke, "and five or six merry
fellows made up his retinue, which paid respect to their god. This game
had begun at the bow of the ship with the noise of plates, speaking-
trumpets, and funnels constituting the music and marking the arrival of
the ruler of the seas. Finally his voice was heard: he asked the name of
the vessel, its destination, and whether it had received Jupiter's permission and so on. Having received affirmative answers, he rose and walked
around the ship; then he approached the captain and greeted him and
those who had been on the first voyage of Vasilii Mikhailovich (i.e., the
voyage with Golovnin aboard the *Diana*—A. A.), calling them old
acquaintances, etc. Those who were crossing the equator for the first
time he wet with a brush and shaved them with a giant razor. The sailors

were doused by the fire pumps, which gave rise to much laughter. The remainder of the day was spent in merriment."[11]

The sloop arrived safely in Rio de Janeiro on 5 November. During the entire trip, the weather was in the sailors' favor. The monotony of the voyage was interrupted only once with the appearance of the English ship *Blossom* which Golovnin at first took for American insurgents and even readied the sloop for battle. It later became clear that the captain of the *Blossom* had thought the same of the *Kamchatka*. On meeting, it turned out that Golovnin and the English captain were old acquaintances from their days of service in the English fleet. For a while the ships sailed together; then the *Blossom* set out on a southwesterly course, and the *Kamchatka* continued south to Brazil.

There it was, the exotic and unknown country! The passage took fifty-eight days. For those days, this was a very short duration. Because of this, Golovnin issued an order of thanks and rewarded all the lower ranks with two months' pay, which was quickly issued in piasters. After setting anchor, giving a twenty-one gun salute and receiving a reply, Golovnin sent two of his officers ashore to see Mr. G. I. Langsdorf, the Russian consul in Brazil. Toward evening that "short, dry man with a nondescript face" came on board ship.

Golovnin and his officers, including Litke, spent all the next day at Langsdorf's country house, resting after a two-month voyage which, though not difficult, was nonetheless exhausting. They relaxed in the company of the consul's wife, the daughter of astronomer Fedor Ivanovich Shubert. Then began the usual bustle of preparing the sloop for continuation of the voyage, especially for rounding Cape Horn. In between work, the officers went ashore with Golovnin's permission. Fedor Litke, too, was given such an opportunity.

Fedor walked around Rio de Janeiro, went on out-of-town excursions, went to the theater and was invited to the court of Juan VI, King of Brazil. On 9 November the officers, accompanied by the consul, rode throughout most of the city. They delighted in its beauty and went to see the long avenue of Volonga where in every house there was a shop where they sold slaves. "There is a street here," wrote Litke, "where they sell Negroes. It consists of houses, a better word for it would be barns, partitioned into two halves: in one they sell the men, in the other, the women. A buyer appears, and the owners show their Negroes, who are forced to move their bodies to prove how healthy they are. Then the buyer looks into their mouths as if he were looking at a horse's teeth. The deal is closed—the poor Negro is someone else's property."[12]

Young Litke was quite upset by the cruel situation of the Negroes: "The Negroes here have taken the place of cattle; they do the work. The Portuguese say that they are necessary, and that to stop this kind of trade would be the same as giving up Brazil. What a regrettable thought that one of the most fruitful countries in the world cannot have a political existence without depriving a certain number of unfortunate people of that priceless and most blessed natural right of freedom."[13] In Litke's diary and Golovnin's book there are many descriptions of the countless natural riches of Brazil: coffee plantations, sugar cane, gold fields, and precious stones. On 12 November the officers of the *Kamchatka*, accompanied by Consul Langsdorf, went to see a waterfall not far from the capital, and on the following day they dined at his house.

A short while before setting sail again, the king and royal family invited the officers of the sloop to court. The court had an unpresentable appearance and looked more like a private home. "The clothes make the man," Litke wrote about the structure, "and this proverb fits the Portuguese court well. The lack of importance of the king is written in his surroundings, not to mention his country place, which looks as much like a palace as the Winter Palace looks like a chicken coop. Looking at his courtiers I imagined I was in some provincial government house and seeing clerks."[14]

On 21 November they weighed anchor at Rio de Janeiro. The sloop held a course for Peru. A visit to this country did not initially enter into the captain's plans, but at the consul's request, Golovnin had agreed to take government papers from the Spanish minister to the Peruvian viceroy and thus show Russia's friendship toward the Spanish court.

The wind was favorable and the sloop, carrying all sails, proceeded south at a speed of seven to eight knots. The sailing was smooth. On 30 November they encountered the Russian vessel *Dvina*, which belonged to the Arkhangel'sk merchant Brandt. Even though the crew consisted entirely of foreign sailors, it was still pleasant to meet a ship flying the Russian flag at the edge of South America. Farther south, at a latitude of 37°, the sailors observed a multitude of flying fish, dolphins, and even large sea turtles. Meanwhile, it was getting colder as the closeness of Antarctica could be felt. Soon the sloop began to encounter large groups of swimming penguins. On 16 December at a latitude of 52° they saw a large three-masted vessel engaged in whaling.

On 19 December the eastern Cape San Juan appeared, whence began the passage round Cape Horn. This is where the sloop's seagoing qualities came to the test, where the sailors proved themselves, where the Golovnin school of training officers and sailors justified itself! The ocean seethed for twenty-five days. For nearly a month the *Kamchatka*'s crew fought the ceaseless storms, rains, hail, and violent winds. Fedor Litke long remembered this voyage. Gazing at the barren cliffs on the unreachable shores, he made the following entry in his diary: "Woe to the seafarer who should ever be wrecked on these barren, terrible, wild shores of Tierra del Fuego. The only fate that awaits him is hunger and a cold death."[15]

They celebrated the New Year of 1818 at Cape Horn. The sailors came up with an original show, written and performed by them. They were all given an extra cup of wine and double pay. Despite the great tossing of the ship, the holiday-making came off quite well. Golovnin was satisfied with his crew: "Nothing helps the physical health of the sailors more than good morale. This is a rule which should be followed, especially on arduous voyages," he wrote in his diary that day.[16]

They rounded Cape Horn on 17 January and soon entered the zone of a constant south wind which quickly brought the sloop along the shores of Chile and Peru. They reached the port of Callao without mishap. As if in reward for their tenacity and steadfastness at Cape Horn, the ocean gave the Russian sailors a rest all along the western shores of South America. During their passage, they caught albatrosses, whose down is quite good; they encountered whales blowing fountains of water; they admired flocks of swallows at play and were ecstatic to see the virtuosity of swordfish slashing the waves.

Despite overcast weather, Golovnin managed to calculate the course to Callao. On 7 February, the *Kamchatka* dropped anchor at the entrance to the port. A boat bearing the Spanish flag approached the ship. The quartermaster told them that two large Russian ships, the *Kutuzov* and the *Suvorov*, had arrived in Callao eight months before them. Those ships were under the Russian-American Company and were sailing to Russian America under the command of L. A. Hagemeister and Z. I. Panafidin.

Rebellions against the Spanish government were taking place in South America at this time. The rebels had taken Valparaiso. Many from the United States were fighting by the rebels' side. In Valparaiso there were six thousand against the crown's seven thousand soldiers in

Concepcion. This was the first news the Russian sailors heard when they reached the port of Callao. Golovnin immediately sent Midshipman Wrangell (not Litke!) to the local authorities, then to Lima with the papers intended for viceroy Joaquim de la Pezuela.

On the following day they sailed into the Callao Roads, saluted with seven guns and received the same number in reply. Soon thereafter, the ship had its first visitors, among them the customhouse director, all of whom were eager to look over a Russian ship. Wrangell returned toward evening, and said he had given the documents to the viceroy, who received him very well.

Then Golovnin and his officers began visiting the captain of the port, the commandant, and the viceroy. Meanwhile, the sloop was undergoing minor repairs, loading up with fresh provisions and barrels of fresh water—everything was being readied for crossing the Pacific Ocean to the shores of Russian America.

The viceroy gave a dinner party in honor of the officers of the *Kamchatka*. It was a wonderful party. The viceroy gave Golovnin assurances that the Russian seafarers would be issued everything needed for the rest of the voyage and that he was always at the captain's service.

Golovnin and his officers repeatedly visited Lima during the month of February and became acquainted with its environs and met people of various classes. Fedor Litke liked the local people and admired their fight for freedom. In general, Litke was sympathetic toward the Peruvian and Chilean rebel cause against the Spanish rulers. "The Peruvian patriots are waiting only for the defeat of the royal troops in Chile in order to declare themselves independent," Litke wrote. "Mexico will immediately follow the example of Peru. And so now Spain is within a hair's breadth of losing all its possessions in the New World."[17]

In Lima Litke inspected the artillery arsenal with interest; he visited the royal mint, Spanish monasteries, among them the largest, the monastery of St. Francis, and the pantheon. These excursions and especially his visit to the ruins of the ancient Indian town Cajamarquilla made quite an impression on the young seafarer. He again thought about the Peruvians' freedom and with sorrow wrote, "The unfortunate Peruvians have been wiped from the face of the earth, and if there are any of them left, it is only to see more clearly the pernicious actions, brutality, and selfish behavior of the Spanish."[18] His diary was filled with such sympathetic lines, which spoke of the nomadic Peruvian Indians who, "because of the cruel, greedy, and bloodthirsty Spaniards," were being forced to pay dearly for a scrap of the land which once belonged to them.

Meanwhile, things worsened for Litke. After an argument with Lieutenant Kutygin in a theater in Rio de Janeiro, he once and for all set Filatov against him. It got to the point that before leaving Callao, Litke decided to feign sickness and sign off the sloop when they reached Kamchatka. He shared his thoughts with Wrangell, but the latter considered Litke's move to be cowardly and advised that he not take such rash steps. As we already know, Fedor took his friend's advice.

During this whole period, Litke kept a diary. Doing this, he soothed his young and offended spirits. Besides keeping a diary, he made excerpts from and translations of foreign books, other than English, and made astronomical observations and calculations. He seriously began to study the English language. "It's true that I studied English at Meier's boarding school," he remembered, "but in ten years I had time to forget it all; however, once sown, knowledge is not entirely lost, but only waits to be watered and cultivated. I had to try. I took Vancouver and a dictionary. Before I finished the third volume of his voyages, I no longer needed the dictionary. Since then I have become fluent in English."[19]

On 17 February the *Kamchatka* left Callao and sailed into the Pacific Ocean. Taking advantage of the trade wind, Golovnin set sail toward the Galapagos Islands in order to pass them from the west and to sail north to 13° latitude; from there he would set course for Kamchatka. There began a boring, monotonous voyage that lasted until the beginning of March. On 8 March the travelers saw numerous gulls; this meant land was not far ahead. After noon on 13 March they saw one of the Washington Islands[a] in the distance. After the sloop passed it, a headwind again began to blow. On 19 March the *Kamchatka* crossed the equator for the second time. Caught by a tailwind, the sloop sailed north at a speed of ten knots.

The sloop gradually left the tropics. It sailed farther and farther north to its native but distant Kamchatkan shores. On 14 April they celebrated Easter. The officers and sailors were marshaled on deck. Golovnin's order was read. He thanked his officers and rewarded his sailors with pay. One of the sailors, Ivan Lebedev, reduced in rank for insubordination, was restored to sailor first class. The Easter celebration brought some animation into the crew's monotonous life.

On 29 April they saw the shores of Kamchatka, but the overcast weather kept the sloop at sea for another three days at the entrance to Avacha Bay. Only on the night of 3 May did the *Kamchatka* enter Petropavlovsk Harbor and anchor. The ship had sailed halfway round the world in eight months and eight days. No other ship out of Kronstadt had ever reached Petropavlovsk so quickly. The ship had been in port for only thirty-four days in all. All the rest of the time it was at sea.

When they awoke in the morning, the inhabitants of Petropavlovsk were pleasantly surprised to see a large Russian ship in their harbor so early in the season. The ice had just left Avacha, and it was still thick in Petropavlovsk Harbor. In order to bring the sloop farther into the harbor, it was necessary to cut the ice. The sloop's sailors and the shore command worked energetically. Those who were not working caught flounder to replenish the food supplies. By 15 May, the sloop was anchored in the harbor for unloading and loading.

By the middle of June all was ready for the continuation of their voyage to North America and new research. Eight thousand puds of ballast and twenty-five cubic sazhens of firewood were loaded on board. The Okhotsk transport *Ioann* was used for that purpose. That task was assigned to Wrangell, who brought all the necessary cargo from Rakovaia Inlet in three trips.

In their free time, the officers and sailors visited Petropavlovsk, went hunting and visited the hot springs.

Despite the fact that the new commander of Kamchatka, P. I. Rikord, had done much to improve life there, this region remained wild. Cheating and stealing from the native population by the merchants and government officials was an everyday affair. But even in these isolated people, Litke could find high moral qualities. "It would be hard, and perhaps impossible," he wrote, "to find a people who could compare with the high moral qualities of the Kamchadals. They are good-hearted, honest, and smart, contrary to what many say." It was with indignation that the young traveler noted what harm was inflicted on the native population of Kamchatka in the raids of the fur-buyers who cheated "the Kamchadal most shamelessly, in one day swindling them out of all the sable furs for which they had worked so hard all winter to catch."[20]

Litke condemned all attempts of the government to change the way of life of the Kamchadals through administrative measures. He condemned the force used to make the natives farm and limit their hunting and fishing. It was with irony that he related his conversation with a Kamchadal who had a "medal for farming." "It's true, we sowed grain," the Kamchadal said, "but we did not have a harvest, so we all went fishing as usual." "Why did they give you a medal?" Litke asked. "The authorities wished it that way," he answered.[21]

On 14 June Litke, along with other officers, was present at the transfer of the remains of James Cook's co-voyager, Captain Charles Clerke, to a new grave. The fact of the matter was that a large church was supposed to be built on the site where his grave had stood along with the graves of astronomer Delisle de la Croyère, astronomer of the Bering expedition, and Collegiate Councilor I. G. Koch, the commander of Okhotsk port. With sadness Litke noted that Clerke's coffin had no lid but "the bones and hair were intact." During the transfer of the remains, a salute was fired.

On 19 June the sloop was taken out of Avacha Bay and Golovnin sailed north to Cape Shipunskii. Initially Golovnin had wanted to begin a description of the Kamchatkan coast, but when it became clear that O. E. Kotzebue, on board the brig *Riurik,* was already doing so, he decided to describe the Komandor and Aleutian islands on the way to Russian America.

These islands were discovered, first described, and put on the map by participants in the expedition of Bering and Chirikov. They were repeatedly visited by Russian navigators and promyshlenniks after that. In the 1760s the Aleutian chain was described by the expedition of P. K. Krenitsyn and M. D. Levashev. Later it was visited by the English navigator James Cook. After him, a Russian government expedition led by J. I. Billings made a great contribution to their study. G. A. Sarychev, later a most outstanding hydrographer, took a very active part in that expedition. Despite such seemingly basic hydrographic work, many islands of the Aleutian chain remained incorrectly placed on the charts. For example, the closest [*sic*] island to Kamchatka, Mednyi Island, was, according to Sarychev, placed 25' too far south on Cook's map.

Golovnin and the young officers of the *Kamchatka* had to work hard to clarify the descriptions of these islands. Charts of the Komandor Islands, Attu, and parts of North America, drawn by Litke, have been preserved.

At the beginning of July they reached the Shumagin Islands, and from there Golovnin set the *Kamchatka* on course for the islands Chirikov

31

[Chirikof] and Ukamok with the intention of getting a true reading of their location. During these voyages they were successful in correcting mistakes made by Vancouver and Sarychev and proving that these two islands were one and the same. Golovnin named it Ukamok.[22]

On 10 July the *Kamchatka* sailed into Chinniatskii [Chiniak] Bay and dropped anchor at Pavlovsk Harbor, Kodiak Island—the cradle of Russian territory in North America, founded by G. I. Shelikhov.[b] Golovnin's detachment spent several days on the island. It was necessary to check the chronometers, to take down a description of the harbor, and to work out "personal matters" of the promyshlenniks working for the Shelikhov [Russian-American] Company ("to look into the actions of employees toward the inhabitants"). The latter task was specifically assigned to Golovnin.

Litke and his crewmates took great interest in looking over the Russian possessions in another part of the world. He was impatient to arrive at the main port of the Russian-American Company. While writing down his impressions, he made detailed observations of the living conditions of the Aleuts and the Russian promyshlenniks; he described the local hospital, school, and charitable home. The school was in bad shape. Litke noticed the unlimited power of the manager of Kodiak: "The native inhabitants of Kodiak are totally dependent on the manager of the Kodiak company office, whose power extends to those living along the Alaskan coast [coast of the Alaska Peninsula] and to the Aleuts of the Fox Islands chain."[23]

On 19 July the *Kamchatka* left Pavlovsk Harbor and set course for the capital of Russian America, Novo-Arkhangel'sk [Sitka]. The crossing was unusually successful, and on 28 July the sloop answered the salute of the fortress on shore and the salute of an American brig that was in the roads. No sooner had the *Kamchatka* anchored, than lieutenants Semen Ivanovich Ianovskii and Iakov Anikeevich Podushkin appeared on board along with office manager Kirill Timofeevich Khlebnikov. The chief manager of the colonies, Captain Lieutenant Leontii Andreianovich Hagemeister, who had replaced Aleksandr Andreevich Baranov, had left for California for grain a month before the *Kamchatka*'s arrival. Baranov was waiting for the opportunity to leave for his homeland.

This is how Litke described his first meeting with this remarkable man: "While we were sitting at the dinner table, Mr. Baranov's arrival was announced. The unusual life and activities of this unusual man had aroused in me great curiosity to see him. He was of shorter than average stature. His age and the hardships he had experienced had left few traces of the zeal that once animated him. His face was wrinkled; he was completely bald; his gait was unsteady; but even so, one would not say that he was in his eighties."[24]

During dinner there were many conversations about the glorious Russian navigators who had visited various corners of the shores of the Gulf of Alaska and the Aleutian Islands long before any foreigners. However, as Golovnin remarked with regret, "our previous navigators were not allowed to disclose their discoveries to the world; their journals and descriptions were turned over to the local authorities who in those days, following the Spanish example, kept everything a secret and thus deprived our navigators of glory."[25]

In their three-week visit to Novo-Arkhangel'sk, the officers had the opportunity to study the life and customs of the local inhabitants. Indians often came on board the sloop as guests. The Russian seafarers hosted their guests with biscuit, molasses, and vodka. The Indians particularly liked these treats. It was with great interest that the crew of the *Kamchatka* examined the structures in Novo-Arkhangel'sk, the fort flying the flag of the Russian-American Company, the houses behind the palisade occupied by the promyshlenniks and sailors in the company's service. At every step, the travelers found traces of the heroic exploits of Russian seafarers and promyshlenniks. And they also felt the strong hand of Baranov everywhere they went. Of course, there were instances when power was abused—that is what Golovnin was to investigate now—but Russian America was flourishing at that time, and Novo-Arkhangel'sk had become an excellent monument to the Russians who had explored and taken possession of the distant American lands.

The weather was overcast the whole time, and it rained often. During such days it was rarely possible to "catch" the time for surveying the environs of Novo-Arkhangel'sk or the Sitka Roads, nor could they get any astronomical readings or check their chronometers. The officers and navigators of the company were a tremendous help to the officers of the sloop. The one who was most helpful was a company navigator, Ivan Filippovich Vasil'ev, who had sailed much around the company's American possessions and had already described the bay. Subsequently Vasil'ev undertook a famous trip into the interior regions of Alaska and returned with a description of the Kuskokwim and Kvikhpak [Yukon] rivers and the lakes located between them.[c]

Golovnin did not wait for Hagemeister's return and decided to meet him in California, at Fort Ross. On 20 August the sloop left Novo-Arkhangel'sk and proceeded south along the American coast. The voyage went very well. At midday on 3 September they saw the famous Fort Ross of California, where the Russian-American Company flag also flew. Soon the sloop was approached by an Aleut baidara with the fort manager, Ivan Aleksandrovich Kuskov, a famous Russian traveler, administrator, and associate of Baranov.

Kuskov remained on board the sloop until evening, entertaining all the officers with his stories about life in America, about the neighboring Spaniards, and about agriculture and gardening which brought abundant harvests. His deep conviction about the need to reinforce Russia's frontiers in California struck everyone. Kuskov said that Hagemeister was in Monterey.

On the way to Monterey the *Kamchatka* met up with the *Kutuzov* on which Hagemeister was traveling. Both ships soon anchored in the port of Monterey. Through an agreement with the local governor, the Russian mariners were supplied with fresh water and firewood; they purchased foodstuffs and made a series of astronomical observations. The officers, naturalists and illustrator made almost daily excursions in the environs of the town and port. Golovnin was occupied with Hagemeister until 10 September, when the latter left for Novo-Arkhangel'sk with a cargo of grain.

On 12 September Litke and other officers were invited to dine at the governor's and on the following day they visited the San Carlos mission. On 16 September the governor and port commander dined on board the sloop. As the guests arrived they were saluted and the governor's colors were hoisted. Two days later the Russian mariners bid farewell to the hospitable Spanish. But before resuming their voyage, Golovnin stopped once more at Fort Ross in order to give Kuskov a letter from Hagemeister and at the same time replenish the ship with fresh water. The officers who were free of watch duty spent their time with Golovnin in the fort and its vicinity.

This area was truly a little corner of paradise. The exceptionally pleasant climatic conditions and the magnificent San Francisco Bay possessed all the necessary factors to have a large population and sea port. Kuskov adamantly complained that the government spared little attention for securing Russia in the southern regions of North America. And it was getting harder for the Russian colonists to live surrounded by Spaniards to whom they sometimes had to turn for help.

The *Kamchatka*'s stay in California was interrupted by strong winds. On 24 September they had to weigh anchor and leave to tack at sea. Within two days they set course for the Sandwich Islands. The storm, which had slightly abated, resumed with new force. They had to sail under harsh conditions. Then the storm ceased as suddenly as it had begun. Accompanied by calm weather, the sloop sailed steadily toward the Sandwich Islands.

On 20 October they dropped anchor near the islands. The king's officials began their visits and the officers of the sloop returned them. During one of these visits ashore, Litke went to the village of Kavaroa [Ka'awaloa]. It was here that the English navigator James Cook had been killed. The present king, Tameamea [Kamehameha I], who had been an elder at the time of Cook's death, told the sailors the details of the circumstances of his death.

The Russians were well received everywhere they went. Litke reacted with liveliness to the surroundings and admired the amazing natural beauty of the islands, not forgetting to make notes on all that he observed.

On 26 October the *Kamchatka* sailed to the island of Ovaigo [Oahu]. They dropped anchor in the picturesque harbor of Honolulu. Together with Golovnin, Litke saw the sights of the island. He saw the remains of the ship *Kad'iak*, which had belonged to the Russian-American Company and had sunk during a storm.

On 30 October the sloop left the island. A new man appeared on board the sloop—a local inhabitant who wanted to work for the Russian-American Company. He was called by a Russian name, Terentii Lauri. Ahead of them were the Mariana and Philippine islands, and then through the Indian Ocean around the Cape of Good Hope to the Atlantic, the Baltic, and then Kronstadt.

Their first stop was the island of Guakhan (Guam), where the *Kamchatka* arrived on 22 November. The travelers stocked their sloop with fresh water and provisions. As usual, the sloop's arrival was marked by visits to the governor, mutual visits and dinners, observations of the settlement, and acquaintance with the inhabitants, who had

had much more contact with European civilization than the people of the Sandwich Islands. The Russian sailors were astonished by the luxuriant tropical vegetation of the island. The land on Guam was quite fertile. This was further promoted by the large amount of rain and a climate that was not too hot, the result of the predominant northeasterly winds which brought freshness and prolonged rains.

From there the *Kamchatka* sailed for the Philippines. There were no particular problems or events on the passage, if one does not count the fire that broke out in one of the cabins at the trip's outset and was quickly extinguished.

On 13 December the *Kamchatka* anchored one mile from Manila. Golovnin decided to remain here longer and to prepare carefully for the difficult passage across the ocean. The crew rested after their long voyage across the Pacific Ocean. They made repairs, fixed the sails, and caulked and painted the planking. They celebrated the New Year of 1819 in Manila. During his stay here, Litke made many notes in his diary. He described the people of the Philippines in detail, made notes on the richness and beauty of nature, made observations on the navigational peculiarities of the port, etc.

On 17 January the *Kamchatka* set out on a continuation of its voyage. The sloop held due course for the Island of St. Helena. The *Kamchatka* crossed the Indian Ocean in two months, went around Africa and entered the Atlantic Ocean. During this part of the journey, they did not land anywhere. On 20 March the sloop anchored by the shores of the island prison of Napoleon [St. Helena]. Naturally, the sailors of the *Kamchatka* wanted to have a glimpse of the awesome conqueror, if only from afar. No one was allowed ashore, however, except Golovnin and Lutkovskii, and that only for a short time. The sloop remained here for only two days.

Golovnin's book and Litke's diary contain many stories about Bonaparte's life and adventures. They were, of course, secondhand. No one was allowed near Napoleon without the governor's permission. Military ships guarded all sides of the island. Only one road led to Napoleon's house in the valley of Longwood. The house was guarded by thirty sentinels and mounted patrols. It is said that Napoleon spent his days dictating his story and played billiards in his spare time.

From St. Helena, where, due to high prices, they could not obtain the necessary amount of provisions, Golovnin set sail for Ascension Island.

They arrived on 27 March. Here the travelers purchased ten large turtles and immediately sailed north. They crossed the equator in the first half of April, after encountering several English ships along the way. Then the sloop entered the zone of equatorial calms and sailed extremely slowly. At the beginning of May they ran out of fresh produce, and were forced to get by on biscuit and salt beef.

This part of the voyage lasted a month and only on 3 June did the sailors see the Azores. They were ecstatic. On 9 June they anchored in the Faial Roads, after completing a seventy-four-day crossing from Ascension Island.

The crew of the *Kamchatka* rested at the Azores and resupplied the ship with necessities. The local authorities and the Russian consul were quite helpful to the crew. The sailors saw the local sights: three monasteries and two convents, a school, churches and the fort. Balls were given in honor of the officers of the *Kamchatka*. Golovnin in turn invited his hosts aboard. Despite his sternness, Golovnin could not help expressing his feelings when he wrote "we had a good time." The captain was happy that "twelve or more sailors went ashore daily without fighting or getting drunk."

They bid farewell to the beautiful Azores on 26 June. Morale was high as they considered themselves nearly home already. Just under a month's passage to England did not seem burdensome, although there were some difficulties. As usual, the Bay of Biscay did not greet the sailors pleasantly; the shaken vessel had to stop in Portsmouth for several days to repair the tackle and spars. But on 4 August, the sailors of the *Kamchatka* were suddenly elated when they saw the sloops *Vostok* and *Mirnyi* sail into Portsmouth. The ships were captained by F. F. Bellinsgauzen and M. P. Lazarev on their way to discover the southern polar regions. They were accompanied by the *Otkrytie* and the *Blagonamerennyi* under the command of M. N. Vasil'ev and G. S. Shishmarev on their way to the northern polar regions.

On 4 September the *Kamchatka* sailed into the Gulf of Finland and on the following day dropped anchor in the Kronstadt Roads. Along with the joy of their return came worries—accounts, turning over of materials, etc. The officers often went ashore. Litke, too, was caught up in the zeal and happiness around him. He was especially ecstatic when on the day following his return he had a very pleasant meeting. This is what he recorded in his diary: "On Saturday, after returning rather late on board

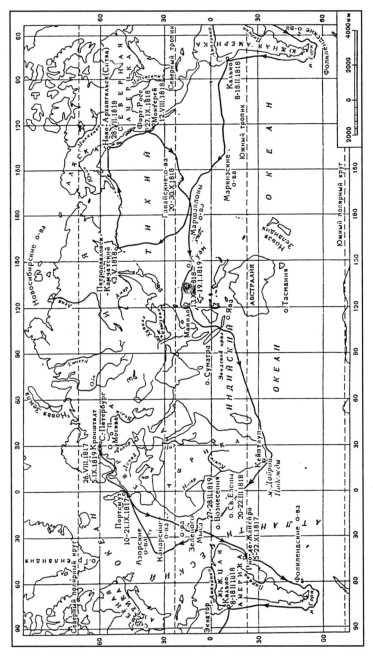

Chart of Litke's voyage on the sloop Kamchatka in 1818 under V. M. Golovnin.

38

the sloop, I entered my cabin and who do I see sitting there but Ivan Savvich [Sul'menev]. This meeting after a two-year absence was unexpected ... You can't imagine how I felt at that moment."[26]

This unusually important event in Litke's life—a voyage around the world under the command of an experienced sailor like Golovnin—had great significance for the youth's future. "Golovnin's school" demanded mastery of navigation skills and experience in commanding; it developed daring, sharpness, and inventiveness in solving the complicated, varied, and quite often dangerous problems which faced the commander of a vessel. Showiness and affectation were alien to Golovnin's method. And Litke, at his own admission, "fully accepted the spirit of this school."

Litke had returned from this voyage having considerably enriched his knowledge and broadened his horizons. The young Litke's diary testifies to a broadening of his mind, a knack for observation and accuracy of description. The diary also speaks of the author's industry. In those years he already had formed the habit of systematic daily work, persistent studies, and an ability to organize his time well. Along with the description of countries, the diary also contains special hydrographic and geographic notes which characterize Litke as a young man of learning; many pages have historical and ethnographic value. There are also thoughts about war, the naval strength of foreign powers and the role of the navy in the life of a country. In the diary we find a poem, apparently recopied from someone else. It characterizes Litke's relationship to the rotting world of the upper class. It is entitled "Christmastide or Today's World":

> Ever since the world became enlightened,
> it has almost always been dressed up;
> It is now under a mask, as they wear even when it is not yuletide,
> and especially where they take their profits and bribes.
> They change their features and
> wear a face not their own;
> Another thinks with a head not his own;
> The well-to-do rent the minds of secretaries,
> and out of weakness allow their own to rest.

Well, live and learn.
All these people wear masks no
matter where you turn![27]

Litke's diary is written in a good literary style. One cannot agree with Bezobrazov that the diary is of no value after the publication of Golovnin's work. Litke's diary not only adds to Golovnin's book, but also recounts many facts about the trip in a different light.

Litke learned much from this round-the-world voyage. He cherished the impressions of what he had seen as a young man for the rest of his life. The successes of the young lieutenant (he had been promoted during the voyage on 26 July 1818) were noted by Golovnin. When it came time for a new task, to explore Novaia Zemlia, Golovnin recommended Litke without hesitation as commander of the expedition.

CITATIONS AND NOTES

1. V. P. Bezobrazov, *Litke. Autobiography ...*, pp. 86–87.

2. V. M. Golovnin, *Puteshestvie vokrug sveta po poveleniiu gosudaria imperatora, sovershennoe na voennom shliupe* Kamchatke *v 1817, 1818, i 1819 godakh* [Voyage around the world ... on the military sloop *Kamchatka* in 1817, 1818, and 1819], part 1 (St. Petersburg, 1822), pp. 1–2. (Hereafter V. M. Golovnin, *Puteshestvie.....)*

3. GIAE, f. 2057, op. 1, d. 453, l. 20 ob.

4. V. M. Golovnin, *Puteshestvie ...*, p. 5.

5. "Dnevnik leitenanta F. P. Litke, vedennyi vo vremia krugosvetnogo plavaniia na shliupe *Kamchatka*" [F. P. Litke's diary kept on the *Kamchatka*]. TsGAVMF, f. 15, op. 1, d. 8, l. 3 ob. (Hereafter, Dnevnik Litke.)

6. V. P. Bezobrazov, *Litke. Autobiography ...*, p. 92.

7. Ibid., pp. 94–95.

8. B. N. Komissarov, "Dnevnik puteshestviia F. P. Litke na shliupe *Kamchatka* v 1817–1819 gg." [The diary of F. P. Litke on the *Kamchatka* 1817–1819], *Izvestiia Vsesoiuznogo Geograficheskogo obshchestva*, vol. 96, vyp. 5, 1964, pp. 414–419. (Hereafter, B. N. Komissarov. "Dnevnik Litke ...," IVGO, vol. 96, vyp. 5, 1964.)

9. G. H. Langsdorff (1774–1852) was a participant in I. F. Kruzenshtern's expedition, then became consul to Brazil, academician, and leader of the first Russian expedition into the interior of Brazil in 1821 to 1829. Cartographic materials of this expedition were brought to St. Petersburg by N. G. Rubtsov, a member of the expedition (see A. I. Alekseev and B. N. Komissarov, "N. G. Rubtsov i ego rol' v issledovanii Brazilii" [N. G. Rubtsov's role in the exploration of Brazil], *Izvestiia Vsesoiuznago Geograficheskogo obshchestva*, vol. 98, vyp. 6, 1966, pp. 500–506).

10. Dnevnik Litke ..., TsGAVMF, f. 15, op. 1, d. 8, l. 29–29 ob.

11. Ibid., l. 30–30 ob.

12. Ibid., l. 37 ob.

13. B. N. Komissarov, "Dnevnik Litke ...," IVGO, vol. 96, vyp. 5, 1964, p. 415.

14. Ibid.

15. Dnevnik Litke ..., TsGAVMF, f. 15, op. 1, d. 8, l. 61 ob.

16. V. M. Golovnin, *Puteshestvie ...*, pp. 63–64.

17. B. N. Komissarov, "Dnevnik Litke ...," IVGO, vol. 96, vyp. 5, 1964, p. 417.

18. Ibid., p. 416.

19. V. P. Bezobrazov, *Litke. Autobiography ...*, p. 93.

20. Dnevnik Litke ..., TsGAVMF, f. 15, op. 1, d. 8, l. 136.

21. B. N. Komissarov, "Dnevnik Litke ..., "IVGO, vol. 96, vyp. 5, 1964, p. 417.

22. "I will call them by the first of these names because it was given by the natives of this archipelago; no one has the right to change the original name, in my opinion," wrote V. M. Golovnin on the matter (V. M. Golovnin, *Puteshestvie ...*, p. 181).

23. Dnevnik Litke ..., TsGAVMF, f. 15, op. 1, d. 8, l. 161 ob.

24. Ibid., l. 175 ob. A. A. Baranov was born in 1746 and it follows that in 1818 he was seventy-two years old. Baranov died in 1819 while returning to Russia. His remains were buried at sea in the region of the Sunda Archipelago.

25. V. M. Golovnin, *Puteshestvie ...*, p. 219.

26. Dnevnik Litke ..., TsGAVMF, f. 15, op. 1, d. 9, l. 156.

27. TsGADA, f. Gosarkhiv, r. 30, d. 53, l. 10–10 ob.

* * *

a. The northern Marquesas Islands (V. M. Golovnin, *Around the World on the* Kamchatka, *1817–1819*, trans. and ed. Ella Lury Wiswell [Honolulu: Hawaiian Historical Society and University Press of Hawaii, 1979], p. 90, n. 5).—Ed.

b. The settlement at Pavlovsk Harbor was founded by Aleksandr Baranov, Shelikhov's chief lieutenant in Russia's North American possessions.—Ed.

c. Ivan Filippovich Vasil'ev, who charted Sitka Sound, drowned at Okhotsk in 1812. Golovnin's account of the voyage of the *Kamchatka* mentions no meeting with Vasil'ev, but merely that the *Kamchatka*'s crew verified the main parts of Vasil'ev's chart of the sound. Recent historical research by Svetlana G. Fedorova also allows us to distinguish Ivan Filippovich from Ivan *Iakovlevich* Vasil'ev. It is the latter who undertook exploration of the Nushagak and Kuskokwim drainages in 1829–1830. He did not reach the Yukon (Richard A. Pierce, *Russian America: A Biographical Dictionary* [Kingston, Ontario, and Fairbanks Alaska: Limestone Press, 1990], pp. 516–519; V. M. Golovnin, *Around the World on the* Kamchatka, *1817–1819*, trans. and ed. E. L.Wiswell [Honolulu: Hawaiian Historical Society and University Press of Hawaii, 1979], p. 122).—Ed.

TO NOVAIA ZEMLIA ABOARD THE *NOVAIA ZEMLIA*

After his voyage on the *Kamchatka*, Fedor Litke received his second order [medal]—the Order of St. Anna Third Class. The young lieutenant, now going on twenty-two, rejoiced.

He spent the winter of 1819–1820 in St. Petersburg. Time was passing quickly. His many acquaintances and his fame after his round-the-world voyage distracted him from business at first.

"Merriment, however, was not the only thing that occupied my time," Litke wrote subsequently, "as was my usual habit and inclination, I also worked a lot. Convinced that I had missed much in my education, I was resolved to study."[1] Thus he began to devote greater attention to the exact sciences so necessary for a naval officer. He even tried to attend lectures at the university, but his formal naval duties prevented him. So, Litke continued to teach himself. He was studying with such zeal and vigor that one day I. S. Sul'menev remarked: "Watch out, brother, that you don't overstudy!"

The round-the-world voyage inspired a love for distant lands in Litke. He literally dreamed of new travels, especially to the polar regions, where the explorer would find much that was mysterious, romantic, and unknown, and where, in his own opinion, he would be of the most use to his country. He submitted a report with a request to be transferred to the Arkhangel'sk naval detachment.

At the start of 1820, Fedor took leave in order to visit his sisters Anna and Elizaveta. Anna lived in Radzivillov with her husband Karl Karlovich Girs, while Elizaveta lived with her husband Rozen in Vilnius. But even during his leave, he took every opportunity to supplement his education. Thus, in Vilnius he became acquainted with several university professors: Boianus, Shpitsnagel, Loboiko, Riustem, and others.

After returning to St. Petersburg, Litke found out that his transfer had been approved. The young lieutenant immediately got his things ready to leave for Arkhangel'sk. The trip there made an indelible impression on him. This is how he described the northern marine gateway of Russia:

Arkhangel'sk "is located on the right bank of the Dvina, at the place where Kuznechikha Stream flows from it … and it consists of a seafront [quay] and two streets; thus, in length or circumference, it is approximately three versts. Along the shore, from one end of the city to the other, stretches a wooden quay where it is pleasant to walk in the summer. The main street is called Nemetskaia [German] because mostly foreign merchants live there. The street is wide, pretty well paved, and consists of pleasant-looking houses, all wooden and single-storied. In the southern part of the city one finds mainly stone buildings, most of them old-fashioned. The house of the town governor is located in the center of the square in the center of town along with one or two other houses belonging to private owners; these houses would be considered beautiful in any city."[2]

Litke's description of Solombala is interesting as well: "It lies on the other side of Kuznechikha, on the right bank of the Dvina. It is what was once in St. Petersburg, a galley settlement; the only people living here are those in the navy. There are five or six narrow streets from north to south and two or three from west to east consisting of small wooden houses or huts, a square with a marketplace and swings, two churches, a cemetery, and the Admiralty. The town is divided by a small stream, across which there are two arched bridges and a third leading to the Admiralty. This, then, is a description of Solombala."[3] There was only one stone building in the village, which contained all the port and other government offices.

The Arkhangel'sk detachment consisted of the ship *Tri Sviatitelia* and the frigates *Patrikii* and *Merkurius*. Litke was assigned to the *Tri Sviatitelia,* commanded by Captain First Class Rudnev. The squadron was getting ready for a trip to Kronstadt. Litke was fourth lieutenant on the ship. He was immediately caught up in shipboard life. He never left the ship; he stood his watch with excellence and continued to study assiduously. He even "preferred a cabin in the crew's quarters which was dark and stuffy, but a place where I was alone and no one prevented me from studying," even though he could have lived in the officers' wardroom.

On 10 June the ships left their winter harbor, Lapominka, and sailed to the island of Mud'iug. Here they were to outfit their ships. On this passage Litke observed with interest the skillful actions of the pilots who knew perfectly the peculiarities of sailing the difficult channels. Litke was pleasantly surprised that "almost all the local pilots spoke

English, and some quite fluently." Their pilot Kottsov also spoke German excellently and amazed Litke with his correct pronunciation.

Despite the fact that the crew worked from three in the morning to nine in the evening daily, it took over four weeks to supply the ships. The rigging, ballast, and cannons all had to be put in place. In addition, they had to load up with complete supplies of foodstuffs and fresh water, and stock up on powder and other things.

During these preparations, Litke became acquainted with the brig *Novaia Zemlia*. "In the morning," he wrote, "the brig *Novaia Zemlia* arrived with the powder. This ship had been built for Lazarev's expedition to Novaia Zemlia, but since Lazarev had declined the offer or something else had happened between them and the College and Sarychev, the *Novaia Zemlia* began its service by carrying powder to various ships and will probably end up carrying water and cast-iron ballast. This wonderful brig is eighty feet long and built much stronger than usual, but perhaps not sufficiently strong for the expedition to which it was assigned. All the ship's fastenings were copper."[4] Litke did not know then that the following year he would be assigned to the *Novaia Zemlia* to go on a polar voyage and then for another three years to describe the shores of the Kola Peninsula (Lapland) and Novaia Zemlia.

Finally on 20 July the detachment sailed on a voyage around Scandinavia. Litke carefully observed the workings aboard the military ship and found many discrepancies and shortcomings. He applied himself in studying navigational handbooks, and noticed that they too contained many disparities with sailing needs.

On 22 July the Arkhangel'sk detachment passed Sosnovets and continued to sail along the Murmansk coast. On the fifth day "in the morning we saw the shores, higher than we had seen earlier, covered with snow in many places. Several capes, all similar, descended sharply into the sea."[5] These were the northernmost capes in Europe—Nordkinn and Nordkapp. Then a storm blew for three days. On 30 July the weather became calm, but the storm was replaced by thick fog. In order not to lose their way, they held a course between the shore and the Shetland Islands.

At the beginning of August the detachment encountered the Russian vessel *Mezen'*. The sailors rejoiced at such an encounter. After exchanging greetings the ships went on their respective ways.

During this passage Litke arranged the notes he had made on Arkhangel'sk, adding information gathered during the voyage. He analyzed these facts carefully and pondered what he had seen. In part he made notes on the local high tides, which bore the name "manikhi." When the shore appeared about thirty miles away on 9 August, they took a bearing on one of its capes. Litke noted with bitterness: "The simple bearing in its intersection with the parallel showed something completely different than shown on the detail map of Skagerrak which is in Kutuzov's *Atlas*.[6] The cape on the map is shown 7' south of its actual position. In general, this atlas leaves much to be desired. I have already mentioned several errors; it is noteworthy that the maps are inaccurately drawn. For example, the parallels are not taken against whole degrees, not a single view is appended, etc...."[7]

However, despite these shortcomings, the voyage continued successfully thanks to the commanders' skills and good weather. On 15 August they dropped anchor at Elsinore [Helsingør].

The Russian consul organized a dinner for the mariners "such as one would expect from a countryman in a foreign country." On the following day Litke brought guests to the ship in two launches and later returned them to shore. On 17 August the off-duty officers were invited to dine at the consul's. Afterwards, they walked through the so-called Royal Garden. "In one corner of the garden," Litke wrote, "which one could reach blindfolded with one's sense of smell, there are four small stone columns surrounded with trees. Here, some say, Hamlet is buried. Others say it is here that the ghost of his father appeared to Hamlet, or the ghost of Hamlet himself to his own son."[8]

On 5 September the Arkhangel'sk detachment anchored in the Kronstadt Roads. The forty-seven-day passage (thirty-eight at sea, nine in harbor) was over. On this trip Litke became very familiar with the navigational conditions in the White and Barents seas; he studied and appraised the navigational manuals of this region and understood the importance of a sailor's knowledge of local landmarks, so well known to the remarkable Arkhangel'sk pilots.

During these years there was serious consideration in naval circles of conducting hydrographic research in the White and Barents seas and in particular by the shores of Novaia Zemlia. Novaia Zemlia, with which ancient Russians had been familiar, had not yet been placed on any chart. Science did not know its outline from either the Barents Sea or the

Kara Sea side. Undoubtedly every Russian navigator sailing in this region had made drawings or charts, but none of them had been preserved. "The details of their voyages," Litke wrote later, "will forever remain unknown to us by reason of the great negligence of the writers of those times.[9] No one bothered to save them from oblivion. And how many of them have not come to our attention at all."[10] Foreigners sailed here also. The expedition of Hugh Willoughby (1553) reached the Murmansk coast, and one of its participants, Captain Richard Chancellor, reached Arkhangel'sk and from there was brought to Tsar Ivan the Terrible's court in Moscow. It was this specific incident that signaled the beginning of the maritime trade between Great Britain and Russia. A Dutch sailor and citizen of Amsterdam by the name of Willem Barents van der Schelling was the first to chart Novaia Zemlia. He sailed with the expedition of Cornelis Cornelisson Nai in 1593–1595 along the shores of Novaia Zemlia; here he wintered and died on its northern island. Later, despite an abundance of voyages, both Russian and foreign, the most precise information necessary to compile a chart of Novaia Zemlia came from Russian sailors: those who participated in the Great Northern Expedition such as lieutenants S. V. Murav'ev and M. S. Pavlov (1734–1735), S. G. Malygin and A. Skuratov (1736–1737), helmsman S. Loshkin, navigator F. Rozmyslov (1768–1769), and navigator Pospelov (1807). Simultaneously with organization of the expeditions of Bellinsgauzen/Lazarev and Vasil'ev/Shishmarev, the Russian government decided to fund a survey of Novaia Zemlia. In 1819 one of the three Lazarev brothers, Lieutenant Andrei Lazarev, was sent to Novaia Zemlia on an old English brig *Katy* which had been renamed *Novaia Zemlia*. His senior officer was Midshipman Mikhail Kiukhel'beker (the brother of Wilhelm Kiukhel'beker), who later became a Decembrist. This voyage was extremely unsuccessful. Despite his repeated attempts, Lazarev did not manage to reach Novaia Zemlia or find Matochkin Shar.[a] The heavy ice conditions and scurvy among the crew forced Lazarev to abandon his task and to return to Arkhangel'sk.

"This expedition, which had such a bad end, did not clear up the doubts and lack of knowledge concerning Novaia Zemlia."[11] New explorations were needed.

At first it was supposed that Lazarev would repeat his voyage in 1820. A new brig *Novaia Zemlia* was built for that purpose (Litke had

47

encountered this ship while serving on the *Tri Sviatitelia*). But due to a series of circumstances, Lazarev was not given command of the brig.

It was then that Golovnin submitted Litke's name to the high command. Litke, of course, accepted the offer. It was really true that twenty-three-year-old Litke became commander of a naval brig and head of a scientific expedition! "Was there anything to think over?" Litke wrote fifty years later. "Subsequently, I realized that I still lacked a lot of experience and character in order to head such an expedition, and its results could have been much more significant if I had been more prepared for the task, though we did accomplish a considerable amount and some of what we did has not entirely lost its value even now, after fifty years."[12]

On 20 April 1821, Litke received order No. 502 from the Minister of the Navy, Marquis Traverse, which stated: "Your orders are not to make a detailed description of Novaia Zemlia, but merely an initial survey of its shores and to find out its size and determine the geographical position of its main capes and the length of the strait called Matochkin Shar, if ice or other obstacles do not prevent you from carrying out your task."[13] Litke was directed not to sail out before July and under no circumstances was he to spend the winter in Novaia Zemlia. But just in case, the brig was supplied with an *izba* [log cabin] and bricks for a stove.

In the name of the Government Admiralty Department, G. A. Sarychev furnished Litke with special instructions for geodesic observations and hydrographic research. In one of the points of the instructions, it was recommended that both chronometers "be set by the height of the sun, making observations several days in a row with sextant and artificial horizon." Sarychev suggested that Litke begin his survey of Novaia Zemlia from the south using two detachments in ship's boats moving from the east and west simultaneously. He advised Litke himself to sail to Matochkin Shar and, if possible, to go around the whole archipelago.

While still in St. Petersburg, Litke expressed great enthusiasm in getting ready for the expedition. He participated in the choice of officers who would go on the expedition; he ordered maps, books, chronometers, and other instruments. At this time he was constantly corresponding with Golovnin, Sarychev, and S. A. Kuznetsov, on all of whom advancement of the expedition's affairs depended. In his letters to Golovnin, Litke expressed his confidence in finding good coworkers, despite the "first unsuccessful campaign (here Litke has A. P. Lazarev's voyage in mind—A. A.) which thoroughly frightened everyone and spread strange and unfounded rumors about this expedition."[14] The composition of the staff officers was not decided until the very end of March. Upon leaving St. Petersburg, Litke sent Golovnin a note informing him of his departure and that "I leave the further choice of officers for the expedition entirely to the higher-ups."

Litke reached Arkhangel'sk by sleigh. It was the beginning of April, but here it was still winter. Before anything else, he went to Lapominskaia Harbor (Lapominka), where the brig was anchored; Litke found it in excellent condition. Thereafter he began to form his crew, and to collect information on Novaia Zemlia and navigational conditions. His papers contain curious notes relating to this period. For example, he noted "Voronin (who had spent the winter on Novaia Zemlia fifteen years earlier—A. A.) reported that in Matochkin Shar the sun shows itself around 4 February and that it would appear sooner were it not for the mountains. Ovodov (another navigator—A. A.) said that when it's dark, they go to bed when the tail of the Big Dipper is northwest."[15]

Litke did not want to limit his research to Novaia Zemlia. He organized a plan to study the Lapland coast, proposing to describe in detail Iokanga, the Nokuev Islands, the Sem' Islands, the bays between them and Olenii Island, Olenii Island itself, Teriberka, Kil'din Island, Kol'skii Bay and its harbors, Motovskii Bay, and the Rybachii Peninsula. In addition to that, he was gathering information about Arkhangel'sk and even began to write a history of that port.

His main occupation, however, was preparing for the expedition. Contrary to his expectations, Litke found many who were willing to go to Novaia Zemlia, and by May had completed his crew. "My crew," he wrote, "the choosing of which was left up to me, has been completed and is now busy working on the rigging. The crew consists mainly of volunteers, of whom there are so many that I foresee no trouble in replacing any unable to go with others no less qualified."[16]

At this particular time Litke's brother Aleksander Petrovich was in Arkhangel'sk. He was a great help to the young commander, coming aboard and directing the supply and arming of the brig. Whenever the weather was clear Litke himself and navigator Ivan Fedorov would make hourly astronomical readings. In this, Litke would sometimes turn to G. A. Sarychev for advice.

Lieutenant Nikolai Alekseevich Chizhov,[17] the senior officer, arrived on board the brig in the middle of May. By that time the big had been moved from Lapominka to the Admiralty wharf for final preparations for the expedition. Litke was satisfied with the brig and thanked its builder, Andrei Mikhailovich Kurochkin, more than once.

Soon after, Lieutenant Mikhail Andreianovich Lavrov[18] arrived in Arkhangel'sk. He had sailed on four such expeditions as senior officer and later would make a round-the-world voyage on the *Krotkii* under the command of F. P. Wrangell. Staff physician Isaak Tikhomirov arrived after him. The entire expedition consisted of forty-three men. It was well supplied with foodstuffs and clothing and it had the newest navigation instruments and hydrographic devices. They loaded 25 cubic sazhens of wood and 350 puds of coal to heat the ship. The brig was equipped with four rowboats. Litke took great interest in his crew's health and morale; therefore he tried to foresee everything in order to prevent any sickness among them.

The *Novaia Zemlia* weighed anchor on 14 July and slowly threaded its way among the numerous channels of the Severnaia [North] Dvina's delta. On the following day they passed the Novo-Dvina fortress, founded by Peter I. They gave it a seven-gun salute and received the same number in reply. At midday the ship crossed the bar. Litke sent the pilot back with the last mail and with full sails and a fresh wind sailed along the Zimnii coast. When the winds calmed, the *Novaia Zemlia* anchored opposite the village of Kuia. At night, however, a steady wind began to blow and Litke decided to weigh anchor and to sail along the coast. The shore was even and low, with sandy beaches. The absence of landmarks made navigation difficult and Litke expressed the idea of placing several towers on these shores. At midday on 17 July they arrived at the village of Intsy, and toward evening passed the island of Sosnovets.

Now the ship had to sail through several shoals which were mapped in various ways on different charts. Litke decided to pass between them. The *Novaia Zemlia* had nearly passed the shoals when the wind suddenly died down and the ship stood still. This had happened on a sand bank while the *Novaia Zemlia* was barely moving. Soon thereafter the brig's bow became firmly stuck in the sand. It was low tide, and the brig was completely out of the water.

"A fully armed ship, stuck on a sandy island, surrounded with breakers, in the middle of the sea, without any boundaries visible on any side, was quite a sight; everyone is busy—some are hanging from the bow, looking under the ship; others are taking astronomical readings; still others are walking unconcerned along the shore, picking up shells and stones; it presented an unusual picture."[19]

Attempts to get off the sandbank before high tide were unsuccessful. Only at high tide did the crew manage, with great effort, to get the brig off the shoals, with loss of two warp anchors Four sailors were hurt in the process, but the crew "endured these hardships with a spirit which only the Russian sailor possesses."

At midday on 20 July everything was ready for them to resume their voyage. The shoals where the brig had gotten stuck were charted precisely. Litke then sailed in a southwesterly direction, after deciding to avoid all shoals from the south and to continue along the Terskii coast. The maneuver was successful and by evening the brig sailed by the mouth of the Ponoi River and reached Cape Orlov where a lighthouse was being built. On the following day they left the inhospitable White Sea channel and sailed into the Barents Sea, holding a course toward the shores of Novaia Zemlia.

The weather did not pamper the sailors: a headwind blew constantly, and there were frequent fogs so that fine drops of water were constantly felt in the air. At midnight on 1 August the first ice was noted. Soon ice covered the entire horizon. Litke decided to sail south around the ice. They sailed in light fog and incessant rain. After sailing south for two hours, the brig again encountered an ice field. Judging from the depths, shore was somewhere close by. Litke noted in his diary: "How I regretted not being able to sail up to it, when we were so close. August had arrived. Though it is the best month for sailing in these places, it is also the last month for such activity, and we had not even begun our real task. With good winds and weather, we could, of course, do a lot even in this short time; but one could not count on that at any time of the year in this region, and therefore the delays began to annoy me with regard to the success of our expedition."[20]

Again they had to change course and sail in a northeasterly direction. They sailed, as it were, by touch, unable to take observations. When the horizon cleared, the sailors again saw ice instead of the expected land.

Litke brought the brig close to the ice field and began to go south around it. In many places the ice was covered with debris and in places it was simply black. This fact told Litke that the ice field had recently broken away from shore. That is why, after going south around it, he hoped to reach Novaia Zemlia and to sail north along its coast. Such wanderings to avoid the ice and rare determinations of position resulted in that after five days (on 10 August), the brig turned out to be in nearly the same place as it had been on 5 August. And not once did they manage to get close to Novaia Zemlia.

Then the commander decided to sail the ship northeast. This time the travelers were lucky. In the evening, finding themselves among sparser ice, they finally saw the long-awaited shore. But they could not get to it immediately. Litke again became anxious: "Our first attempt to reach the shore was not successful and this proved that, in general, this would not be so easily accomplished as we had first thought. The hope we had cherished began to wane, because if the shore was still completely surrounded by ice in the middle of August after nearly a month of strong easterly winds, then when and for how long will it be free of ice? And with the obstacles so great at a latitude of 71°, what could we expect farther north?"[21]

Judging from the chart, the brig was situated near the Gusinyi coast, by [the strait] Kostin Shar. For several days Litke attempted to sail through the floating ice to the shore by changing course and constantly tacking. All his attempts failed. "In general, the only fruit of all our labors and efforts was the discovery that from a latitude of nearly 72°, there stretches a solid wall of ice which makes the shore unreachable."[22]

And so, Litke changed his plans by sailing north. Soon the *Novaia Zemlia* moved away from the edge of the ice and sailed full speed ahead. They saw ice floes with many walruses and black gulls floating by them. On 15 August they saw the shore in the distance. That evening they saw a polar bear swim by the ship even though it was at least twenty miles from shore. The following days were just as unsuccessful. They encountered only ice. Litke decided to make one last attempt, and if he failed, he would return to Arkhangel'sk.

On 22 August an ice-free shore opened unexpectedly before them. Noncommissioned officer Serebrennikov, who had been to Novaia Zemlia before, was called on deck, but he did not recognize the area they were in. Litke sailed north along the shore, hoping to reach [the strait]

Matochkin Shar. At midday on 23 August they took readings of their position. It appeared that the brig was on the parallel of the mouth of Britvennaia Bay. They continued to search for an entrance into Matochkin Shar, without going too close to shore because of strong winds. Near each visible cape, which might prove an opening into Matochkin Shar, the brig would stop and take observations.

The coast was high and mountainous. While making observations, Litke named the most prominent capes. He named one of them Cape Lavrov, in honor of his senior officer, and to a rather high mountain, which had a conical shape, he assigned the name of Sarychev. On 24 August the brig, judging from the chart, had already sailed sixteen miles north of Matochkin Shar. However, not trusting those previous map readings, Litke continued to sail north to 74°10'. Here the travelers saw a huge mountain, which they named Golovnin. Then they turned back and by evening drifted with the wind.

On the morning of 26 August the *Novaia Zemlia* continued sailing south and by midday reached a latitude which was already seventeen miles south of that of Matochkin Shar. They had failed to find an entrance into the strait for a second time. Litke decided to use the remaining time to describe the coast seen and to determine its position precisely. On shore they saw the house and bathhouse of fur hunters and noticed their landmarks erected to mark the entrances of the various inlets.

On 31 August Litke sailed the brig toward the White Sea channel in order to reach Arkhangel'sk before the river froze. The passage was successful. On 8 September the brig reached the bar and arrived safely in Arkhangel'sk two days later.

Unloaded, the brig was transferred to Lapominskaia Harbor for the winter. For the next two months Litke put his journals in order and compiled charts. While comparing his notes with Pospelov's chart, Litke recognized the shore and found the place where they had passed the entrance into Matochkin Shar.

Lieutenant Litke was overcome with unhappy thoughts as he rode into St. Petersburg at the beginning of December, whither he had been summoned by order of the Minister of the Navy. The expedition had failed to fulfill its main task, that of measuring the length of Matochkin Shar. Basically, Litke had only managed to make rather superficial observations of the shores of Novaia Zemlia. True, the voyage had shown that the shores of Novaia Zemlia are not closed by ice all year round and that Matochkin Shar could still be found. Litke had made regular and careful meteorological observations which he had presented in diagram form. In his diagram, compiled for each month, he recorded the daily readings of latitude, longitude, declination of the compass, strength and direction of the wind, fog and cloud cover.

Litke found out from Golovnin that the Minister of the Navy had a grudge against him. In a letter dated 8 October 1821, Golovnin informed Litke that at first the minister "was very dissatisfied that you had not seen Matochkin Shar, but I wrote him a note and explained that you cannot be blamed for that." Golovnin's note explained that according to F. Rozmyslov's readings, Matochkin Shar is located at latitude 73°40', while on other charts it is shown at 74°30'. Golovnin wrote that Litke had looked for the bay between 72°30' and 75°, but because the readings were so far from being exact, there was possibility of error. Golovnin recommended to the minister that the expedition be repeated. Then he wrote to Litke: "I am convinced that, after judging this matter by yourself, you will not allow anyone else (two unclear words—A. A.) and that you will agree to try again."[23]

The intercession of V. M. Golovnin and G. A. Sarychev led to Litke's assignment, at the beginning of 1822, to continue the description of Novaia Zemlia in the next navigation season. While preparing the new expedition, Litke corresponded intensively with Sarychev concerning hydrographic matters. In particular, Sarychev wrote special instructions for Litke's second voyage:

"This summer you are again assigned as commander of a brig and are being sent to survey Novaia Zemlia and determine both its extent and its latitude and longitude; and since experience has proven that the shores are not free of ice before the end of July, you can use the time before that to survey the Lapland coast, from [Cape] Sviatoi Nos to the mouth of the Kola River. In this area there are numerous anchorages protected from the sea; some of them were visited by Russian navigators, such as the anchorages beyond the islands of Sv. Nos, beyond the Sem' Islands, beyond Olenii Island, beyond the southeastern end of Kil'diuin [Kil'din], and near the mouth of the Kola River beyond Ekaterinskii Island. Even though these anchorages are included in the Naval Atlas published in 1800 by G. L. Golenishchev-Kutuzov for navigating from the White Sea toward the English Channel, there are no detailed descriptions which might help navigators to find entrance to them.

"For each anchorage, the surrounding shores should be surveyed by baidara with exactness according to the rules of marine geodetics, their depths should be measured, and samples of the bottom should be taken. Find the lunitidal interval and observe the height of the high tide and the direction of the sea current during it. At every convenient opportunity, you are to take sightings of the shores and carefully note the alignment of capes and other prominent places by which any navigator could recognize the coast and safely enter the anchorages."[24]

It was recommended that Litke reach the northern end of Novaia Zemlia, then turn back toward Matochkin Shar. In these extensive orders,[25] he was given methodical problems and a sequence of tasks to perform. He was again categorically forbidden to spend the winter on Novaia Zemlia. Thus, Litke was given the responsibility of getting a detailed description not only of the coast of Novaia Zemlia, but also of the Murmansk coast, which had "never been described in a proper manner. All the charts of this coast were based on incomplete and sometimes erroneous information scattered in many old books." Thus, the fulfillment of this program, outlined by Litke himself, suddenly rested entirely on his shoulders.

Preparations for the new expedition took a long time. It was necessary to order new instruments to replace the old ones. For equipment, they had at their disposal two chronometers, three copper sextants, a telescope, a barometer, a log, two inclinometors, and an aerometer. Litke arrived in Arkhangel'sk on 31 March. Here again, a crew had to be assembled, supplies and instruments checked. The crew consisted of forty-eight men, among them Lieutenant Mikhail Lavrov, Midshipman Aleksandr Litke, navigators Stepan Sofronov and Grigorii Prokof'ev, and Doctor Nikita Smirnov. In addition to them, there were three assistant navigators, a doctor's assistant and a skipper's mate. There were twenty-eight sailors.

It was necessary to set sail as quickly as possible since their tasks were extensive. Besides, the Severnaia Dvina's ice broke unusually early, on 11 April. This circumstance also hurried the brig's departure. Despite some delay with inspection of the brig's bottom, on 10 June they were ready to sail. But now the weather was not on their side, as northern winds began to blow. Only on 17 June did they manage to weigh anchor and only on the fourth day did they sail out of the river beyond the bar.

In the White Sea they were met by a storm. For two days they were forced to tack near shore. When the storm passed, they set their course. The brig quickly passed the island of Sosnovets, the mouth of the Ponoi River, and Cape Orlov, and reached Cape Sv. Nos, to the north of which the Iokanga River flowed into Sviatonosskii Bay.

Litke, Lavrov, and Sofronov made astronomical readings and a description of the bay. The researchers did not forget to observe the inclination [dip] of the magnetic needle. In his notes, Litke made detailed descriptions of the Iokanga Islands and observations on the life of the local inhabitants, the Lopars [Laplanders]. Describing a summer Iokanga camp, Litke mentioned that "it consisted of eleven shelters where sixty Lapps of both sexes live. Their shelters are made of brushwood, twigs, and covered with sod and moss; they are cone-shaped and measure from three to four arshins at the base and two and one-half to three arshins in height. A small opening, level with the ground, serves as window and door; another opening above serves as a chimney. In the center of the shelter are stones which form the hearth where the Lapps warm themselves, cook, and bake their bread."[26]

On 2 July the brig sailed toward Kanin Nos. Litke wanted to determine its exact coordinates, but the weather prevented the researchers from carrying out their observations. They had to cut their readings short and sail toward Nokuev Island and Nokuev Bay, which were described and measured by Litke himself. On 8 July they crossed to the Sem' Islands, where during one of the high tides, the brig almost washed up on the shoals. Only Litke's quickness and the sailors' courage saved the *Novaia Zemlia* from damage. On the following day the officers became acquainted with the Lapps of the Sem' Islands, whose lifestyle did not differ from that of the Iokanga Lapps. Lavrov busied himself with description of the shore, while Sofronov measured the roadstead. After replenishing the ship with fresh water and completing their assigned tasks, they set out along the Murmansk coast on 13 July.

In the second half of July the explorers described and measured the coast at Olenii Island, Porchnikh and Teriberka inlets, Kil'din Island, and the Kil'din Roads. Incidentally, Litke corrected the transcription of the name given to the island. "It is Kil'din Island, not Kil'diuin, as we have called it up to now, like the Dutch," he wrote. He performed a full series of observations everywhere, including astronomical determinations and study of the tides.

On 26 July the brig entered Kol'skii Bay and soon found itself in Ekaterinskaia Harbor. On the following day they began their hydrographic work and observations and astronomical determinations. On 30 July Litke, accompanied by his brother Aleksandr, Prokof'ev, and Smirnov, went to Kola. On the following day the travelers arrived at the capital of Lapland. The mayor received them. They quickly made arrangements for fresh provisions and for dispatching their accounts and letters to St. Petersburg. Then the officers spent all day looking at the city and attended dinner parties, to the great satisfaction of the local inhabitants. The mariners found this city quite likable. Litke noticed the cleanliness of its orderly streets and the attractive way in which the houses were situated. There were 800 inhabitants in Kola. Their basic occupation was fishing (cod and halibut), while the women gathered tasty northern cloudberries.

But, they had to hurry back to the brig. August was beginning and they still had their main task ahead—Novaia Zemlia. All night and all day Litke and his companions sailed through Kol'skii Bay and by the evening of 1 August they were aboard the brig.

On 3 August the brig weighed anchor. The weather was fair and a tailwind was blowing. The brig was flying with full sails toward Novaia Zemlia. On the fifth day the island was already in sight. Above it rose a mountain which was the first thing they had seen on the last voyage as well. Litke had named it Pervousmotrennaia [First Seen]. There was no ice near the shore.

The fur hunter Smirennikov, who had been to Novaia Zemlia before, immediately recognized Bezymiannaia Inlet south of the mountain. Still farther south was Gribovaia Inlet. Litke sent his navigator there to get a description. He precisely identified the place. Orienting himself on it, literally not letting his sextant out of his hands, Litke sailed north in search of the entrance into Matochkin Shar. On that day the travelers recognized the islands of Pan'kov and Mitiushev and Cape Stolbovoi. This reassured Litke that he was nearing his goal. By evening the brig reached the mouth of the long-awaited Matochkin Shar.

Before describing and exploring Matochkin Shar in detail, Litke decided to sail the brig north of the strait. The brig moved slowly along the shore, while the officers tirelessly labored over a description. Soon

Traverse Bay, Cape Sofronov (in honor of the senior navigator), Cape Litke (in honor of Aleksandr Litke), Cape Smirnov (in honor of the ship's doctor), Cape Prokof'ev (in honor of the second navigator), Vrangel' Island (in honor of F. P. Wrangell), and Sul'menev Inlet (in honor of Ivan Savvich Sul'menev) all appeared on the chart. By six o'clock in the evening on 9 August the brig reached the area where the previous year's expedition had ended. Before the sailors lay the long, low-lying island which Barents had named Admiralty Island. Beyond the island lay another shore, just as even, but sharp and precipitous. Litke named one of its prominent mountains Mount Kruzenshtern. At midday on 10 August the navigators completed a description of Berkh Island, Krestovoi Island, and the Pankrat'ev Islands. At this point the coast of the archipelago turned sharply east.

Small pieces of ice began to appear. The weather was fair, but the barometer was falling and announcing unpleasantness. "With each new cape which opened before us," Litke recalled, "we expected to see the northern end of Novaia Zemlia which, according to the chart, could not be far ahead of us."[27] How the navigators desired to round Novaia Zemlia and then sail south through the Kara Sea. But their wish was not fated to come true. They soon encountered thick ice, and the shore was enveloped by fog. "At that time we were surrounded by ice and driftwood along with whole stumps from thick trees. This wood could only have come out of Siberian rivers and served as undoubted evidence of the nearness of the Siberian Ocean and, consequently, that the last cape we had seen was really Cape Zhelaniia."[28]

A whole day was spent tacking in the thick fog among the grinding of ice. When the fog lifted the next day, they saw before them a thick wall of ice stretching across the horizon all the way to Novaia Zemlia. "Thus our pleasant dream was shattered," Litke wrote, "and we were unable to pass into the Kara Sea; we retraced our path back to Matochkin Shar."[29]

From 13 to 15 August, the brig sailed only a short distance; ice and fog interfered. A lifeless, icy desert lay all around. The sailors encountered no signs of life. "The emptiness all around surpasses all description. Not a single animal, nor a single bird broke the cemeterial silence."[30] In addition, it was damp and cold. They were surprised by the unusual clearness of the water; a white disk could still be seen at a depth of twelve sazhens.

On the morning of 17 August visibility improved and the brig immediately sailed to Matochkin Shar. Litke did not bother to describe the strait since Navigator Rozmyslov had already performed that task. The commander of the brig decided to use the time left to describe the southern coast of Novaia Zemlia and, as possible, Vaigach Island. That same day Litke and his officers went ashore and visited an abandoned Old Believers' settlement situated near the mouth of the Matochka River. It was quiet and deserted here. On the shore stood a house in ruins next to a rotten barn and bathhouse. There were overturned barkazes [boats] and three crosses stood in memory of expeditions that had been here. True to this tradition, the mariners of the *Novaia Zemlia*, too, placed a cross with an inscription on the northern shore of the strait, in honor of their visit. The navigators determined the coordinates of their anchoring place, while the officers took mineral samples, and observed the tides.

On 21 August they sailed out into the sea, but because of a complete calm, they had to drop anchor. While anchored, they killed a young walrus which weighed over 320 kg, from which they rendered 96 kg of fat. By the morning of 27 August the brig was near Gusinyi Cape. Litke named the bay between the northern and southern ends of the cape "Moller Bay" in honor of the Minister of the Navy. The winds grew stronger, but did not turn into a storm. It did, however, prevent them from making descriptions. Litke waited three days, but "seeing that the storm would not relent, and that there was no reason to expect a change for the better in the weather any time soon, I was forced, finally, to abandon further attempts and set course for the White Sea."[31]

The weather was stormy throughout the return trip, but the brig arrived safely in Arkhangel'sk on 6 September and was transferred to Lapominskaia Harbor for the winter. Here the crew of the *Novaia Zemlia* expected mail. Litke received numerous letters. His comrades in the navy had written and, what was very pleasing to the young traveler, so had Golovnin, Kruzenshtern, and Sarychev. As usual, he received warm greetings from Ivan Sul'menev and his sister Natasha. His brother Evgenii, sister Anna in Radzivillov, and Teofil and Vladimir Pankrat'ev all sent their regards.

Having prepared his data, journals, and charts, Litke went to St. Petersburg. The trip in the winter seemed short. Litke was soon being embraced by relatives and friends. Then he presented his reports to the Minister of the Navy and to the head of the Russian hydrographers, G. A. Sarychev.

The well-known scholar F. Shubert praised Litke's scientific findings, especially the astronomical determinations. At a session of the Government Admiralty Department he declared:

> At the behest of the department, I have carefully examined the observations and calculations of Lieutenant Litke, which are herewith returned. Having completed the task, I have the pleasure to report to the department that the diligence and precision with which Litke made and calculated his observations are deserving of praise and do him great honor. During his stay in Arkhangel'sk from 15 April to 19 July and from 9 to 27 September, he did not miss a single chance to observe the corresponding height of the sun for checking his chronometers or a single chance to observe the lunar distance from the sun for determining the longitude of the place. And he continued to perform these tasks during his voyage so that by observing the height of the sun at noon and three to four hours before or after noon, he could daily determine both the longitude and latitude of a place, and also the declination of the compass. In addition to that, throughout the voyage he kept a detailed meteorological journal and made interesting observations concerning the inclination of the magnetic needle and the degree of magnetic force, observations of deviation of the magnetic needle from iron which was kept on board ship, and observations of the specific gravity of sea water at various latitudes and depths. In particular, the internal consistency of his observations proves the great skill of the observer and his efforts are praiseworthy. And since I found no error in his calculations, this proves his knowledge of mathematical and navigational sciences. I therefore consider it my duty to assure the department, which asked for my opinion in this matter, that Lieutenant Litke distinguished himself on this voyage and that he deserves to be rewarded.[32]

The navigators' services were rewarded by the government: Lieutenant Lavrov received the Order of St. Vladimir Fourth Class; Midshipman A. Litke received the Order of St. Anna Third Class, and the rest of the participants in the expedition all received a sum equivalent to a year's base pay. Litke himself was promoted to captain lieutenant.

Despite the great successes attained by Litke's expeditions to Novaia Zemlia and the Murmansk coast, this region of the Arctic still had many blank spots. The region west of Kol'skii Bay, where old maps referred to Rybachii Island, had not been explored or studied in the least. The location of Cape Zhelaniia on Novaia Zemlia had not been fixed. A description of Matochkin Shar had not been renewed. And there was almost no information concerning the southern coast of Novaia Zemlia and nothing was known about its eastern coast, either.

These and other tasks were assigned to the expedition of 1823, which was again headed by Litke. On 9 February the head of naval headquarters gave orders to organize such an expedition. Litke presented to the Government Admiralty Department his proposed project of describing the Lapland coast. This proposal was fully incorporated into the Admiralty Department's order No. 298 of 2 April 1823. The order stated:

> 1. Repeat the calculation of the difference in longitude between Capes Sv. Nos and Kandenois (Kanin Nos—A. A.); determine the correct latitude and longitude of Kolguev Island.
> 2. Complete the description of the Lapland coast begun in 1822, up to the Russian border with Sweden, as stated in your proposed project.
> 3. Reaffirm that Cape Zhelaniia, which you saw and which is shown on your chart of Novaia Zemlia, is truly Cape Zhelaniia as you suppose, and not Cape Oranskii; perhaps Cape Zhelaniia is farther to the northeast as shown on old Dutch charts.
> 4. Find out whether navigator Rozmyslov correctly determined the length of Matochkin Shar, as shown on his chart, of which you have a copy.
> 5. Examine Iugorskii Shar and Vaigachskii Strait and describe Vaigach Island; if time and circumstances permit, you are to sail around Cape Zhelaniia, pass through Matochkin Shar or Iugorskii Shar into the Kara

Sea, and describe the eastern part of Novaia Zemlia. You are to accomplish these tasks using your best judgment, depending on the time and local conditions and your experience and skills which are already known to the authorities based on your journals and the charts compiled on the basis of your previous voyages to those same places.[33]

At Litke's request, Lieutenant M. A. Lavrov, Midshipman A. P. Litke, Assistant Navigators Fourteenth Class Semen Efremov and Rodion Vikulov, and noncommissioned officers Iakov Kharlov, Koz'ma Zalesov and Aleksandr Seliverstov were again assigned to the 1823 expedition.

Litke tried to supply his ship with the best instruments. He wanted to leave St. Petersburg as quickly as possible, but he managed to get away only on 11 March. The road turned out to be arduous. He had to ride on sleighs and a carriage, all the while trying to safeguard the astronomical instruments. Within twelve days he arrived in Arkhangel'sk. About three weeks later the navigators assigned to the expedition arrived with the rest of the instruments and devices.

Litke was delighted to hear that the participants of the second expedition had all agreed to go with him on the third. Lieutenant Nikolai Irinarkhovich Zavalishin and navigator Semen Efremov were assigned to go instead of the ailing navigators Prokof'ev and Sofronov. Litke was also successful in recruiting pilots. Pavel Otkupshchikov, son of the famous navigator Aleksei Otkupshchikov (who in the eighteenth century had gone to the tip of Novaia Zemlia), was assigned to the *Novaia Zemlia* as helmsman. The famous Arkhangel'sk mariner and hero Matvei Gerasimov agreed to go on the brig during the voyage along the Murmansk coast. Otkupshchikov and Gerasimov were of great service to the expedition and made no small contribution toward its success.

On 11 June the brig weighed anchor. A strong northwest wind hindered the ship's movements. The brig went aground twice. Skillfully tacking in light, variable winds, within three days Litke sailed the ship beyond Cape Sv. Nos, toward the Iokanga Roads. Here Litke took astronomical readings of the islands' position, while the officers checked the previous year's survey and repeated a detailed description of the shore.

While working, Litke noticed the strange names that appeared on the old charts. "One of the features of these charts is a strange distortion of names due to the fact that they are based on Dutch charts. Almost all the names on them are Russian, but they are so distorted that for many of them it was impossible to find out their Russian origins. For example, is it easy to guess that Svetennois, Kandenois, Lambaska, Panfalotski, and Svane Krist are actually the Russian names Sviatoi Nos, Kanin Nos, Lumbovka, Panfilovka, Ivanovy Kresty and so forth? These monstrous names were driven from the White Sea by Lieutenant General Kutuzov's chart; it was now up to us to drive them from the shore washed by the ocean."[34] Litke boldly dealt with these names and corrected them on his charts.

Having successfully completed one part of their assignment, the expedition sailed to the Sem' Islands on 19 June. No sooner had the brig dropped anchor than strong northern winds began blowing with icy rain. Nevertheless, Zavalishin and a detachment set out to describe the western coast and fulfilled their orders with precision.

On Matvei Gerasimov's advice, Litke made his next stop at Teriberka Inlet. This section of the coast was not only undescribed, but in general was not even on the chart. Therefore Teriberka Inlet especially interested Litke's detachment. According to Gerasimov, this inlet was a pleasant place to anchor the ships. The *Novaia Zemlia* made its passage to it in dense fog which lifted only in Teriberka Inlet itself. They dropped anchor in Korabel'naia Bay and on 2 July began their survey. Lavrov, Zavalishin, Efremov and Litke worked on separate sections of the assignment, which went quickly. Meanwhile, the sailors built a real steam bath on shore.

It took only a week for the researchers to make their initial survey and first chart of Teriberka Inlet. In addition, they made valuable astronomical determinations, determined the lunitidal interval, and made observations on the inclination of the magnetic needle.

The crew of the *Novaia Zemlia* was especially interested in the fishing camp located at the entrance of the bay. Usually eighty men would gather in the summer to fish for cod, flounder, and halibut. These sea people would come to the bay in boats from afar, from their permanent settlement. Later Litke made detailed accounts of the life of the *pomory* [sea folk], their fishing habits, and the economic conditions in general. He was repeatedly enraptured by their skills, knowledge of the sea, and bravery as they sailed twenty to thirty versts from shore in fragile-looking boats. "One cannot imagine," Litke wrote, "with what difficulties and danger these people fish in open boats in the rough polar sea!"

Listening to the stories of Gerasimov and the other *pomory* about the destruction of Teriberka and other settlements by the English in 1809, Litke felt his heart fill with anger and hatred toward those land-grabbers. "Who would have ever thought of that?" he wrote. "According to the accepted national rights, one can take enemy territory; all consider that a good prize for the winner. But to burn and destroy, without any aim in mind, the poor shelters of peaceful, defenseless fishing people is an exploit which a Norman of the ninth century would have shunned."[35]

Litke then decided to explore Motovskii Bay and Rybachii Island. This region of the Arctic had also been ignored. Despite the bad weather, Matvei Gerasimov brought the brig successfully into Motovskii Bay. The sailor and hero Gerasimov was so popular that Litke wrote "up to now we had not met a man along these shores who was not a relative or friend of his."

The brig anchored in the northern part of Motovskii Bay on 11 July. That same day Lieutenant Zavalishin set to the task of describing the bay. The part of the bay where the brig stood at anchor was named Novaia Zemlia Harbor and described in detail. The navigators determined that Rybachii Island was actually a peninsula. Litke thought that perhaps in the olden days Rybachii might have been an island, because it was so low and narrow—its isthmus was only half a verst wide. In Litke's opinion, this supposition "is all the more probable in that a lowering of the waters of the northern Arctic Ocean has long been noted by many and is scarcely in doubt any more."

In Motovskii Bay the sailors of the brig saw many whales, and on the shore of Novaia Zemlia Harbor lay piles of their remains.

Zavalishin completed his description of Motovskii Bay on 16 July. Litke sailed the brig along the coast of the Rybachii Peninsula and described it. On the way the explorers stopped at Pechenga and visited the small and secluded monasteries of this Lapland Mecca. The expedition was successful in charting the entire peninsula and in tying its description in to surveys of Varde Island. Then the Murmansk coast was described right up to the border between Russia and Norway.

On 18 July, as soon as they finished the work in the vicinity of the Murmansk coast, Litke sailed directly for the shores of Novaia Zemlia. The voyage lasted more than a week. A weak wind accompanied them, while the current carried the brig south and slightly east. Nevertheless, at midday on 27 July they saw the northern Gusinyi Cape. Litke's first thought was to reach Matochkin Shar and to begin charting and describing it. However, a strong wind was blowing from the strait and the current was against them. Litke decided to search first for the northern cape of Novaia Zemlia.

The brig set a direct course for Admiralty Island, and reached it on 29 July. There the ship sat to the end of the day, becalmed. On the following morning they gradually made their way north by tacking. They passed Vil'gel'm and Berkh islands. The area was not as deserted as the last time. A multitude of birds—gulls, loons, and others—flew about the ship. On 1 August the brig reached a latitude of 76°30', and Litke was already counting on reaching the northern cape of Novaia Zemlia.

But that very evening the *Novaia Zemlia* was stopped by an ice field. In the distance they could see the cape which Litke had taken for Cape Zhelaniia the last time he had been here. As a result of careful study, Litke concluded that this cape was Cape Nassau. He then renamed the Oranskie Islands and the Barents Islands, the previous descriptions of which had turned out to be surprisingly accurate and corresponded to Litke's descriptions.

While sailing to the northern end of Novaia Zemlia, Litke discovered a current flowing from south to north up to 76° latitude and then in the opposite direction from 76° latitude. At the northern shore of Novaia Zemlia the researchers noticed another current, this one flowing west. Linking up with the first current, it formed a new one, which flowed in a northwesterly direction.

The return trip to Matochkin Shar took several days. They had to tack away from shore in the fog. On 6 August the brig dropped anchor at the mouth of Matochkin Shar, beyond Cape Baranii. On the following day Mikhail Lavrov set out in a launch to describe the strait, while Semen Efremov took to describing its mouth.

Lavrov completed his voyage along the shores of the strait in several days. Together with his crew, he spent the nights on shore—driftwood served as fuel for the research team. In the strait and at its exit into the sea, Lavrov saw large groups of walrus. On one of the days they killed a polar bear. The Kara Sea was clogged with ice. Individual floes were encountered with regularity even in the strait.

Meanwhile Litke and the remaining officers made astronomical readings on shore. The sailors checked the sails, supplied the ship with fresh water, and tried to hunt, but were unsuccessful.

On 11 August Lavrov returned to the brig after completing his description of Matochkin Shar. The rest of the tasks had just been completed at the mouth of the strait: its location had been astronomically determined (latitude 73°19'33", longitude 54°20'06"), and they had three days of tidal measurements and magnetic readings. The results of Lavrov's research forced them to abandon their initial decision to go around the southern island of Novaia Zemlia. It was decided to sail south.

Early on the morning of 12 August the *Novaia Zemlia* weighed anchor. The brig encountered strong winds and fought the waves all day long. On the following morning the wind died and only on the following day did a light east wind begin to move the brig on its course. On 16 August they saw the southern Gusinyi Cape.

After beginning a survey of southern Gusinyi Cape, the researchers described Kostin Shar and the islands of Podrezov, Iartsev, and Mezhdusharskii. On the following day the crew of the *Novaia Zemlia* observed Strogonovskaia Inlet. According to legend, the Strogonovs, Novgorodian settlers, had lived here during the reign of Ivan the Terrible. The remains of their settlement were near Cape Muchnyi. The navigators then described Chernaia Inlet, famous for the fact that the Painachevs, an Old Believer family, perished in it. Pilot Otkupshchikov had heard the story from a hunter who found their remains. In Sakhanikh Inlet the travelers discovered many islands and several good harbors.

A strong wind pushed the brig along. They quickly sailed by Sakhninskaia Inlet and soon found themselves within sight of Nikol'skii Shar and Kusovaia Zemlia. The winds became stronger and the sea more turbulent. When they passed Cape Kusov at the southeastern end of Novaia Zemlia, Litke was faced with a dilemma: should he sail through [the strait] Karskie Vorota and into the Kara Sea, which was free of ice as far as the eye could see, or should he go by his orders and describe Vaigach and Kolguev?

An unexpected event decided things for him. The *Novaia Zemlia* was sailing in deep waters. Suddenly the brig received a hard knock on its bow and then on its stern. Then the ship shook from numerous poundings. It had washed on a rocky bank. Soon it lost its rudder, the planking around the stern flew off, and pieces of the keel were floating around the ship. The vessel was on the verge of coming apart. Litke was ready to cut the cables and masts loose when a large wave lifted the brig over the bank and brought it back down in deep waters.

The immediate danger had passed, but the vessel could not be maneuvered. It was not easy to replace the rudder at night, especially during a storm, but the well-organized crew performed this arduous task in an hour and a half. The ill-fated bank was named after the navigator— Prokof'ev Bank. There could be no more talk of further explorations. No matter how hard they had tried, the sailors of the *Novaia Zemlia* had not replaced the rudder properly, and the shaken hull of the brig could begin leaking at any moment. And they did not even want to think about encountering ice floes. It was necessary to return to Arkhangel'sk, for which they set their course.

Around midday on 23 August they saw the northern shore of Kolguev Island. Litke, taking a risk, sailed near it. He fixed the coordinates of its prominent cape and described its shore until late evening. On the following morning the sailors saw the Kaninskii Peninsula and at seven o'clock Litke determined its longitude to be 43° 16' 40" by the chronometers.

At the moment when the brig was rounding Kanin Nos, another unfortunate incident occurred. A strong wave again knocked out the rudder. With great difficulty the crew lifted the rudder on deck. There was not a single intact hook on it—they were all eaten away with rust and had broken in the places of greatest corrosion. But the crew did not lose faith. On sailor Abrosimov's suggestion, they organized a smithy and made two replacement hooks for the rudder. Litke wholeheartedly thanked his officers and sailors and ordered that the crew be issued an extra portion of vodka.

The brig continued on its way and on the morning of 31 August arrived in Arkhangel'sk.

The difficult voyage, which yielded significant scientific data, had ended successfully. The brig was transferred to the Solombalka River, where it was put up for repairs. Litke and his officers, as usual, put their notes in order and compiled charts, and then traveled to St. Petersburg.

The naval authorities were satisfied with the actions of the brig's captain. On 18 January 1824, F. Shubert, at a meeting of the Admiralty Department, read the following comment about Litke's work on this expedition:

> Careful analysis of his work has brought me great pleasure. In examining Litke's observations in the course of several years now, I have found that both his zeal and his skill in observation have increased with every year; along with them has grown my respect, which this outstanding naval officer has truly earned. In a word, I must say that his work brings Lieutenant Litke great honor. The tables of meridian points and the meteorological journal of the *Novaia Zemlia* can serve as an example of order and clarity. For the three summer months, they contain barometric readings, thermometer readings for every four hours, wind velocity and direction, and weather conditions. Extracts from this meteorological journal deserve a place in our *Zapiski* [*Notes*, a publication of the Admiralty] because it contains conclusions which deserve the attentions of physicists; for example, that the thermometer did not go below 0° [Réaumur?] during the trip all the way to 31 August, that at 70° latitude in the middle of July it read +20° at midday and +15° at midnight, that at 74° latitude in the middle of August the air temperature was not less than +4° or +5° at midnight , and so on.
>
> His observations of inclination of the magnetic needle are no less important. Observations of the opposite sides of the incline usually differed from the mean by ½°, and never 1°; from these it is clear that there is a gradual increase in inclination from Arkhangel'sk to 73° 19' latitude. Whoever is aware of the difficult task of getting such information will appreciate the care and precision with which the above-mentioned work was done. The information is important to physicists who

study the earth sciences and deserves to be made public through our *Zapiski*. It would also be desirable that such detailed observations be repeated in other parts of the Arctic Ocean.

The astronomical observations, apart from a large number of comparisons of the chronometers with each other, consist of: (1) 680 corresponding heights of the sun to determine the correctness of the chronometers and the correct time of day; (2) 725 similar sun readings to define latitudes and azimuths; (3) 84 distances between the sun and moon, to determine longitudes. The great internal consistency in the observations proves the diligence and precision with which they were done. In the corresponding heights of the sun, the difference from the mean rarely exceeds $\frac{1}{2}$ second; only three or four times does it exceed 1 second and only once (on 14 July) does the reading exceed 2 seconds. I did not find a single mistake in any of his calculations. In lunar distances, the readings differ from the mean by 35 seconds at most, and usually by much less.[36]

Since the western and southern shores of Novaia Zemlia had now been described, it was decided to try once more to do what previous expeditions had not accomplished. The new expedition was assigned two extra detachments for special tasks. Litke was again appointed head of the entire expedition. "Three expeditions had been enough for me," he wrote later, "but I did not refuse a fourth, although I did not understand what else was wanted. It seems that even the Admiralty Department was not entirely clear on this, because it ordered me to write my own instructions, for which I naturally thanked it."[37]

In the orders of 18 March 1824, signed by G. A. Sarychev, it said: "(1) Try again, if circumstances allow, to go around Cape Nassavskii (Nassau—A. A.) and to determine the position of the shores stretching northeast from the cape to the northeastern end of Novaia Zemlia. If there is no ice in the way, try to sail along the eastern shore of Novaia Zemlia to Matochkin and on to Vaigachskii Strait. But if ice should prevent you from going around the northern edge of Novaia Zemlia as it has in previous years, then sail south." Litke was also ordered to "try to describe not only the eastern side of Novaia Zemlia, but also the southern and eastern shores of the sea from Belyi Island to Obskaia Inlet."[38]

Litke was responsible for supplying the brig *Ketti* with provisions and instruments for the expedition. That vessel was commanded by one of Litke's old friends, P. A. Demidov. Captain Lieutenant Domogatskii had done research aboard this brig in 1823, but at that time he was not officially subordinate to Litke. Now Litke also had to be in charge of the work done by the detachment of navigator Ivan Ivanov,[39] which was describing the Pechora River and the Pechora coast. Thus Litke became the head of the hydrographic expedition of the Barents, White, and Kara seas.

The following men were again invited to participate in this expedition: Lieutenants N. I. Zavalishin, M. A. Lavrov and A. P. Litke; Navigator's Assistants Semen Efremov (Fourteenth Class) and Iakov Kharlov and Aleksandr Seliverstov (both noncommissioned officers); and as steward, Sailor First Class Pavel Krupennikov. The rest of the *Novaia Zemlia*'s crew remained nearly unchanged.

Litke left St. Petersburg on 15 March along with his brother Aleksandr and sailor Pavel Krupennikov. At first everything was going smoothly; the horses, harnessed in tandem, moved briskly along a good winter road. But on the night of 19–20 March there was a heavy snow storm. The road, which lay between ravines, was completely covered. On one steep slope the carriage toppled over and trapped the passengers and coachman. With great difficulty the coachman climbed out from beneath the carriage and freed the Litke brothers. Fedor was hardly breathing; he had almost been crushed under the load of the carriage. After a while they found Pavel Krupennikov, but despite their efforts, they could not revive him. Thus, at the very outset of the expedition, Litke was deprived of a very necessary crewman.

Nothing else happened during the rest of the journey, and on 25 March Litke arrived in Arkhangel'sk, where preparations far above the normal amount began for the expedition. Everything had to be prepared for Ivanov's detachment, which was leaving on 2 April. Ivanov was no novice in polar explorations, as he had already described the Pechora coast in 1821 and 1822. He was now assigned to complete that survey and also to describe the mouth of the Pechora. Litke wrote detailed instructions for Ivanov. But even after that detachment had left, Litke continued to guide its activities, as attested by Ivanov's reports from Mezen' (6 and 30 April) and from Pustozersk (12 June). Ivanov, calling Litke the leader of the northern expeditions, wrote: "I received your most esteemed letter of 16 April along with my orders and your explanation on how to read latitudes using the distance between the sun and the moon. I received it on 30 May, for which I am much obliged."[40] From this letter, one can conclude that Litke kept track of the detachments of his expedition and was ready to help them in any way.

After seeing off Ivanov's detachment, Litke put all his energy into preparing the brigs *Novaia Zemlia* and *Ketti* to sail. Lieutenant Demidov, aboard the *Ketti,* was to continue hydrographic investigations of the banks in the White Sea channel. Demidov's predecessors, Petr Grigorkov and Dmitrii Domogatskii, had described the Terskii coast and several banks; Abrosimov and Ivanov, participants in the expedition of Golenishchev-Kutuzov, had defined astronomical points in several places along the coast in 1798–1801. The entire White Sea from Kanin Nos to Sviatoi Nos, divided into sixteen sections, had been described by various hydrographic parties. As a result of this work, Golenishchev-Kutuzov had compiled the "General Mercator Map of the White Sea," which was published in 1806. This map did not include any features of the sea, however, and lacked the banks discovered by Grigorkov and Domozhirov.

Therefore, beginning in 1821 when the *Novaia Zemlia* washed up on the shoals of the White Sea channel, investigation of these sandbanks commenced. The *Ketti,* under the command of Captain Lieutenant Dlotovskii in 1822 and under Captain Lieutenant Domogatskii in 1823, was engaged in sounding the White Sea channel and investigating the banks. During these voyages the researchers discovered and charted two banks. This, however, was just the beginning. Demidov was assigned to describe the Severnye Spits [*koshki*] and to conduct a whole series of soundings in the White Sea channel. With him were Lieutenant M. F. Reineke, Midshipmen Shatilov and Bubnov, and navigators Poriadin and Churkin.

During these spring months Litke carried on a lively correspondence with Golovnin, Kruzenshtern, and Sarychev. To the latter, who was engaged in writing a history of Russian ports, he sent a description of Arkhangel'sk Port on 17 May. Sarychev thanked Litke in his letter of 2 June, in which he wrote: "Although I already had a description of this port prepared, it was not as complete as yours. I therefore will use it. I hope that, as you promised, you will do me the favor of furnishing a description of those Arctic bays you visited in previous years."[41]

Lieutenant Demidov arrived in Arkhangel'sk at the end of May after the preparations for the expedition had been completed. Both brigs were brought into the roads at the beginning of June. On 17 June the ships sailed into the sea. On the following day the *Novaia Zemlia* sailed away from the *Ketti* toward the Zimnie Hills. Litke's officers determined the coordinates of several places along the shores of the White Sea channel and mouth.

On 2 July the brig anchored in the Iokanga Roads in order to check the chronometers, which took three days. During that time the sailors supplied the ship with fresh water, bartered salmon from the Lapps, and took a steam bath. Everything was ready for the voyage to resume. On the morning of 6 July Litke sailed toward Novaia Zemlia for the fourth time.

The weather was calm. The southeast winds were constant. At midday the explorers were already able to see the Terskii coast and the Kaninskii Peninsula, and by evening were able to determine the longitude of Kanin Nos as 43°16' 30". Then the *Novaia Zemlia* returned to the White Sea channel. Litke wanted to determine the coordinates of Cape Konushin. However, he only managed to describe the Kaninskii coast up to the mouth of the Kiia River. By the longitude of the mouth of the Kiia, which lay on the same meridian as Cape Konushin, the researchers also determined the longitude of the latter. This was accomplished in several days.

Litke again sailed north, figuring first to reach a latitude of 74° or 75° and from there to sail for Cape Nassau. On 12 July they had an unexpected meeting. At latitude 69°28' the brig encountered six English ships. One of the captains came aboard Litke's brig and told him that they were headed from London to Arkhangel'sk and that the prevailing northeast winds had forced them to stay away from the shore. In addition, the British were off by three degrees of longitude in their calculations and were off course. Litke used this occasion to send reports on his voyage to Arkhangel'sk.

The brig sailed farther north. The weather got colder; the rigging became iced over and the air temperature fell below 0° [Réaumur?]. They could feel the cold breath of the Arctic. At midday on 20 July the brig was at a latitude of 74°55'. On the following morning they encountered the first ice. Among the ice were zones of clear water, and Litke sailed the brig in these openings in an attempt to push as far as possible in an eastern direction. The brig tacked unsuccessfully through the ice until 25 July. It became clear that in such conditions they could not even reach Cape Nassau. Then Litke tried to sail north between Spitsbergen and Novaia Zemlia. Only on the evening of 27 July did the brig sail into clear water within sight of Cape Spidvel'.

Sailing along the ice edge, the *Novaia Zemlia* slowly moved west, then north. The ice became more severe; its height reached 2.5 meters, and they saw individual ice hummocks nearly 21.4 meters high. On 30 July the brig was at a latitude of 76°5' and a longitude of 42°15'. Further sailing along the ice edge was becoming dangerous. Litke concluded from his own and others' voyages that it was difficult to sail at high latitudes between Spitsbergen and Novaia Zemlia.

The *Novaia Zemlia* then sailed toward Kostin Shar. On the way, on 3 August, they encountered ice 35 miles from the shore. It stood as a solid wall to the south along the shores of Novaia Zemlia. It was impossible to approach Kostin Shar. Litke then decided to try his luck in other areas, but his repeated attempts were unsuccessful. The brig found nothing but ice floes. Litke decided to sail to Vaigach Island.

At midday on 13 August the brig reached the western coast of the island. The researchers described this section of the coast and determined the coordinates of Cape Voronov. Then the *Novaia Zemlia* went into the strait toward the Kara Sea "almost completely assured that within a few hours we would be able to describe a shore as yet unseen by any other navigators. But no sooner had we traveled a mile in that direction, than we were faced by a wall of ice which covered the whole horizon from east to west as far as we could see. This unpleasant encounter dashed in an instant all the hopes we had begun to cherish."[42]

Litke decided to wait a week in hopes that the wind would change and carry the ice away from the eastern shore of the island for a few days, and then they would be able to survey it. On the following day they encountered two boats near the island. At first they all thought it was Ivanov and his detachment returning, but they were Nenets[b] fur hunters going to Novaia Zemlia. They told Litke that from Vaigach Island, the whole Kara Sea was covered with ice and that Ivanov had sailed to Vaigach. The Nentsy also communicated to the explorers much valuable information about the natural environment on the island, the names of capes and islands, the number of people living on the island, and the number of reindeer there.

Meanwhile, a strong northeast wind began to blow, taking away all hopes of sailing into the Kara Sea. Litke decided to leave Novaia Zemlia. On 19 August the brig sailed for Kolguev Island. Within four days they were near the island. The weather became changeable. The winds grew strong one moment and stilled the next. A thick fog hung in the air, it was overcast, and it sometimes rained. They could not even think of conducting a survey. For six days the *Novaia Zemlia* cruised aimlessly near Kolguev. All they could do was hope for a chance. This was not the way of a young mariner, but of one who was experienced. On 30 August Litke decided to return to Arkhangel'sk. The voyage ended on 11 September in Solombal'skaia Harbor.

Taking stock of his voyages, Litke did not think that he had done everything that had to be done. He made plans for future expeditions to survey all of Novaia Zemlia with two ships "which could boldly go into the ice without subjecting themselves to any danger and which could remain for the winter wherever God saw fit.[43] If such an expedition were really to take place, the commanding officer, upon reaching the northeastern end of Novaia Zemlia, must not miss the opportunity to establish the existence of previously unknown lands northeast from this cape. Discovery of these islands or proof of their existence would be as important as description of the eastern shore of Novaia Zemlia."[44] The reader is well aware of the existence of the Central Kara Rise which stretches northeast and east from Cape Zhelaniia, and also the existence of the island of Vize and the northern islands of Severnaia Zemlia. The young mariner and scholar Litke wrote about the possibility of finding these lands nearly one hundred years before their discovery.

The voyages of the brig *Ketti* and Ivanov's detachment had been more successful than that of the *Novaia Zemlia*. Litke had maintained contact with Ivanov as long as that was possible.

Demidov arrived in Arkhangel'sk slightly earlier than Litke. In his report he wrote that from 19 June to 19 August he took soundings near the Terskii coast, paying special attention to the Orlovskie Spits, the banks near Sosnovets and the Tri Islands. As a result of the measurements by Domogatskii and Demidov in the White Sea, they charted eleven banks.

Portrait of F. P. Litke,
made in Arkhangel'sk on
4 December 1823
(the earliest known
picture of the scientist).

Ivanov's detachment described the mouth of the Pechora River; after determining its latitude in several places, he took various astronomical readings and compiled the first "Mercator Map of the Mouth of the Pechora River and Adjacent Shores." P. K. Pakhtusov made excellent astronomical readings, determining astro-points on Bolvanskii Nos, the Chernaia River, Medinskii Zavorot, Dolgii [Island], Iugorskii Shar, and Pustozersk village. Thus the mean latitude of Iugorskii Shar was 69°39' 35" 3, and its longitude, in the time measurement, was 4 hours 2 minutes 39.13 seconds from Greenwich. When on 5 February 1825 Ivanov reported his findings to Litke in St. Petersburg, he asked that Pakhtusov and Pogozin be rewarded because they "had conducted themselves well during the expedition and performed their assigned duties with enthusiasm." Litke sent Ivanov's report to the Government Admiralty Department and included the following: "Having examined these documents in detail, I have the honor to report to the Government Admiralty Department that Mr. Ivanov has fulfilled all the most important points of his instructions with exactitude."

The results of Litke's fourth expedition turned out to be very important: the western part of Novaia Zemlia was described; a detailed chart

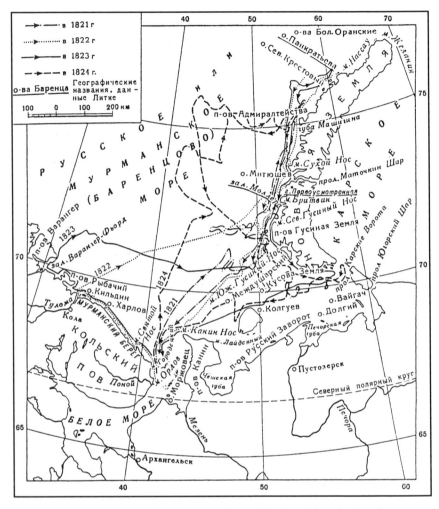

Chart of F. P. Litke's voyages aboard the brig Novaia Zemlia.

of the Murmansk coast was compiled; the White Sea channel and the mouth of the Pechora River were researched; significant hydrographic observations were made, which allowed definition of a series of laws concerning the conditions of the Barents Sea; a general picture was obtained of tidal phenomena of the White and Barents seas; and they obtained valuable data on air temperature at high latitudes and on ice

76

conditions. Finally, they made systematic observations of the inclination of the magnetic needle and declination of the compass, the results of which were very important for navigators.

ЧЕТЫРЕКРАТНОЕ ПУТЕШЕСТВІЕ

ВЪ СѢВЕРНЫЙ ЛЕДОВИТЫЙ ОКЕАНЪ,

совершенное по повелѣнію

ИМПЕРАТОРА АЛЕКСАНДРА I,

на военномъ бригѣ

НОВАЯ ЗЕМЛЯ,

въ 1821, 1822, 1823 и 1824 годахъ,

Флота Капитанъ - Лейтенантомъ

Ѳедоромъ Литке.

Съ присовокупленіемъ путешествій Лейтенанта Демидова въ Бѣлое море и Штурмана Иванова на рѣку Печору.

———— • ————

Une volonté forte et une persévérance active ne suffisent pas toujours pour surmonter les obstacles. A. Humboldt. Relation historique. Jntroduction. p. 7.

————

Издано по Высочайшему повелѣнію.

ЧАСТЬ ВТОРАЯ.

〰〰〰〰〰〰〰〰〰〰〰〰〰〰

САНКТПЕТЕРБУРГЪ.

Въ Морской Типографіи, 1828 года.

Title page of Litke's book Chetyrekratnoe puteshestvie v Severnyi Ledovityi Okean…[*Four voyages to the Arctic Ocean…*].

During these expeditions Litke proved himself to be an experienced sailor, a knowledgeable hydrographer, and a promising scholar-geographer. Thus it is not by chance that he was asked to head a fifth expedition to the Arctic Ocean. Even though Litke turned down the offer, he continue for a while to conduct all business concerning the expedition. Thus, in March of 1825 he suggested that the Pechora expedition be divided into a western and an eastern detachment, and over Ivanov's objections, got him assigned "to finish the descriptions of the Pechora River and Vaigach Island and the shores of Novaia Zemlia" (order No. 276 of 13 March, from the Admiralty Department, had Litke's name attached to it).

Having refused immediate participation in any further voyages to Novaia Zemlia, Litke asked to be assigned to the Admiralty Department so that he could work under G. A. Sarychev and bring his notes on the Novaia Zemlia expeditions together so that they could go to print. Litke recommended Mikhail Frantsevich Reineke (the future talented Russian hydrographer)[45] for continuation of the hydrographic study of the White and Barents seas. Headquarters concurred with Litke's wishes.

CITATATIONS AND NOTES

1. V. P. Bezobrazov, *Litke. Autobiography ...*, p. 95.

2. TsGADA, f. Gosarkhiv, r. 30, d. 54, l. 2 ob.–3.

3. Ibid., l. 3.

4. Ibid., l. 12.

5. Ibid., l. 7.

6. The subject is charts compiled as a result of surveys in 1798–1801 and published in 1806 under the leadership of L. I. Golenishchev-Kutuzov.

7. TsGADA, f. Gosarkhiv, r. 30, d. 54, l. 9 ob.

8. Ibid., l. 11.

9. This line ("by reason of the great negligence of the writers of those times") is in English in the original text.

10. F. P. Litke, *Chetyrekhkratnoe puteshestvie v Severnyi Ledovityi okean sovershennoe po poveleniiu imperatora Aleksandra I na voennom brige Novaia*

78

Zemlia v 1821, 1822, 1823 i 1824 [F. P. Litke's four voyages to the Arctic Ocean in 1821, 1822, 1823, and 1824], part 1 (St. Petersburg, 1828), p. 4. (Hereafter, F. P. Litke, *Chetyrekhkratnoe puteshestvie.*)

11. Ibid., pp. 118–119.

12. V. P. Bezobrazov, *Litke. Autobiography ...*, pp. 99–100.

13. TsGADA, f. Gosarkhiv, r. 30, d. 55, l. 89.

14. TsGADA, f. Gosarkhiv, r. 30, d. 57, l. 113.

15. Ibid., l. 76 ob.

16. Ibid., l. 115.

17. N. A. Chizhov (born either in 1799 or 1800, died in 1848), Decembrist, exiled to Yakutsk and Irkutsk provinces, then became a private in Tobol'sk (1826–1833). In 1843, he returned home to Tula province.

18. He died in 1882. Year of birth unknown.

19. F. P. Litke, *Chetyrekhkratnoe puteshestvie ...*, part 1, p. 178.

20. Ibid., p. 186.

21. Ibid., p. 193.

22. Ibid., p. 199.

23. TsGADA, f. Gosarkhiv, r. 30, d. 57, l. 133 ob.

24. TsGADA, f. Gosarkhiv, r. 30, d. 55, ch.1, l. 175–176.

25. It was first published in entirety in *Zapiskakh, izdavaemykh Gosudarstvennym Admiralteiskim departamentom otnosiashchikhsia k moreplavaniiu, naukam i slovesnosti* [Notes published by the Admiralty, dealing with navigation, science, and literature], part 5 (St. Petersburg, 1823, pp. xlii–li). The instructions for the officers assigned to describe the White Sea were also published here.

26. F. P. Likte, *Chetyrekhkratnoe puteshestvie ...*, part 1. p. 244.

27. Ibid., p. 306.

28. Ibid., p. 307.

29. Ibid.

30. Ibid., p. 309.

31. Ibid., p. 319.

32. *Zapiski, izdavaemye Gosudarstvennym Admiralteiskim departamentom ...*, part 6. (St. Petersburg, 1824), pp. xi–xii.

33. TsGADA, f. Gosarkhiv, r. 30, d. 55, ch. 1, l. 267 ob.–268.

34. F. P. Litke. *Chetyrekhkratnoe puteshestvie ...*, part 2 (St. Petersburg, 1823), p. 13.

35. Ibid., p. 32.

36. *Zapiski izdavaemye Gosudarstvennym Admiralteiskim departamentom ...*, part 7 (St. Petersburg, 1824), pp. ii–iv.

37. V. P. Bezobrazov, *Litke. Autobiography ...*, p. 103.

38. TsGADA, f. Gosarkhiv, r. 30, d. 55, ch. 1, l. 316–316 ob.

39. Navigator Twelfth Class I. N. Ivanov was born in 1784. He sailed abroad under Captain Ratmanov on the frigate *Legkii* in 1818. His assistant, Nikolai Rogozin, was born in 1803, also from the artisan class like his chief (TsGADA, f. Gosarkhiv, r. 30, d. 56, l. 65–67). Assistant navigator of sub-officer rank Petr Kuz'mich Pakhtusov also participated in the work of Ivanov's detachment; subsequently, he became a well-known explorer of Novaia Zemlia.

40. TsGADA, f. Gosarkhiv, r. 30, d. 56, l. 74.

41. Ibid., l. 168.

42. F. P. Litke, *Chetyrekhkratnoe puteshestvie ...*, part 2, p. 130.

43. Ibid., p. 141.

44. TsGADA, f. Gosarkhiv, r. 30, d. 56, l. 28 ob.

45. On M. F. Reineke (born 10 November 1801, died 17 April 1859), see: K. A. Bel'chenko, "M. F. Reineke, ego zhizn' i nauchnaia deiatel'nost' v oblasti gidrografii" [M. F. Reineke, his life and work in hydrography]. *Trudy Instituta istorii estestvoznaniia i tekhniki AN SSSR* vol. 37, vyp. 2, *Istoriia geologo-geograficheskikh nauk* (Moscow: AN SSSR, 1961), pp. 118–127.

* * *

a. The strait separating the northern from the southern island of Novaia Zemlia.—Ed.

b. A northern people; in the plural, Nentsy.—Trans.

SCIENTIFIC EXPLOITS

At the beginning of December, 1824, Litke arrived in St. Petersburg, where traces of the destructive flood that had occurred in November were still visible. He was deeply moved, but his impressions became especially real when he heard stories from his relations and friends about the trials of the citizens during the storm.

As soon as Litke arrived, he met with his friend Ferdinand Petrovich Wrangell, who had just returned from an expedition to the shores of the Arctic Ocean.[1] The friends rented a small apartment and divided their time between scientific pursuits and socializing. (Aleksandr Litke, who had been transferred to the Guards, lived with them.) They had a great deal to do. By decision of the Admiralty Department, Litke was to present for publication a full description of his travels to Novaia Zemlia. Wrangell was also working on a book about his own expedition.

Litke was now corresponding with many Russian scholars. He had an especially lively correspondence with Academician K. M. Ber,[a] who himself wanted to go to Novaia Zemlia and, as is known, later completed the trip, sailing with A. K. Tsivol'ka.[2] Satisfying Ber's curiosity concerning the results of the voyages, Litke wrote to him in June 1825 (Ber wrote in German, while Litke answered in Russian): "my voyages perhaps served somewhat to obtain precise knowledge of that region in respect to hydrography, but it was of no use for natural history since I could not stop in any one place for more than a few days and besides, I did not have a naturalist on board."[3] Later he set forth his opinions to Karl Ber concerning organization of a natural science expedition to Novaia Zemlia. These views, along with the latest interesting and entertaining stories by Tsivol'ka, laid the foundation of the program of Ber's expedition.

In the summer Litke and Wrangell moved out of town into a summer house on the bank of the Neva, not far from the Olenin summer home in Priiutino. After nine years of wandering, it was gratifying to feel the calmness and sweetness of a hot summer, the quiet of the Neva forests and the light waves of the beautiful Neva River. Litke's happiness was interrupted by the departure of Wrangell, who had been assigned command of the sloop *Krotkii,* which was sailing for Russian America. Fedor Matiushkin, their mutual friend from their voyage on the *Kamchatka,* was sailing with Wrangell. So was the navigator Prokopii Tarasovich Koz'min, a friend of Litke from the voyage on the *Kamchatka* and a companion of Wrangell and Matiushkin in their exploration of the northeastern coast of Siberia.

Litke found time to work on his "Four Voyages to Novaia Zemlia." In September he moved back into town, where he rented a room on Vasil'evskii Island in Marsh's house, opposite the Naval Corps. He worked diligently on his book and spent his free time at his sister's in the Sul'menev household. He could not put Novaia Zemlia out of his mind.

In the Admiralty Department on 30 November 1825, the academician V. K. Vishnevskii, who had taken the place of Shubert (now deceased), read Litke's memorandum on the necessity of a new, detailed description of Kol'skii Bay and several adjacent areas. Litke had looked into the matter of forming a small expedition with that aim. "One naval officer or a navigator, and two assistants," Litke wrote, "will take off for Kola in the winter, where, for a low price, they can hire two boats and the necessary number of workers for the summer. As soon as the water opens they are to begin their work; they will tie Kol'skii Bay in with a chain of triangulations and determine by chronometer the difference in latitude between Kola and Ekaterinskaia Harbor. After that, they are to form two detachments and go about making descriptions of Ura and Ara inlets—and finally, making the most exact readings possible of latitudes and longitudes by chronometer as well as by astronomical bearings and angles, they will determine both the geographical and the relative position of the northwest extremity of Kil'din Island, the southeast extremity of the Rybachii Peninsula, and Cape Pogan-Navolok. If any time remains, they will proceed in one boat to the head of Motovskii Inlet, cross the Volok [portage] between Titovskaia and Volokov inlets, and then proceed to the Pechenga River. We know by hearsay that the Pechenga is deep enough to accommodate large vessels; it only follows then that it should also have good harbors."[4]

The department approved Litke's suggestion and asked him to write up detailed instructions for an expedition to describe the Murmansk coast in general and, in 1826, Kol'skii Bay in particular. M. F. Reineke was assigned as head of the expedition.

Litke did not participate in the activities or the revolt of the Decembrists, although, as he himself wrote, he came off untouched only by chance, since he "was acquainted with many of the rebels, including the Bestuzhevs, close friends since childhood. In the winter of 1824–1825, Wrangell and I were often guests in their circles. Later we remembered that we alone did not end up as Decembrists. Never did they make the slightest attempt to draw us into their activities, except by allusion. Apparently they did not trust us. At that time, it was popular to blame the government; there was no other conversation among the young. It was somewhat chic to behave in such a manner and there were many occasions for it."[5]

Litke found out about the Decembrist revolt from his manservant. That whole memorable day Litke spent looking for his brother Aleksandr, who was serving in the Guards, which had sided with the Decembrists. Even though his brother did not participate in the revolt, he was deprived of the tsar's favors for the rest of his life.

In order to understand Litke's relationship to the Decembrists, we introduce here an excerpt from a letter he sent to Wrangell on 12 January 1826 (Wrangell was on a distant voyage at that time). Litke wrote that passions had just died down after the death of the tsar "when 14 December disclosed an unheard-of and terrible plot which, by the special mercy of Providence, was completely unsuccessful. One bubble of that pernicious thought, which had already been fermenting for several years, had to burst on that day from all the firing on Isaakiev Square. The plotters were all exposed and—good God! Whom do we see among them? I hope you can stand the shock, dear Ferdinand, when reading Bestuzhev's name, that singular man, that cream of the navy, pride and hope of a glorious family, idol of society, my friend of fifteen years."[6]

It was at that time, in the winter of 1825–1826, that the idea to organize an expedition arose in government circles. Its goal was to "describe in detail the previously described shores of northwestern America and Northeast Asia."[7]

Such an expedition was considered indispensable because in 1826 Russia concluded conventions with England and the United States[b] "on trade between their respective subjects, on navigation and fishing in the Pacific Ocean, and on the borders of mutual possessions on the Northwest Coast of America."[8] Along with this, it was also apparent that the vast Russian coast on the Pacific Ocean was not well researched and even less so were the ocean expanses and sea regions which bordered the continents of Asia and America. These areas were perforated in many places by the sharp spires of the Kuril and Aleutian islands as well as by the mountain ranges of the Shantar and Japanese islands, and mysterious Sakhalin.

The previous expeditions into this region by I. F. Kruzenshtern and Iu. F. Lisianskii (1803–1806), V. M. Golovnin (1807–1809, 1817–1819), M. P. Lazarev (1813–1816), O. E. Kotzebue (1815–1818), and M. N. Vasil'ev and G. S. Shishmarev (1819–1822) had accomplished much, but left many questions unanswered. Thus, Sakhalin Island remained an enigma and the problem of the Amur River had not been studied. As before, some parts of the Asian coast were poorly described, for example, the part north of Avacha Bay up to Cape Dezhnev. The shores of America, too, were poorly described, even though much had been done by officers and officials of the Russian-American Company (the voyages of N. A. Khvostov and G. I. Davydov, the explorations of I. F. Vasil'ev, and others). Hydrological, magnetic, and meteorological observations were made as the chance arose.

The commander of the sloop *Moller,* Captain Lieutenant M. N. Staniukovich, was named head of the expedition. The command of the sloop *Seniavin* was given to F. P. Litke. In a letter to Wrangell dated 1 March 1826, Litke stated that he already knew about his assignment and duties. He described the sloops *Moller* and *Seniavin* in detail and bid a long farewell to his friend. "My old and constant wish had come true," Litke wrote in his autobiography.

Nothing prevented Litke from going on such an alluring voyage. At this time he had completed all work on his book concerning his travels to Novaia Zemlia. He sent his book to the press of the Admiralty Department for printing. After Litke's departure, G. A. Sarychev wrote to A. V. Moller on this matter on 20 December 1826: "In a general meeting of the Admiralty Department on 1 May 1825, after deciding that a full description of the travels by Fleet Captain Lieutenant Litke, a respected member of this department who was in the Arctic Ocean four times, and also of the travels of Lieutenant Demidov in the White Sea and of navigator Ivanov on the Pechora River, would make a very interesting book, I assigned Mr. Litke to prepare such a description and to present it to the department for review and publication.

"After Captain Lieutenant Litke compiled the description, he submitted it to the department along with maps and drawings on 23 July 1826. After looking over his work, the department decided to print 1200 copies, out of which half would be turned over to the author, following the department's decree ... Because of the author's long absence, he has agreed to allow Rear Admiral Kruzenshtern to correct the maps and drawings while Department Head Eighth Class Nikol'skoi will proofread the descriptions of the voyages themselves."[9]

The sloops for the expedition were built at the Okhtenskie shipyards under the supervision of master shipbuilder Strok. On 14 May 1826, both sloops were launched. The length of the *Seniavin* reached 30 meters and the vessel had a displacement of nearly 300 tons. The sloop was armed with sixteen cannon and had good maneuvering ability. By comparison, the *Moller* sailed better and its living accommodations were more elegantly finished. The ships were brought to Kronstadt at the beginning of June for final preparation for the voyage.

Despite the fact that both sloops comprised a single expedition, which was officially led by a single leader, they have to be viewed as two independent scientific detachments. In completing the various tasks, they participated in separate voyages, the results of which naturally differed in many ways, especially in their scientific findings. M. N. Staniukovich's instructions were "to split up the expedition" as soon as they arrived at the Aleutian Islands (Unalaska Island), and Staniukovich was "to describe the shores of America and the islands lying near the mainland, while Captain Lieutenant Litke [is to describe] the Asiatic shores."[10]

According to his instructions,[11] Litke was to "describe the eastern lands of the Koriaks, the shores of Kamchatka (which up to now have not yet been described by anyone and are known only from the voyage of Captain Bering), the shores of the Sea of Okhotsk, and the Shantar Islands, which are known to us but have not been sufficiently described."[12] It was recommended that Litke begin his survey from Bering Strait and proceed south. On the way to East Cape (as Cape Dezhnev was then called) Litke was to describe St. Matthew Island, and while describing the eastern shores of Asia, he was to pay particular attention to Anadyrskii and Oliutorskii inlets. During the second year Litke was to describe the Sea of Okhotsk, including the Shantar Islands and

Sakhalin. During the winter Litke was to leave for the tropics, where his duties were to observe and describe the Caroline and Mariana islands and the Bonin Sima [Bonin] Islands.

In addition, G. A. Sarychev, with Litke's approval, gave him the following order: "1. In addition to the observations which you are supposed to make on such voyages, it is recommended that you make exact observations on the inclination and declination and deviation of the magnetic needle; for that purpose you are to stop in England and buy a Gilbert compass along with Professor Barlow's instrument. 2. In every place, if feasible, you are to observe the pendulum, and for that purpose you are to equip yourself in England with two or three instruments, including that of K. Kater [?], which is considered the best."[13]

In connection with decisions on equipping the expedition, many wrote to Litke with requests concerning the expedition's crew. Aleksei Spiridov asked that Midshipman Bodisko and Lieutenant Aboleshev be included; M. N. Vasil'ev recommended Midshipman A. L. Iunker, Lieutenant P. Naumov, and Navigator Twelfth Class V. E. Semenov; and N. I. Zavalishin himself addressed his old friend with a request to accompany him on the voyage. Litke very much wanted his brother Aleksandr to accompany him as he had earlier, but the Minister of the Navy, A. V. Moller, turned the request down because "the Guards are under the government's suspicion,"[14] and not yet recovered from the Decembrist revolt.

Finally Lieutenant Mikhail Aboleshev of the Thirty-seventh Detachment, Lieutenant Ivan Ratmanov of the Fourth Detachment, Midshipman Nikolai Butakov of the Sixth Detachment, Midshipman Gotlib Glazenap of the Second Detachment, Midshipman Pavel Kruzenshtern of the Guards (the son of the famous navigator Kruzenshtern), Lieutenant of the Corps of Fleet Navigators Vasilii Semenov, technicians of the Corps of Fleet Navigators Gavriil Nozikov and Dmitrii Orlov, and Doctor Andrei [Karl-Heinrich] Mertens were assigned to the *Seniavin*. The senior lieutenant on the ship was Nikolai Zavalishin. Naturalist Aleksandr Postels and artist-ornithologist Kittlitz also sailed on the *Seniavin*. Court Councilor Nikolai Prokof'evich Shcheglov, an esteemed member of the Naval Scientific Committee, wrote out instructions on the subjects of zoology, botany, mineralogy, and geodesy for the naturalists. In his instructions he stated: "So far nothing much is known about the Kuril and Shantar islands and Sakhalin, and therefore you are to gather everything possible. They say that on the southern Kuril Islands there exists one species of palm and that at the mouth of the Amur there are many bamboo bushes which are an obstacle to vessels trying to enter it. These stories must be checked for their authenticity."[15]

This testifies how little we knew about the [Russian] Far East at the time and what fairy tales were in circulation about it.

Aleksandr Postels, a graduate student at St. Petersburg University, was given the basic task of making observations on mineralogy and geognosy (geology). He also had a talent for sketching and was a very useful member of the expedition.

From the Minister of the Navy Litke received an order to help in every way possible the leader of the first Russian expedition to Brazil, Academician G. I. Langsdorf.

Thanks to Litke's efforts, the *Seniavin* was outfitted with a good library and the latest collection of maps. He had at his disposal the latest publications (books by Sarychev, Golovnin, Lisianskii, Davydov and Khvostov, Cook, Vancouver, and atlases of voyages). Litke also gathered copies of journals of the voyages of Shel'ting, Sindt, Khmetevskii, Shakhovskoi, Chaplin, and Fomin, which were undoubtedly a great help to him for a voyage to many places. Subsequently, he also acquired books from abroad.

The participants were anxious to sail into the Malyi Roads long before they had been equipped. "There is no other moment in sea travels that is more impatiently awaited by all without exception, and especially by the commander, than the trip from the harbor into the roads."[16] Thus Litke began his narrative of the *Seniavin* expedition. They sailed into the Malyi Roads on 4 August. Within ten days there was a ship's inspection and Litke was given permission to sail.

At midday on 20 August[c] the *Moller* and *Seniavin* weighed anchor. Along with them sailed many merchant vessels on their way to different parts of the world. Because of the fires that raged that burning summer on the southern shore of the Gulf of Finland, the air was heavy with smoke. They had to observe caution, keep an eye on what the merchant ships were doing, and execute their maneuvers as if they were sailing through fog. They carried on in such a manner until they reached Gogland Island.

When they passed the Tolbukhin lighthouse, Litke mustered his crew in formation on deck and addressed his men, wishing them a successful voyage and expressing his conviction that each sailor would uphold the honor of the flag of the Russian navy. Following that, he gathered the officers in his cabin and informed them of his views on disciplinary punishment. After reminding them that the crew was made up of chosen men, Litke told them to avoid the use of corporal punishment. "I am far from the thought of limiting your rights, granted to you by naval disciplinary regulations, under which you can punish guilty sailors by hitting them with a rope, but I am sure that you will agree with me that, because of our cultural development and progressive ideas about humanity, it is better not to use such primitive methods. As enlightened, humane leaders you will be able to find a civilized way of dealing with each guilty man. In the long run, this will be of more use to the service than coarse and humiliating punishment."[17] Jumping ahead, it must be stated that, during the entire voyage of the *Seniavin,* there was not a single incident of mistreatment of the sailors, unlike on the *Moller.*

On 26 August the sloops left the Gulf of Finland, and that night passed Cape Dagerort; accompanied by a fresh tailwind, they sailed quickly past the Baltic shores toward the southern straits. Everything was going smoothly until the winds changed, and a storm blew up. The sloops became separated and lost sight of each other. Not even ten days after beginning, the travelers got a taste of everything the sea has in store for those who dare to take it on. "At the beginning of a voyage, nothing is usually in place—everything falls and breaks, water leaks in, and the greater part of the crew is seasick. Even though these things are unpleasant, they have their advantages: the qualities of the ship are put to the test, many of its shortcomings are discovered and are corrected, and those unaccustomed to the sea become familiarized. After that, everyone looks at the vast field before him with calm and self-assurance."[18]

Everything ended well. On 6 September the *Seniavin* reached the southern cape of Gotland Island. From there they reached Copenhagen in two days, accompanied by still-strong east winds. Here they encountered the *Iezekiil'* and other ships on their way from Arkhangel'sk to Kronstadt; they were under the command of Captain Second Rank M. P. Lazarev, future hero of the Battle of Navarino. Litke sent letters, greetings, and official reports home with him.

Within three days the *Moller*, which had taken refuge from the storm in Arensburg Bay, behind Ezel' [Saaremaa] Island, arrived in Copenhagen. Its arrival delayed their joint departure for several days. For some reason, Staniukovich decided to supply his ship with rum in Copenhagen. On 15 September they finally sailed. The *Moller*, which moved better, sailed ahead and disappeared from the *Seniavin*'s sight when they entered the North Sea. Thanks to favorable winds the S*eniavin* reached the English shores within a week and within another few days was brought into the Spithead Roads. The pilot was the same man who, nine years earlier, had shown the way to Golovnin's *Kamchatka*. They found the recently arrived *Moller* already in the roads.

It was late fall, and they had to hurry to leave, but there was a great deal to do in London. Besides that, Litke had to make observations of the fixed pendulum at the Greenwich Observatory. English scientists and captains gave Litke active assistance in organizing this serious scientific experiment.

Litke returned to Portsmouth on 15 September. Loading of the sloop was in full swing. Everyone was impatient to sail as soon as possible, but they had to spend another week in loading and repairs. They could not very well leave without fresh water and spare anchors! Only on 22 September did the *Seniavin* leave the roads. The *Moller* had sailed somewhat earlier. When it had sailed by, Staniukovich yelled though the speaking trumpet that the *Moller* would wait at sea. But the *Seniavin* was parted from it for a long time, because, when they did get to sea, the *Moller* was no longer in sight.

By evening the last European lighthouses had vanished. The *Seniavin* found itself in the power of the Atlantic Ocean and a large swell which caused the sloop to pitch violently from side to side and simultaneously from stem to stern. But, knowing that the sloop was rapidly moving on course made the rocking less hateful. Accompanied by a strong wind, the sloop reached Tenerife Island, where it was to meet the *Moller*, in a very short time. At dawn on 2 November the sloop's crew saw the Santa Cruz Roads.

After the formalities associated with the arrival of a foreign ship in the roads, the naturalists were among the first to rush onto the island and soon disappeared into its interior. It became apparent that no one had seen the *Moller*. This worried Litke greatly because not long before their arrival a strong hurricane, unprecedented in these parts, had raged here, during which more than three hundred people had perished and many vessels had been wrecked. The wreckage of ten ships was found on one of the Canary Islands alone. Litke and his companions were extremely worried about the *Moller*'s fate.

Because of his worry, Litke decided to continue his voyage the next day, a choice which did not particularly please the naturalists. After the necessary visits to the governor and other officials, Litke strolled about town and saw traces of destruction all around: torn up roadways, destroyed streets and houses, the cries and laments of the inhabitants.

Soon after setting sail, the sloop encountered a period of dead winds. The swell, the lack of wind, and the forced general idleness wore on the crew and scientists for ten days. If Litke had not stopped at Tenerife, he would have managed to avoid this period as, they learned later, Staniukovich had done. Only on 15 November did the sailing somewhat pick up and after coming into a trade wind, the *Seniavin* quickly passed the Cape Verde Islands in rainy weather. Not far from the equator, however, they again encountered a period of dead wind which caused them to remain there for two weeks. It was extremely boring and the sailors suffered from the lack of wind and the tropical heat: "Every little cloud on the horizon was met with happiness, as a forerunner of wind, but it always disappeared, not bothering to defend us from the burning sun. The eternal emptiness around us aggravated the boredom of our situation: only rarely did a greedy shark and even more rarely a frigate bird or a petrel break the silence which reigned about us."[19]

But there was not a single sick man on board. This was due to the care shown by the commander, doctor, and officers. A strict routine, the right food, variety of occupations, and relaxation were all aimed at preserving the health of the sailors. Only on 13 December did the sailors manage to cross the equator. It had taken forty days from the Canary Islands. It seems that not a single ship, not a single one of Litke's predecessors, had ever taken longer on this route.

As they crossed the equator, Neptune, surrounded by a half-naked retinue, gaily appeared on deck. Loudly he asked the traditional questions and received satisfying answers. His retinue sprinkled water on all those crossing into the southern hemisphere for the first time. "That day was also remarkable for us," Litke wrote, "because of the unusual agitation of the sea which contrasted highly with the emptiness of the equator. Bonitas and albacores chased flying fish and sharks swam after the bonitas; large schools of flying fish jumped through the air while bonitas jumped after them, splashing on all sides, like the ricocheting shots during a sea battle."[20]

Sailing away from the equator again became monotonous, although the *Seniavin* now moved slightly faster. On 26 December they saw the entrance cape to the capital of Brazil and on the following day the sloop set anchor in the Bay of Rio de Janeiro, where the *Moller* had been waiting for ten days. It turned out that Staniukovich had decided to bypass the Canary Islands and thus avoided the hurricane and "beat" the crew of the *Seniavin.*

As in London, Litke spent much time in Rio de Janeiro making astronomical and magnetic observations, including observations of the fixed pendulum, in addition to preparing his sloop for the rest of the voyage. These observations were made from 1 to 4 January in Praia Grande on the northeastern end of Krys [?] Island in an enclosed area. The apparatus was placed on a brick foundation two feet above the ground. The results were satisfactory and, in the words of Academician Vishnevskii, "they attest to the outstanding zeal of this skillful officer. They are his first and rather successful experience in a new field which demands not only vigilant work but vast knowledge and great skill in observation."[21]

Naturally Litke at that time did not yet know about this flattering mention of his work. In his own words, he did not see anything in Brazil, met scarcely anyone, and only went to town twice on business. All that time in port, he was busy making observations and on 8 January he moved back aboard the ship. Within three days everything was ready for the voyage to continue.

Staniukovich decided to sail around Cape Horn, which is so famous for its storms and was so well remembered by Litke from his trip on the *Kamchatka.* This route was considered more dangerous than the one around the Cape of Good Hope, but it was undoubtedly the shorter of the two.

On 12 January the sloops sailed into the sea. A tailwind was blowing. The sloops traveled within sight of one another. The farther south they went, the more noticeable the wildlife became. The naturalists increased their collection of various species of fish, including flying fish. On 2 February they sailed past the Falkland Islands. On the following day they began their trip around the ill-famed Cape Horn. This time, too, it was true to its notoriety. The sailors encountered a harsh west wind with driving rain and heavy seas. Soon the sloops became separated. The *Moller* again pulled away. The sailors of the *Seniavin* grew somewhat anxious. They were suddenly alone amid a raging ocean, in sight of the gloomy extremity of the American continent.

For ten days the sloop was blown about near the cape, and only on 13 February did it manage to round it. But the weather remained as cold and icy as before. A storm would often pass over them, the rain changing to hail, and a thick fog enveloped them most of the time. Everyone on board froze. In his cabin, Litke was coldest of all. The temperature did not rise above five or six degrees, [Réaumur] but no one complained and no one got sick. The crew efficiently carried on its arduous naval duties.

Having gone around Tierra del Fuego, the *Seniavin* entered the waters of the Pacific Ocean. The captains had not agreed earlier on a meeting place should they become separated. Litke set a course for Concepcion Bay, as recommended in his instructions. It slowly grew warmer, calmer, and clearer. On 4 March the sloop met dawn not far from shore. According to Litke, "It [dawn] presented us with a spectacle of indescribable greatness and beauty—the jagged, sharp-peaked chain of the Andes strikingly lined the blue sky lit by the sun's first rays! I will not increase the number of those who have been lost in painstaking efforts to convey to others their feelings at the first sight of such pictures of nature. They are as inexplicable as the splendor of the sight itself. The abundance of colors, the gradual brightening of the sky and clouds with the rising of the sun, are all beyond comparison."[22]

Litke did not sail the sloop into the bay, but decided to go ashore in the ship's boats to find out about the *Moller*. By then, evening had come and they had to postpone their landing until the next morning. The naturalists, in their impatience to set foot on dry land after a long and, for them, generally unfruitful voyage, decided to go ashore that night. In the morning Midshipman Ratmanov was sent ashore and was followed later by Litke.

It became apparent that Staniukovich had not stopped here. According to the general instructions, Litke's sloop was to accompany the *Moller* to Russian America. Not losing a single moment, he set out for the next possible meeting place, Valparaiso. It goes without saying that the naturalists amicably but completely unsuccessfully attempted to attack Litke and to convince him to remain in the bay. After Brazil, this area seemed rather poor to the Russian sailors, but they all admired the people of this country, whom Litke called "the friendliest and gentlest people in the world." The inhabitants rendered the travelers all possible aid and assistance, but did it delicately, unobtrusively, and with a sense of personal dignity.

Leaving on 6 March in a calm south wind, they soon found themselves in a northeast squall; they lost the warp anchor they used at night. This occurrence caused them to lose two days. Only on the evening of 8 March did the sloop approach Valparaiso Harbor, but the fog prevented the *Seniavin* from entering. On the following day when the sloop sailed into the harbor, the first thing they saw was the *Moller,* which was weighing anchor and setting sail. It became apparent that it had already repaired all damage and resupplied itself in the twelve days it had been there. The meeting of the sloops was brief. The *Seniavin* continued to sail into the harbor while the *Moller* was entering the ocean.

First Litke visited the governor; then he accompanied the naturalists into town "but they soon dragged me into such a place that I could not go back or forward; I therefore left the naturalists with a companion and bid them to come home safe and sound, but as I was climbing down I thought that I would lose my own head a thousand times."[23] Then they looked over the Chilean admiralty and visited the fortress of San Antonio. In the city Litke met a friend from his Arkhangel'sk days, a Frenchman, who now occupied the post of French consul general in Peru.

Litke chose a convenient place at the edge of the suburb Almendral for making his astronomical and magnetic observations. The naturalists, too, were billeted there. Not far from here it was possible to take on a supply of water.

Preparation for continuation of the voyage went smoothly, and the observations were completed in a week's time. But Litke was in no hurry. He was counting on going straight to Russian America without any more stops, and for that reason he decided to give his crew a good rest and allow the naturalists time to make their observations.

The time was used to visit the city of Quillota, which lay fourteen miles northeast of Valparaiso. On 30 March the sailors went there along the shore and reached the mountains of Seven Sisters, which were covered with forest. From there they came out on a plain. This area was covered with sand and rocks, and there were few trees; the only thing that grew here was brambles. It was hot, dusty and stifling. They arrived in Quillota tired. But after a tasty meal at an Englishman's house and a rest in his shady garden, their fatigue lifted and the sailors went to look over the town.

The city is situated not far from the tallest mountain in South America—the Aconcagua, and thanks to the Concon River, it is "drowned" in luxuriant vegetation. As with most South American cities, it was well laid out. There was a large garden near each house. It is no wonder that the inhabitants of this city supplied Valparaiso with fruit.

The travelers appeared wild to the eyes of the local population, who brazenly looked them over and accompanied them wherever they went. They expressed particular curiosity at the sight of the artist sketching.

Around noon the following day the sailors returned to the Seniavin. Their route passed through Lima [Limache], where they took in the sights. Leaving Lima [Limache], their guide lost his way and only in the morning did the travelers returned to the sloop.

Their departure had to be postponed for two days due to the lack of fresh provisions. Taking advantage of this unforeseen chance, Litke described the city and port of Valparaiso in detail.

According to Litke, the city, situated in the mountains, is not without beauty. The two-storied houses with large verandas are made of brick and have flat roofs. The inhabitants do not build taller houses because of frequent earthquakes. The Russian sailors witnessed traces of the last earthquake (1823): buildings still lay in ruin everywhere and the fort of San Rosario was completely destroyed. Litke could not help but notice the depressed condition of the Chilean navy which consisted of one frigate and two brigs. To make up for it, the Russian sailors were fascinated by the passionate dances and songs they could see and hear in the city at night.

The Seniavin set sail on 3 April. Ahead of them lay an ocean voyage nearly a third of the earth's circumference in length. Litke was having second thoughts and was especially bothered by his late arrival at the place of his main work. His misgivings were not in vain. Spring was beginning in the northern hemisphere and the researchers' tasks for the summer were many. Litke wanted to think that the long haul would be quick and successful. But the start of the voyage did not herald anything good. They encountered a strong northeast headwind which held them at the same parallel as Valparaiso until 14 April. On that day the sloop finally met a trade wind and sailed north.

All during the voyage, the weather notwithstanding, they made regular observations of the magnetic needle, changes in air pressure, and conditions of the air and sea. They paid particular attention to astronomical determinations, without which one cannot sail in the open ocean. Litke set a course from 10° S latitude for the Sandwich Islands; no other sailor had yet followed this route. Litke hoped to discover new lands; in addition, it was important to make magnetic and other observations in this region.

But Litke's suppositions did not come true. There were no new islands in sight, no matter how hard the sailors stared into the void, hoping to get the reward set by Litke for the first man to yell "Land ho!" "The discovery of supposed islands, the existence of which I do not doubt despite our failure, awaits a much luckier navigator," Litke wrote.[24]

But for all that, Litke made successful magnetic observations in this region which were important for theories of the earth's magnetism. The *Seniavin* crossed the magnetic equator three times at various points, and established its position relative to the geographic equator. These direct magnetic observations reinforced the conclusion that the level of magnetic force is stronger in the Pacific Ocean than at the same latitudes in the Atlantic.

On 8 May the *Seniavin* crossed the geographic equator for a second time and entered the northern hemisphere. They were met with heavy rains, which allowed them to supply themselves with fresh water, wash their laundry, and wash themselves in fresh water, a luxury rare in the midst of the vast, salty ocean. The weather became overcast. The naturalists were dismayed with their visit to the tropics: the ocean for some reason was not rich in fish or marine animals. But as soon as they crossed the Tropic of Cancer on 27 May "many different sorts of marine worms began to appear, which interested not only the naturalists, who busied themselves with studying them, but also us, the laymen. The unusual variety of form and build, the grace of movement, beautiful colors and tints of these barely animate beings forces us to be surprised at the inexhaustiveness and even capriciousness of the creations of nature, even greater, perhaps, than in the elephant and hippopotamus."[25] Litke noticed that some of the marine animals, forming long, ribbon-like bands, were always arranged in a single direction in parallel lines, independent of the movement of the ship and the direction of the wind or waves. This indicated the presence of a current in this region.

Fort of Novo-Arkhangel'sk with the flag of the Russian-American Company.

The rest of the voyage was tranquil. According to Litke, he had never sailed so tranquilly in the ocean before. The *Seniavin* experienced no rocking at all. On 11 June, in the distance, they saw Mount Edgecumbe, which is used to orient entrance into Sitka. On the following day, the *Seniavin*, accompanied by a Russian pilot, sailed into the Sitka Roads, and anchored in the inner harbor of Novo-Arkhangel'sk. This is how Litke described his arrival:

> A navigator seeing the northwestern coast of America for the first time is impressed by its picturesque wildness. The high, peaked mountains covered with virgin forests from summit to foot drop steeply into the sea. Upon entering broad Sitka Sound, on the left is Mount Edgecumbe, an extinct volcano (2800 feet above sea level); on the right and straight ahead is a chain of islands close to the main shore. Everything appears

96

The Admiralty of Novo-Arkhangel'sk.
Ships of the Russian-American Company can be seen in the Sitka Roads.

quiet and wild. Nothing foreshadows his approach to the port. The launches and baidarkas that have appeared among the peaks and hurry toward him are his first hint of it. After passing this labyrinth of islands, the picture before him suddenly becomes lively: a Russian flag flies proudly above a fort situated on a high cliff; palisades with watchtowers surround the large house of the director, stores, and barracks; at the right is a church; farther along the shore is a series of houses and gardens; on the left is a shipyard and a large settlement of [Native] Americans; in the harbor and in the roadstead there are several ships, unloaded and rigged,[d] often including foreign ships; everything presents an orderly picture, one of activity, prosperity, a pleasant contrast to the gloomy picture presented by the surrounding nature.[26]

A scene from the Russian colony at Novo-Arkhangel'sk.

The inhabitants of Novo-Arkhangel'sk and the manager of Russian America, Captain Second Rank Petr Egorovich Chistiakov, welcomed the sailors warmly. Unfortunately, almost the entire male population had left on business and no one could help the sailors unload the sloop. They themselves unloaded the company cargo which lay at the very bottom of the hold and replaced it with thirty-five tons of rock ballast. They themselves repaired the sloop during their five-week stay, as well as carrying on with a multitude of other necessary activities.

Litke, his officers, and the naturalists occupied themselves with research activities. Postels, Mertens, and Kittlitz traveled about in baidarkas in the vicinity of Novo-Arkhangel'sk, while Litke labored over the magnetic and astronomical observations of which he was so fond. For the first time (in distinction from St. Petersburg, Greenwich, and even Valparaiso) the pendulum was set up in a tent and placed on three large stones dug into the earth (the rocky ground prevented piles from being driven for a foundation).

The mariners found time to look around Novo-Arkhangel'sk. It consisted of a fort, suburb, and a small settlement with a church. The

Novo-Arkhangel'sk, showing the church.

settlement had in all about twenty-five houses, which looked clean and well built. It appeared that the inhabitants were satisfied with their lot and that they were not lacking in the necessities for life and work. In the port could be counted fifteen ships with a water displacement of from 60 to 350 tons. At the local shipyard, which out of pride was called the Admiralty, new ships were being built. They even made ploughs and cast bells for churches and made copper vessels [dishes] for the local inhabitants. In a word, the Admiralty was simultaneously a factory, a workshop, and a shipyard.

Litke gathered quite a lot of material on the physical geography, ethnography and history of Novo-Arkhangel'sk. He set forth these accounts in articles which have great historical and geographical value. For the Russian and European readers of that time, this was sensational material, since little was then known about the distant Russian lands. It was thought that the area was dark, uncivilized and covered with impassable mud. Suddenly, Europe discovered that the other side of the world was growing and that a remarkable Russian colony was flourishing.

Interior of a Kolosh [Tlingit] dwelling near Sitka.

During his stay in Sitka, Litke did not relent in his meteorological and hydrological observations. In addition, he carried on a series of magnetic observations and astronomical readings. Through Chistiakov, he sent a report to St. Petersburg about his voyage from England to America. To his report, Litke appended his "Observations of the fixed pendulum, performed in Valparaiso and Novo-Arkhangel'sk; the conclusions from astronomical observations performed in Novo-Arkhangel'sk and conclusions from observations of the magnetic needle."[27]

On 19 July the *Seniavin* set sail on a course for Unalaska Island. There, Litke was supposed to take aboard baidarkas and Aleuts who had agreed to accompany the expedition to the tropics and to the northern part of the Bering Sea. At Chistiakov's request, the sloop carried a load of wheat to Unalaska.

Until 7 August they sailed primarily against the wind, handling the choppiness with difficulty. In order to gain time, Litke sailed to the island by taking a shortcut, not via Unimak Pass, but instead via

Housing on Unalaska.

dangerous, narrow Unalga Pass. On the evening of 8 August, the *Seniavin* approached the entrance of the strait. In the morning they were enveloped by a thick fog, a strong wind pressed the sloop toward shore, and the barometer continued to fall. To remain here was impossible— the sloop would have been thrown on the rocks. It was just as complicated and dangerous to enter the strait under the prevailing conditions, but that is what Litke decided to do.

At times it seemed that the sloop was being carried directly into the breakers on shore. But by some sailor's instinct, Litke avoided catastrophe and maneuvered the *Seniavin* into the quiet waters of the strait. The sloop entered Captains Harbor towed by large baidaras, and was welcomed with a salute from the settlement of Iliuliuk. It anchored near the island of Amaknak. Litke did not want to stay in Iliuliuk very long. He made his observations in a very short time, the wheat was unloaded, and the Aleuts with one baidara [*sic*] came on board. Everything was ready for them to sail. However, a fresh northwest wind began to blow and ruined their plans. They had to wait for a favorable wind.

During this forced inactivity, the naturalists and Litke became well acquainted with the island and Captains Harbor. The harbor was named in honor of Captain Lieutenant M. D. Levashev, a member of P. K. Krenitsyn's expedition who had wintered here in 1768–1769. The priest Innokentii [Ivan] Veniaminov proved to be a good guide [for Litke], not only with regard to Unalaska and the Fox Islands, but for the whole Aleutian chain. This man, successfully mixing propagation of the Christian faith with study of the natural sciences, had an excellent knowledge of the customs, language, and life of the Aleuts, garnered during his long stay on those islands.

On 19 August the *Seniavin* left Captains Harbor with a tailwind, bound for the Pribilof Islands and St. Matthew Island. On the following morning the travelers were admiring the wonderful view of the high volcanoes of Unimak Island. The conical Shishaldin volcano especially stood out among them. A light white smoke rose from its peak. They sailed by Akutan, and on the morning of 21 August Litke made out one of the Pribilof Islands, the island of St. George. It had a completely flat surface with one single hill. After a cannon shot from the *Seniavin*, two baidarkas were sent from shore. Riazantsev, who had been running the island for more than twenty years, came on board. He told the navigators many stories and spoke warmly of Baranov. Litke was very pleased with the order of things in the Russian-American Company. "Never overlook anything and be ready for everything was Baranov's rule; the spirit of this unusual man still, it seems, watches over the establishments he founded."[28]

These islands (St. George and St. Paul) were discovered by navigator G. L. Pribylov aboard the vessel *Sv. Georgii* [*St. George*] in 1786. Since that time they have been known as excellent fur seal rookeries. In two years, Pribylov procured more than two thousand sea otters, forty thousand fur seals, and six thousand blue arctic fox on the islands. But then there began a mass slaughter of animals. Litke brings up a striking example of such wasteful, criminal behavior in the fur hunt. In 1803 there was an accumulation of eight hundred thousand fur seal skins on Unalaska which had been badly prepared and remained unsent to Okhotsk (they simply had not had the time!). They decided to destroy (burn and cast into the water) nearly seven hundred thousand skins in order to keep the market price from falling.

Petropavlovsk, Kamchatka, second half of the eighteenth century.

Litke did not manage to stop at St. Paul due to a wind which the *Seniavin* weathered out at sea. On 25 August the sloop approached St. Matthew Island. This island had been discovered as early as 1766 by Lieutenant I. Sindt, but it had not been studied or described. It was no wonder, for approaches to the island were very difficult. The naturalists of the *Seniavin* also failed to get ashore there during the week spent in surveying the island. The survey was conducted from the vessel. The mariners obtained some information about the island from promyshlenniks who had once lived there.

Fall came. At the beginning of September Litke had to put a visit to Bering Strait out of his mind. Strong winds turning to storms became frequent at sea. Wind velocities varied, but the winds all blew in an easterly direction. Therefore, Litke set course directly for Kamchatka. On the way, they looked over Bering Island with the aim of finding a suitable place for landing some Aleuts the following year.

The *Seniavin* set a course for Avacha Bay. By the evening of 12 September they saw Maiachnyi Cape. "It had just become dark and

Houses of Kamchatka.

lights were being lit on Maiachnyi Cape and on another cape inside the bay so that even at night we could very easily have sailed into it, had the wind been favorable. Sailing from Europe to such places, where a navigator finds safety only in his own caution, it was pleasant to encounter an establishment which was solicitous of his peace of mind."[29] In the morning the sloop entered Avacha Bay and anchored in Petropavlovsk Harbor.

Voluminous mail awaited Litke and his crew. In particular, I. F. Kruzenshtern related how glad he was of his son's work on the *Seniavin*. Further, he wrote Litke that "the arrangements for the publication of your book have long since come to an end; Appolon Aleksandrovich (Nikol'skii) will notify you of this himself. At this time the money for printing your book has not yet been received and that is why it has not been published yet." After opening Nikol'skii's letter, Litke became convinced that the printing of his book was being delayed solely for monetary reasons: "Can you believe it? Your book has not been published yet," Nikolskii wrote. "Despite Kruzenshtern's efforts and care and my frequent requests to the cabinet, the money is not yet allocated,

Catching birds in Kamchatka.

and it will not be paid out in one lump sum, but in two equal payments."[30] From these and other letters Litke learned that Sarychev had been promoted to commander of Kronstadt Port, and that Ivan Savvich Sul'menev's father had died. Mikhail Frantsevich Reineke wrote regularly to Litke on the progress of hydrographic work in the Barents Sea.

The *Seniavin* remained in Petropavlovsk Harbor until 19 October and set to sea when the Kamchatkan shores were already covered with snow. The sailors had spent a pleasant time ashore in the company of soldiers and cossacks from the Kamchatka garrison. The naturalists made frequent trips to the surrounding areas; the officers did not forget their duties in regard to the ladies, and the first chance they had they waltzed at evening parties organized by the commandant of Kamchatka. In a word, there was work and entertainment enough for all. From Petropavlovsk Litke sent a report to the Admiralty Department concerning his voyage from Novo-Arkhangel'sk to Kamchatka and a general report about the progress of his expedition, the condition of his crew and ship. He also forwarded all the personal letters to St. Petersburg.

The *Seniavin* set a course for the Caroline Islands. But first Litke wanted to visit the island of Iualan [Kosrae] and make observations of

Inhabitants of the island of Pouynipet [Ponape], with their boats.[e]

his pendulum there. On the way, he decided to check the accuracy of the coordinates of Colunas Island—according to mariners, it was supposed to be in the vicinity of latitude 28°9', longitude 128°. The island was not even near those coordinates.

On 10 November the *Seniavin* crossed the Tropic of Cancer. Thereafter the explorers looked over the Brown [Enewetak] Islands. They were all of coral origin. Soon Iualan appeared on the horizon.

A calm prevented the sloop from approaching the island right away. Soon, however, the island's inhabitants came out toward the *Seniavin* in boats. The mariners greeted the friendly islanders well. The inhabitants willingly showed them how best to enter La Coquille harbor. Due to rain, fog and headwinds, however, the *Seniavin* did not enter the harbor until 27 November.

On shore the Russian sailors were received quite hospitably. The travelers and the islanders immediately established friendly relations. And when Litke went ashore to find a suitable place to make his pendulum observations, the inhabitants offered their advice. Finally, Litke chose the small island of Matanial. Because of an excessive

On Iualan [Kosrae] Island. On the shore one can see the tent used for pendulum observations, surrounded by a boarding net.

display of curiosity on the part of the islanders, the area where the observations were taking place was surrounded with a boarding net. Two tall sailors guarded the net. These measures were not excessive— the excessively curious islanders were interested in literally everything concerning the white travelers. By custom, Litke became brother of one of their chiefs, Nena, and received his name. From then on Litke was Nena to the islanders, and the iuros' (chief) was now called Litske (Litke).

After completing his pendulum observations and astronomical determinations, Like made several excursions on Iualan and the surrounding islets. On 14 December Litke, Mertens, Postels, Ratmanov, and Kruzenshtern, along with three sailors and an Aleut, took a trip to the island of Lella [Lele]. They were also accompanied by local inhabitants who carried their instruments and other baggage.

At first they walked along the shore on the northern side of the island. The shore was sandy and broken by many shallow lagoons. On the way, the researchers conducted a survey, sketched the surrounding countryside and hunted wildlife. At dusk they saw the island of Lella. The

Map of Iualan [Kosrae] Island, based on the survey of N. I. Zavalishin.

inhabitants were already waiting on shore to take them by boat to the island itself. There Litke and his companions met the local chief, Sipe, who greeted them politely and led them to rest in a separate hut. In the morning Litke visited the head chief and then began going around the lagoon. He was surprised that nearly the whole shore was protected by high breakwaters. "We were astonished by the large size of the stones in the walls: some about four feet in all dimensions, and thus containing no less than sixty cubic feet of material, and weighing no less than 150 puds," Litke wrote. "We could not understand by what means the inhabitants could have lifted such large stones to a height of five to six feet. Many of the uninhabited islands are surrounded by such walls. The canals crossing the middle of the island in various directions were also especially remarkable. At first the canals were just ordinary streams between the mangroves, but the inhabitants later reinforced their banks with stone walls and thus turned them into real canals three to four feet deep; these canals now greatly facilitate communication."[31]

After spending several days on the island the travelers returned via one of the canals to the *Seniavin*. They had to ready the sloop for the continuation of their voyage. Once on the sloop, Litke sailed around the island once more, lay to near the island of Lella, and for the last time exchanged presents and farewells with the hospitable inhabitants. On 22 December the mariners "finally left this interesting island, which had left us such pleasant memories."

In order to determine the intersection point of the magnetic equator and the meridian of the island of Iualan, Litke held a course south for some time. After finishing his observations, he turned the sloop north again and began his description of the Caroline Archipelago. In order not to miss any of the islands, Litke would stop sailing for the night. Only once did he break this rule, and the *Seniavin* calmly sailed all night in places where three navigators had already sailed before Litke, and where there probably was nothing new to describe. "All night long we sailed calmly under light sail and at dawn we saw before us an elevated piece of land. We could hardly believe our eyes; such an interesting discovery had seemed to us to be unrealizable."[32]

The island appeared tall. As it was later found out, this was the highest and largest of the Caroline Islands. It was surrounded by coral reefs and thickly covered with luxuriant groves of coconut palms. The islanders here were not friendly. They were not at all like the inhabitants of Iualan and spoke a different language. They were open about their dislike of travelers. The first of the islanders who bravely stepped on board fell upon Litke and began to take his sextant away. Litke nonetheless decided to send a ship's boat ashore with Zavalishin as the leader of the party. The natives fell on the crew, but thanks to Zavalishin's decisive actions (as one of the natives threw a javelin at them, he fired above their heads) it avoided any unpleasantness. Taking advantage of the confusion among the attackers, the sailors pulled hard at their oars and safely reached the sloop accompanied by threatening yells of the natives and the summoning calls of Triton's horn.

After such a reception, the sailors did not try to anchor near this island and continued to sail west and north along its shore. On the way the navigators encountered several small coral lagoons, so shallow that trees seemed to grow out of them. When the *Seniavin* approached the northern side of the island, Litke decided to try again to find a suitable place to harbor. With this aim he sent two ship's boats ashore with Zavalishin and Ratmanov. For greater safety, a falconet was mounted on one of the boats.

They found a small bay suitable for anchorage, but the sailors were not even able to enter it. They were soon surrounded by native boats which had been waiting in ambush up to that time. With great difficulty, the ship's boats returned to the *Seniavin*. Individual shots from the boats and from the cannon of the *Seniavin* made no impression on the natives. Of course, a decision to teach them a lesson about the strength of firearms could have been taken, but "I considered such a measure too cruel and was ready to give up the pleasure of setting foot on this island rather than buy that pleasure at the cost of not only the islanders' blood but, in all likelihood, the blood of our people as well,"[33] Litke remarked on this occasion. The angered sailors baptized this convenient bay the Port of Bad Reception.

Later, in a new place, Litke again tried to send a boat ashore, but this area did not have a good anchorage. Thus ended the description of the largest of the group of islands discovered, without them being able to set foot on shore.

This island was nearly fifty miles in circumference and was completely covered with vegetation which hid the habitations of the natives from view. The island's inhabitants differed from the inhabitants of Iualan not only in their behavior, but also in appearance. They had flat faces, thick lips, protruding eyes, and curly hair—all of these features made them akin to the Papuans. The mariners had seen only slings and spears or javelins. Apparently, these were their only arms. Litke supposed that they had not yet become acquainted with Europeans.

Again Litke sent a ship's boat to that island after they had described the surrounding smaller islands. This time they were greeted by a friendly and sensible bunch of islanders. They approached the *Seniavin* in two large boats and shared their knowledge about the islands. In particular, they told the mariners the names of almost all the islands. The largest was named Pyinipet [Ponape]. Litke named the entire group of islands in honor of Admiral Dmitrii Nikolaevich Seniavin [the Senyavin Islands].

After that the *Seniavin* continued its voyage among the Carolines. During this time Litke tried to describe and more correctly chart the islands already known to mariners. On 13 January the *Seniavin* approached the Lugunor [Lukunor] Islands. The explorers counted eight islands. The islanders gave the *Seniavin*'s sailors a warm reception. They came on board the ship willingly and without fear, accepted gifts, exchanged coconuts and chickens for axes and nails, and invited the sailors ashore as guests. They answered quite sensibly the questions put to them. From conversations with the local inhabitants, the travelers were able to find out in detail about the relative locations of the islands.

Constantly tacking among the reefs, Litke looked for a suitable place to anchor. On 22 January, in calm winds, the *Seniavin* was towed beyond the reefs and anchored at the island of Lugunor. The deck was soon filled with noisy Lugunor inhabitants. The mariners continued to gather information about the islands. The islanders tried to help in every way. One of them, an old man, not only named for Litke all the islands he knew of the Caroline Archipelago but even drew them on a piece of board with chalk. Another old man, who had traveled much in the archipelago, corrected the drawing in places. Litke redrew this original chart and later used it often in his survey.

The officers of the sloop made a careful description of Lugunor. They named its concave part Chamisso Harbor. Litke, of course, carried on astronomical and magnetic observations, and when he had finished, took a small trip about the island. The island made quite an impression on him. He noticed that the abundant coconut palms and breadfruit trees made the life of the islanders self-sufficient. "One becomes lost in astonishment," he later wrote, "at the wisdom with which Mother Nature supplied man with two trees which furnish not only drink and food, but also all the necessary materials for houses, boats, clothing, household utensils, etc. And in them you can also protect yourself from the vertical rays of the sun and breathe cool air."[34]

The hospitable inhabitants invited the travelers to their huts and readily showed their rooms and decorations. But they did not allow the sailors anywhere near the fair sex. "If we were inclined toward malicious gossip," Litke remarked, "then we could note that it is apparent that the men here have been taught by experience that their wives' chastity is safe only behind the protection of shields and matting, and that to keep peace in the house it is best not to subject it to temptation."[35]

The inhabitants of Lugunor were taller than average, their skin was chestnut colored, and their faces were flat with broad, turned-up noses and thick, protruding lips. On their shoulders they wore cloaks like raincoats which covered their heavily tattooed bodies. They were all distinguished by an unusual agility and liveliness. The sailors observed with curiosity and admiration how quickly the islanders climbed palm trees which were up to eighty feet tall. Sailors experienced in climbing the shrouds could not catch up with the islanders. The mariners were quite interested in the boats used by the inhabitants for very distant trips. These boats with a beam—a counterweight—held well on the water, carried much cargo, and in general were distinguished by their lightness and durability.

On 27 January the sloop weighed anchor and set sail. On exiting the lagoon, they encountered a three-masted vessel, an English whaler. Its captain visited the *Seniavin* and told Litke about his voyage. Toward evening the Russian officers returned the visit. They became acquainted with the ways and means of whaling and the equipment on board.

After that the mariners continued their observations. Within a short time they concluded their description of the Namoluk Islands, and observed and described the high and dangerous island of Rug [Truk], which is surrounded by low-lying islets. The Russian sailors also became acquainted with the natural environment and inhabitants of the beautiful and picturesque group of Namonuito Islands.

On the evening of 14 February they saw the island of Guam. On the following morning the sloop, in a calm wind, entered the harbor without a pilot. The forts of Santa Cruz and Santiago seemed dead: no flags could be seen, pilots did not meet the sloop. The governor of the island was a certain Medinilia,[f] with whom Golovnin and Kotzebue had met and whom Litke knew and remembered well. Several days were spent writing letters to him in order to get permission to investigate the island.

113

Litke did not waste much time and managed to locate a suitable place ashore in which to carry out his pendulum observations. The area was located on the southern shore of the harbor La Coldera de Aira [Apra] on the Orore [Orote] Peninsula at Sume's [Sumay's] farm. Here, too, he had to emplace his instruments on coral sand, on piles in a tent.[36]

On Sunday, 19 February, Litke and a group of officers visited the capital Agaña and dropped by for an official visit to the governor. The governor received the Russian mariners in a friendly manner on the palace veranda and promised to help them in any way he could. After an abundant dinner at the governor's, the officers of the *Seniavin* went for a walk through town. Litke visited the traveler and naturalist Don Luis Torres. A friendly conversation took place between the two scholars. Torres related to Litke many interesting facts about the natural environment and inhabitants of the Caroline Islands. After their walk, the Russian mariners went to see the cockfights which were so popular on the island.

On the following day Litke began his magnetic and pendulum observations. Meanwhile on the sloop, the sailors made repairs, and resupplied with provisions and fresh water. The naturalists roamed the island, climbed the hills and cliffs, bartered with the inhabitants for small artifacts, and described and made drawings of the local flora and fauna.

Litke concluded his observations on 4 March. He would have finished earlier if it had not been for unfortunate happenings which had dire consequences. One of his assistants, wishing to dry out the notes which contained the results of his observations, placed them too close to the candles and the notes burned up. Litke therefore had to spend several days in repeating his observations. This was not the only misfortune, however. While on an evening hunt, the commander of the sloop accidentally shot himself in the right arm at the elbow. For a month and a half Litke could not write, and he had to rely on his memory and the log book to make notes in his diary.

On 7 March the governor visited the sloop. Because of his wound, Litke was unable to give him an official reception, but the *Seniavin* greeted and saw off its guest with the prescribed salute. After the visit by the governor of Guam, the sloop left this island.

The mariners held a course toward the islands which had not yet been investigated or described. They soon put the Swede [*Shved*] Islands (consisting of three groups of islands) on the map. On one of them—the eastern group of islands, Zlato [Elato]—the mariners became acquainted with the local inhabitants. According to Litke, they differed from the population of the other islands because of their well-proportioned bodies. But for some reason the inhabitants of Zlato [Elato] were very hungry and constantly asked for food.

From here the researchers moved to the Uleai [Woleai] group of islands and described the Farrolaip [Faraulep] Islands on the way. Litke decided to make magnetic observations on this island. Zavalishin located a suitable place. Accompanied by a large number of local boats, the sloop entered the lagoon and anchored across from the northern end of the island of Raur. Now Vasilii Semenov exclusively made the astronomical observations while Dmitrii Orlov, under Litke's supervision, made magnetic observations.

The inhabitants of Uleai turned out to be not as hospitable as those of Lugunor and Guam. They knew the price of goods very well. Even the boys, who gathered sea urchins and other animals for Mertens, demanded payment. But for all that, they did not hinder the mariners in their work, hunting, and observations. They gladly sold and exchanged everything they could for things made of iron. Litke exchanged an axe for a small boat, and for three axes he got a large boat and full gear.

The basic work of the descriptions rested on the shoulders of Zavalishin, Semenov, Nozikov, and Orlov. In a short time they described the entire group of twenty-two islands of coral origin. These low-lying lagoon-type islands were all of the same form, horseshoe-shaped, and were distinguished by rich, tropical vegetation. Only Uleai [Woleai] Island was an exception to this standard. Its shape did not resemble a horseshoe. It occupied a large area and had a hilly surface. The breadfruit trees and coconut palms were no more common here than on the other islands, but on Uleai they were taller and bore more fruit.

The *Seniavin* remained in the Caroline Archipelago until 3 April, when, having implemented in full the Admiralty Department's orders, the expedition sailed to its native northern lands. At first the weather was conducive to sailing: it was warm, a light wind blew, the ocean was calm. But in the middle of April, the weather became noticeably colder—the temperature did not rise above 17° [Réaumur]. Clouds hung over the ocean and the air became damp. At times it rained and a dank wind blew.

On 19 April the *Seniavin* was in the region of the Bonin Sima [Bonin] Islands. Captain Beechey, who had sailed in this area on the sloop *Blossom*, had already described these islands in 1827. Therefore Litke decided to limit himself to physical geographical investigations of this region and to make astronomical determinations and magnetic observations.

The sloop sailed into the harbor which Beechey had named Port Lloyd. The mariners became acquainted with the shelter built by English sailors who had saved themselves after their whaling ship was wrecked. This was the only dwelling on the island. Here they also admired a large herd of pigs. These new Robinson Crusoes showed the Russian sailors their two-year-old haven with great zeal and led them about the island.

Litke placed his observatory in Pendulum Bay. He carried on his observations in a tent. He placed his instruments on an even, firm basalt foundation. Around the tent were tall trees, thanks to which the air temperature did not drastically change. Meanwhile on the sloop, the sailors repaired damage and fixed newly found leaks. Ratmanov and Zavalishin described the harbor. The English sailors moved aboard the ship. Later one of them, Peterson, entered the service of the Russian-American Company while another remained on the *Seniavin* as far as London.

On 3 May, after finishing all their work in Port Lloyd and having examined two more groups of islands of the Bonin Sima Archipelago, the travelers sailed for Kamchatka. A tailwind blew and the sloop made good speed. On 23 May the shores of Kamchatka appeared in the distance. All evening the mariners admired the wonderful view of the Kamchatkan volcanoes which were sharply silhouetted against the setting sun's rays. On 1 June they anchored in Petropavlovsk Harbor.

Mail was waiting for everyone. A. A. Nikol'skii wrote Litke about the reforms in naval circles. He wrote that from 1 October 1827, "an Admiralty Council, under the chairmanship of the minister or chief of staff, would take the place of the [Admiralty] College. Its members would be: the Hydrographer General (G. A. Sarychev), the Commissary General (V. M. Golovnin), the General On Duty (M. I. Ratmanov), I. F. Kruzenshtern, F. F. Bellinsgauzen, and G. Ia. Machkov. Out of the Admiralty Department (may it rest in peace!) were formed (it goes without saying that the number of officials has increased) the Administration of the Hydrographer General and a Scientific Committee. Besides having a chairman (L. I. Golenishchev-Kutuzov—A. A.), the committee has four permanent members: Kruzenshtern, Bellinsgauzen, Golovnin, and A. S. Nikol'skii."[37] He also informed Litke that his book was finally going to press. Litke was also quite pleased to hear that he had been chosen as honorary member of the Naval Scientific Committee.

They began preparations for the continuation of their voyage. The preparation of letters and preliminary accounts, the loading of flour and baking of bread, and replenishment of supplies took two weeks. In addition, Litke had to bid farewell to his experienced assistant and friend, Lieutenant Nikolai Irinarkhovich Zavalishin, who, on the doctor's advice, had to return to Russia. Along with him Litke sent Sarychev exerpts from his astronomical and physical observations, and a very detailed report of his voyage to the Carolines, to which he appended "sixteen sheets of Mercator maps and plans and five sheets with drawings of them." Skipping ahead, we will say that when Sarychev had received and studied these materials, he immediately requested (No. 2186 of 1 November 1828) that A. V. Moller reward the officers of the *Seniavin* for their excellent survey. Baron Kittlitz remained behind on Kamchatka temporarily. He considered it much more useful and interesting to make several trips about the peninsula itself than to sail into fruitless northern regions.

On 15 June the *Seniavin* was again at sea. Now it was headed north to the far shores of Chukotka and Bering Strait. Visibility was excellent and their descriptions were made in a short time. Navigators Semenov, Orlov, and Nozikov and officers Ratmanov and Aboleshev, who became senior officer of the sloop after Zavalishin's departure, worked especially hard. Taking advantage of the excellent visibility, Litke decided to determine as precisely as possible the coordinates of the most important capes and volcanoes, to tie them together, and later make a detailed description of these regions.

The visibility was so excellent that the sailors could see Avachinskaia, Koriakskaia, Zhupanov, and Kronotskaia volcanoes all at the same time. The peak of the latter was covered with snow. Litke carefully determined its height—3,372.9 meters. On the following day they could see the enormous Kliuchevskaia volcano. Its height equaled 4,402 meters. Litke determined its position. Drawings of the coastal features were made, along with navigational notes. On 22 June they could see Karaginskii Island.

Litke sailed the *Seniavin* into the strait in order to observe the western shore of this as yet undescribed island. As soon as it became dark, they anchored at the very entrance of the strait. In the morning, Ratmanov went to look for a bay about which he had heard from sailors in Petropavlovsk. Litke and the naturalists went ashore. "This part of the island forms a spit," he later recalled. "It is covered with dry tundra, alder bushes, and rather rich vegetation. A deep and rapid stream, shallow at the mouth, winds along this tundra. We encountered a multitude of geese, ducks, and snipes on its banks, but to our surprise, they were so wild that our hunters were not very lucky."[38] They had better luck on the cliffs, near the seashore bird colonies. The travelers saw traces of bear and red fox.

Litke set up on the island for observations, but "clouds of mosquitoes made work most unbearable. During astronomical observations, two men constantly had to whip my face and hands with branches. The magnetic observations could only be carried out by making a fire out of brush and turf inside the tent so that the acrid smoke drove out the insects and sometimes the researcher himself."[39] The observations were also made difficult by unusually strong refraction.

On the following day around noon Ratmanov returned and reported that he was unable to locate any bay within twenty miles. It became clear that Karaginskii Island was much larger than navigators had supposed up to that time and depicted on charts. Litke decided to sail farther into the strait. After weighing anchor the travelers spent the entire day describing the strait, tacking from shore to shore. Toward evening they saw a large spit which indicated the presence of the mouth of the Karaga River. They anchored nearby and in the morning Midshipman Ratmanov and navigator Semenov went off to describe the river's mouth. Meanwhile the sailors spent their time catching fish. They had a bountiful catch. They not only had enough fresh fish for the entire crew, but even salted several barrels of it. They caught mostly humpbacked salmon, flounder, and other salmon.

Boats with officers were sent out daily from the sloop in order to describe the coast. A chart of the whole western shore of the island and the adjacent mainland coast was made. The weather was favorable for hydrographic work. By the evening of 3 July Semenov reached the

Chukchi.

northeast end, which he had already reached from the southwest. Thus it was the first time that the description of such a large island was made.

Then the sloop set a course for Verkhoturskii Island. It was thought to be located five miles from Karaginskii Island, but it turned out that the distance was ten times as far. They approached the island at night, and until morning admired a totally effective spectacle—a forest fire, of unknown cause, raged on the mainland opposite Verkhoturskii Island. According to Litke, "a large portion of the forest which covered the nearby mainland shore was in flames: the streams of fire darted quickly in all directions along the resinous bushes. Sometimes the flames swirled upward, sometimes it appeared as a straight row of fires, quite like artificial lighting."[40] In the morning they made a description of this small island, which was nearly eight miles in circumference. The southern and eastern sides of the island were steep. The others had low-lying features. In some places on the shore they found the remains of yurts and shacks, but encountered no inhabitants at all.

From here Litke sailed for Oliutorskii Cape, hoping to finish his observations there quickly. But the weather suddenly changed. Winds began to blow and a storm brewed, bringing darkness, fog, and overcast skies. In order to continue hydrographic work, Litke decided to sail to Cape Chukotka (Cape Dezhnev).

The *Seniavin* sailed in fog, which rarely lifted. When it did, rain took its place. Then, as the sun shone through a gap, they saw the shore. Through the openings in the fog, the sailors saw the mountains on St. Lawrence Island. On the morning of 15 July they discovered that they were in the midst of a large, unknown archipelago. Their misunderstanding dispersed with the fog. It seems that they had mistaken the mountains and prominent capes of both America and Asia (including the islands of Bering Strait) for an archipelago.

As soon as they became aware of that fact, they immediately "put things in order" on the charts, too, after describing and determining the position of [the] Diomede Island[s], Cape Dezhnev and other places. Then the sloop sailed for St. Lawerence [Sv. Lavrentiia] Bay, where the sailors intended to repair damage inflicted by the storm, check the chronometers, and make magnetic observations. Right at the entrance to the bay, the wind died and they had to anchor there. The sailors were met by friendly, smiling Chukchi. They continued to visit the sloop all day. The entire village had probably visited the *Seniavin* and every guest received a present.

On the following day, winds began to blow and the sloop sailed farther into the bay. The Chukchi helped the mariners in various ways and were interested in their work. They were particularly curious about the captain's "sorcery" with the magnetic and astronomical instruments. The sailors of the sloop spent most of their time among the Chukchi and became acquainted with their way of life and customs. To supply themselves with fresh meat, they purchased six reindeer from them. Baidarkas [*sic*] continuously jostled around the sloop and there was brisk trade. "All this day, as on the previous one," Litke said about the last day in the harbor, "we were surrounded by baidaras; the trade in small articles, and the stories, jokes, and songs did not stop. Those who came on board, whose number we finally did not limit, behaved most properly. These where not the same Chukchi we had envisioned from previous accounts of them."[41]

After concluding a description of the bay and the necessary observations, the travelers resumed their voyage on 20 July. Accompanied by a still wind and fog, the *Seniavin* weighed anchor and, moving "in driblets," reached the entrance of Mechigmenskii Bay by the evening of 27 July. They anchored there. According to Litke, the slowness of their voyage was due to the nearly total lack of wind and the constant fog. No sooner had they anchored than Chukchi in baidaras made their appearance. Among them were some from St. Lawrence Bay who had managed to get here overland. Some of them wore medals given to them by G. S. Shishmarev, who not long before had sailed to this area on the sloop *Blagonamerennyi.*

After describing Mechigmenskii Bay, Litke sailed farther south. Near midday of 28 July the travelers found the entrance to the bay. It stretched for quite a distance among high mountains. A careful study of the area refuted an old idea. The bay was actually a deep strait which separated the island of Arakamchechen from the mainland. This was a great discovery. Litke sailed the *Seniavin* into the strait, anchored, and commenced the necessary investigations. During this time the travelers often went ashore, and Litke even climbed the highest peak on the island "from which I had a wide and beautiful view of the surrounding areas from the mountain of St. Lawrence toward the north to St. Lawrence Island toward the south; the strait with all its bays and its island lay clearly before us."[42] The researchers unanimously gave this mountain the name Afos [Athos] (in honor of Mount Athos, within sight of which, on 19 June 1807, the Russian navy, under the command of D. N. Seniavin, fought a Turkish squadron); they named the strait itself Seniavin Strait.

On 6 August they concluded their descriptive work. The following areas were placed on the chart: Glazenap Harbor, Cape and Mount Postels, Aboleshev Inlet, and Cape Mertens. The naturalists made a series of interesting excursions about the island and gathered a large amount of data on nature. The sailors constantly encountered a friendly reception from the Chukchi. Very often the sailors whiled away the time in their camps, listening to their songs, watching their dancing and even shamanistic sorcery.

After bidding farewell to the hospitable inhabitants, the mariners made a description of the shore from Cape Mertens to Cape Chaplin. On 10 August, at midday, the *Seniavin* found itself in the same spot where V. I. Bering had been one hundred years before. Litke marked the event by naming a nearby cape "Cape Stoletiia [Centennial]."

Not far from Preobrazhenie Bay the sailors met some baptized Chukchi. They were all dressed like Russians, the men in sheepskin coats, "the women in kamleikas [parkas] and head kerchiefs. They constantly crossed themselves and could not remember their own [Christian] names. And only when a Chukcha showed a small book which was given to him by the Kolyma priest Vasilii Trifonov upon his baptism did he remember that he had taken on the priest's name: 'Vasilii, Vasilii,' our guest cried out, remembering his name which, however, we had to repeat to him several times before we left. To our question as to whether he knew what was written in the book, he openly answered that he did not. Of what use is this book to you? The Chukcha did not know. He had been given it without being asked whether he wanted it and therefore thought it was supposed to be that way."[43] For answering these questions, Litke remembered, the Chukcha had asked for vodka.

While continuing his research of Anadyrskii Bay, Litke mapped capes Bering and Chirikov, which had no previous name. He also described a major portion of the shore of this bay. On 16 August the *Seniavin* approached the entrance to Kresta Bay. A Chukchi settlement was located on the spit and it was from the inhabitants that the sailors gathered initial data on the bay. Following the directions of one of the young Chukchi (Khatyrgin), Litke sailed into the bay and anchored. After that, he visited the settlement situated in Nochen Inlet. Here, to Litke's surprise, he discovered that the mouth of the Anadyr' River is only one and a half days' voyage from this place. Litke was truly amazed because on all previous maps, the distance measured a good hundred miles.

On the following day a group of sedentary Chukchi arrived, led by an elderly man called Imlerat. They confirmed that the Anadyr's mouth was nearby and gave a detailed route to it. Litke decided to explore that mouth and Kresta Bay simultaneously. However, an incoming storm changed the plans of the expedition's leader. With fall in the offing, he considered it too risky to send a boat party to the mouth of the Anadyr'. In two teams, Ratmanov and Semenov began to describe Kresta Bay.

Meanwhile, the rest of the crew continued to become acquainted with the lifestyle and customs of the Chukchi and with the natural environment of their country. In turn, the Chukchi intently looked over the Russians. For a long time, they could not understand why the Russians would not buy walrus tusks from them. Imlerat was especially surprised by this fact. The mariners explained to him with great difficulty the true aims of the expedition. On 23 August a baidara arrived with Chukchi who hunted wild reindeer at the mouth of the Anadyr'. From them, Litke found out that a sloop could enter it easily. He again made up his mind to go to the Anadyr'.

Meanwhile, the parties of Semenov and Ratmanov managed to describe a twenty-mile strip of coast in a relatively short time. This allowed Litke to bring his sloop into the deep waters of the bay and to anchor in a bight found by Semenov. Litke went ashore to make his observations.

September brought good, clear weather. The rest of the coast was described. On 5 September both detachments returned to the sloop. That same day, after finishing his pendulum observations and astronomical determinations, Litke also returned. They immediately weighed anchor and continued the voyage. Litke was obsessed with visiting the mouth of the Anadyr' River. "I very much wanted to examine the mouth of the Anadyr'," he wrote, "the position of which on previous charts was so much in error, but I decided not to sail to an unknown shore with the wind blowing straight from the sea, in horrible weather, and in such a vessel, in which one could not hope to move away from a leeward shore. I was forced to sail by the wind south."[44]

The mouth of the Anadyr' remained unstudied. Despite that, a great deal of work was accomplished in this area. The shores from Anadyrskii Bay to Kamchatka had been drawn. New names appeared on the chart: Cape Navarin, Mt. Geiden (the sailors of the *Seniavin* found out about the glorious battle of Navarino when in Petropavlovsk and thus were the first to imprint this heroic event in Russian naval history on a geographical map), Archangel Gavriil Inlet (in honor of Bering's ship), and Cape King (a member of Cook's expedition).

When the sloop approached Cape Oliutorskii, the weather worsened. A strong wind began to blow mixed with fine rain, the typical [Russian] Far East *bus*. During one gust, Pavel Zherebchikov, one of the best sailors, was torn from the foretop. The crew took the loss of their comrade quite hard.

The constant stormy northern winds drove the sloop south. On 17 September Kliuchevskaia volcano appeared on the horizon. Within two days they passed Shipunskii Cape. All the while fighting the storm, they drifted another two days near the entrance to Avacha [Bay]. They then sailed into the bay and anchored at Petropavlovsk. The sailors of the *Seniavin* had a happy reunion with the crew of the *Moller*, who had returned here a month earlier.

It was with great satisfaction that the sailors of the *Seniavin* read about the details of the Battle of Navarino. Zavalishin wrote quite a lot about it from Okhotsk. The new commander of Kamchatka, Captain Second Rank Arkadii Vasil'evich Golenishchev, shared interesting news with the officers of the sloop. He had also brought the latest letters from relatives and friends in St. Petersburg. Litke even received a letter from P. E. Chistiakov in Novo-Arkhangel'sk, who in particular complained: "Ach! How unfortunate it is that I did not ask you to describe the Aleutian chain. Our respected Mikhailo Nikolaevich Staniukovich will probably give very little work to our hydrographic depot."[45] This exclamation contained a clear hint of the lack of professionalism on Staniukovich's part. This fact was underscored several times in journals and was also mentioned in the publications of scholars.

No matter how pleasantly the time was spent in Petropavlovsk Harbor, no matter how glad they were to be among their own countrymen, the sailors of the sloops kept thinking about returning to Kronstadt and began readying for their forthcoming voyage across three oceans. The approach of winter could already be felt in Kamchatka. The preparations on the sloop took five weeks.

As always, Litke wrote letters to his acquaintances and friends and sent in his official reports on his voyage. In a letter to his bosom friend Wrangell (18 October) he remarked: "My work is complete: spare me, my dear friend, from having to give you an uninteresting description of our survey of Chukotka. What can this mostly prosaic work in the most romantic country in the world give to the imagination?" Litke suggested that Wrangell read his report to Hydrographer General Sarychev. Litke remembered his youthful years in St. Petersburg, Radzivillov, and Kronstadt. He recalled his love for a certain Minna and added that if at all possible he "would not hesitate to share my future life with that of Minna." Up to now nothing has been uncovered about Litke's first serious love, except that she was a plump little blonde with whom he had become acquainted at a ball at Girsov's and that he was so enamored of her, that he even wrote about her to Wrangell.

On 28 October, when winter had arrived in Petropavlovsk and its vicinity, the *Moller* and *Seniavin,* accompanied by a Far East blizzard, left Kamchatka. They continued to sail together until 5 November. They sailed straight south, intending to examine the northern part of the Caroline Archipelago and to reach Manila in the Philippine Islands by the new year. On 5 November waves and overcast weather separated the two ships. Again Litke sailed the *Seniavin* alone to the Carolines.

Exactly one month later, the mariners saw the shore of coral islands surrounded by reefs. Immediately two local boats approached the ship. In one of them sat a man with red hair and light skin. In good English, he asked for permission to come aboard. The red-headed islander turned out to be the English sailor W[illiam] Floyd, who had left a whaling ship and had lived on these islands for two years. Litke decided to take the poor man all the way to London. While navigating through the Caroline waters, Floyd sometimes helped the Russian mariners as an interpreter. He told Litke much that was interesting about the inhabitants and natural environment of the islands.

The *Seniavin* found itself by the group of Murilo Islands. The Fananu Islands were located approximately ten miles from this area. The weather was excellent and the sloop sailed slowly among the numerous islands. Sometimes it lay adrift in order to welcome islanders on board, with whom the crew carried on endless conversations and lively trade. From these two groups of islands Litke sailed his ship to the Namonuito Islands, which the expedition had visited the previous year. Soon after they approached the island of Onoun. Old acquaintances came aboard and conversations and dances began.

From here the sloop sailed to the Farrolaip [Faraulep] Islands. The researchers checked the precision of the results of their previous survey and then sailed to the Uleai [Woleai] Islands to make astronomical determinations to serve as a control. Upon seeing the Russian mariners, the inhabitants of Uleai expressed wild enthusiasm. Now they did not at all leave the sides of the officers who were carrying on observations. They crowded onto the ship or sailed around it in their boats from morning to evening.

On 8 December the crew of the *Seniavin* was already at Fais Island. The naturalists made an excursion ashore and gathered a series of interesting data about the natural environment of this hospitable island.

Passage to the Philippine Islands was completed successfully. The sloop sailed slowly. Instead of the expected storms and typhoons, they had nothing but complete calm which long delayed their arrival in Manila. The *Seniavin* arrived at this beautiful port on the eve of the new year of 1829. The crew of the *Moller*, not at all busy with scientific research, had been waiting here for their friends for a long time already.

The *Seniavin* anchored next to the *Moller*, one-half mile from the mouth of the Pasig River, on whose banks lies the city of Manila. Litke and his crew readied the sloop for their further voyage, repairing damage and loading provisions, etc. During their free time, the sailors roamed through the city with great pleasure, as they admired the peculiar beauty of Manila and were amazed by the customs of the inhabitants. The main street of Manila, Espolote, was comparable to any in a European city. It had stores, stalls, and crowds of scurrying inhabitants, sailors, and priests. The sailors looked over the beautiful, gracious, dark-eyed Spanish women and the short local women, the Tagalogs, full of fire and passion. Along with the townspeople, the Russians grew obsessed with the cockfights. They admired the architecture and historical monuments, visited the fort, went to a local operetta, and looked over the tobacco factories which manufactured the famous Manila cigars. It goes without saying that they could not pass up the most famous and favorite spectacle of the Manilans—the bullfight.

On 18 January the sloops left the hospitable Manila Roads and sailed into the Sunda Archipelago. It was unbearably hot. Even those accustomed to such weather were uncomfortable. Traces of moisture remained on everything, no matter how many times they were wiped away, and they had to wear half-wet undergarments. Before entering Sunda Strait, sailor Pavel Zherebchikov died. Everyone felt pity for this good and conscientious man. According to naval custom, his body was buried at sea with a lowering of the flag.

The sloops anchored near Sumatra Island. The naturalists immediately went ashore, where they gathered priceless collections of animals and vegetation.

On 11 February, after sailing ten days through the strait, the sailors who had suffered from the heat and humidity gladly welcomed the vast Indian Ocean. It met them pleasantly. A constant southeast tailwind brought both sloops safely to the Cape of Good Hope, without the least inconvenience. The only thing that happened was on the *Moller* when sailor Vetoshkin fell overboard. The sloops immediately lay to and lowered the ship's boats. The crew of the *Seniavin* was the first to reach the drowning man and brought him to the *Moller*. On the following day, following Vetoshkin's example, a monkey from the *Seniavin* jumped into the ocean, and it, too, was saved. During this operation, the monkeys on the sloop suffered the most. It was impossible to drag them away from the side until the one that had gone overboard had been returned to them.

On 24 February, before reaching the Cape of Good Hope, the *Seniavin* again separated from the *Moller*, which set its course for Cape Town. Litke sailed for the island of St. Helena and on 18 April the *Seniavin* stood in the Jamestown Roads. The sailors looked at the sights connected with the great exile [Napoleon], while Litke was taking advantage of the politeness and help of the island's governor to make his pendulum observations. He placed his instruments on the eastern bastion of the city, on a stone platform where a large-caliber gun stood.

On 26 April the *Moller* arrived in port and within two days both sloops set a northerly course. On 10 May the sloops crossed the equator for the fourth time. "Now our native Kronstadt is within reach," the sailors said.

In order to get fresh provisions, the sloops stopped for a day at Port Faial (the Azores). From 17 to 30 June they ploughed the waves of the Atlantic Ocean. Soon after, they could see the shores of Europe. On 4 July the *Moller* and *Seniavin* saluted the French nation and sailed into Le Havre. The senior French military ship in the roads replied with the required number of shots. The ships anchored. They began to visit, bargain, load supplies, repair damage, and of course, stroll through the crowded Havre. Here they became acquainted with France and its cheerful people.

In a letter to Wrangell dated 24 March 1830, Litke admitted that he could have gone straight to London where he had to make a second set of observations on his pendulum at Greenwich and could have avoided stopping at Le Havre. But he took advantage of the fact that he was sailing with the *Moller*, because he, the officers, and the sailors all wanted to visit France. Out of the three weeks they spent there, Litke managed to visit Paris for two weeks, where he became acquainted with the well-known French scholar Cuvier, with navigators Dumont d'Urville and Frément and the artist Gérard.

The Russian sailors left Le Havre on 21 July. Staniukovich sailed straight for Russia while Litke went to London, to Greenwich, where he remained until 11 August. Litke and his officers were busy most of the time at the observatory. And the sailors visited London and the Naval Museum, strolled across Waterloo Bridge, looked at the monument to Nelson on Trafalgar Square, and admired the paintings of famous artists in the Picture Gallery.

The closer they got to their native shores, the faster each sailor's heart beat. They cleaned, scoured and washed the *Seniavin*, ready for inspection in Kronstadt. The sloop anchored in the Kronstadt Roads on 25 August. The round-the-world voyage, which had lasted three years and five days, had come to an end. There was not a single sick man on board. Everyone looked healthy, strong, and ready to sail to the edge of the world again. On 4 September the tsar visited the sloop and was quite satisfied with its performance.

The entire crew of the sloop was rewarded. F. P. Litke was promoted to captain first rank and was given the Order of St. Anna Second Class. All the officers were given orders [medals] and promoted. A letter written by Litke to Wrangell on this topic is quite curious. "As the first captain lieutenant on the list, I have been promoted to first rank, while the rest received the usual promotions. In addition, in an amusing way, I received a diamond ring for the two monkeys which His Majesty liked so much, and which he took from me to send to the tsarevich in Warsaw."[46]

In addition to these rewards, the Inspector's Department of Naval Headquarters declared on 25 November 1829 that the tsar "on 21 September of this year, has declared: (1) Staff and upper officers and the lower ranks who were on the sloop *Seniavin* during its voyage around the world in 1826, 1827, 1828, and 1829, are to receive, if they remain in the service, an extra year's salary according to their ranks at the time they returned from the voyage. (2) This campaign is to be considered as two for the receipt of the Order of St. George for all staff and upper officers of the line. For all the lower ranks, three years of service will be added toward their retirement."[47]

This is not the place to discuss the details of M. N. Staniukovich's voyage on the *Moller*. However, we will mention that its results were small in comparison to the amount of work done by the officers of the *Seniavin*. We have already mentioned P. E. Chistiakov's opinion, expressed in a personal letter to Litke. We shall add that Sarychev was also quite dissatisfied with Staniukovich's work. Thus, on 18 January 1830, he wrote to the commander-in-chief of the port of Kronstadt that Staniukovich "has yet to furnish me with the journals of his surveys," while Litke "gave me a full report of his activities on 10 September." Finally, on 22 January Staniukovich presented his material, and by 23 January Sarychev related to F. F. Shubert that "having found many mistakes in it, I have returned the material for correction and completion. In the same manner, I have requested that he redraw his general chart of the extension of the Sandwich Islands, of which some were newly discovered by him and others were studied."[48]

In general, Staniukovich's voyage was not very successful, although it was marked by geographical discoveries. It was also unsuccessful due to his cruelty, which resulted in the use of corporal punishment, thus turning the crew against him. Tyranny and lawlessness ruled his sloop. It is no wonder that upon its return to Kronstadt the sloop was placed under arrest until an investigation was completed.

While waiting to be called to St. Petersburg, Litke lived in Kronstadt on Shkiperskaia Street in Sedel'nikov's house. Finally he received his orders to leave. On 3 October, after bidding farewell to his crew with whom he had lived for three years, he moved to the capital. First he visited his sister. By that time, life at the Sul'menevs' had undergone changes. In connection with the reorganization of the educational system, Sul'menev was dismissed from the Naval Corps and remained without work for a year. After that, he was given the job of Auditor General. He remained in this position for the rest of his life.

Litke immersed himself in work. First, he gave a detailed report on his voyage. As early as 10 September, he presented Sarychev with forty-nine journals of descriptions and twenty-two charts on fourteen sheets. On 14 September he gave him the log book of the *Seniavin* which was kept from 4 August 1826 to 5 September 1829. At the orders of A. S. Menshikov, Litke presented to the Academy of Sciences everything "which relates to the sphere of natural history ... in addition to those things which relate to navigation and nautical sciences."

Litke wanted to publish all the material dealing with his expedition. "My only aim and wish was to occupy myself exclusively with this matter until completed. I saw that now, because of the changed circumstances and new views on service, this (that is, scientific pursuits—

A. A.) would not lead to a shining career. But, satisfied for the first time in this respect and having grown passionate for this work which has occupied me exclusively for three, better say nine years, I wanted only to continue further on this path, hoping that my activities would be of some use."[49]

Hydrographer General G. A. Sarychev, after receiving Litke's reports and material on 13 September, decided to help him by addressing himself to the head of Naval Headquarters, A. S. Menshikov: "It being necessary that Captain Lieutenant Litke remain here to complete his descriptions and observations, I beg to ask your Highness to allow Mr. Litke to remain in St. Petersburg for the reasons stated above without any other duties."[50]

The request was approved. Litke immersed himself in processing the vast amount of observations he had collected. After his expeditions to Novaia Zemlia, he had already been recognized in scientific circles. He constantly corresponded with Academician K. M. Ber. Now he became one among equals in the circle of academicians to which Ber belonged, along with M. V. Ostrogradskii, A. Ia. Kupfer, V. K. Vishnevskii, and P. N. Fus. Corresponding member of the Academy of Sciences G. A. Sarychev supported him in every possible way. That winter (1829–1830) Litke became acquainted with the German naturalist and geographer Alexander Humboldt, who had just returned from a trip to the Urals and Western Siberia. The venerable scholar complimented the young traveler and scholar in his address before the members of the Academy of Sciences. Moreover, at a reception at the tsar's, Humboldt mentioned Litke's talents. It is not out of the question that such a high recommendation played a decisive role in Litke's appointment as tutor of the tsar's son, Grand Duke Constantine.

After processing the material on the *Seniavin*'s voyage, Litke turned to A. S. Menshikov on 14 April 1830 with a request to publish in separate editions the descriptive and scientific parts of his navigations, and an atlas. The government approved an estimate of "20,128 rubles and 12 kopeks" for such a publication in the 1831 budget.

At this time Ferdinand Wrangell was in Sitka, where he had moved in November [September] of 1830 with his family in the capacity of chief manager of the Russian-American Company. Wrangell spent five years there. All this time Litke wrote to him and advised him not to waste an opportunity, but to occupy himself with scientific research, especially magnetic and hydrological research. "The Academy is sending you," Litke wrote him on 10 February 1831, "wonderful magnetic instruments and it is expecting great things from you. Magnetic observations in Sitka, given the high inclination [dip], high degree of force, and the site's great distance from other observation posts, give us important data for the theory of magnetic phenomena. Using your vessels which sail along the American coast north and south of Sitka, it would be easy to determine the inclination and magnetic force in many places in relation to Sitka, which I have already connected with other places. Such observations are a simple thing. Patience and accuracy are the main thing. Many of those in your service could learn to make such observations. The [company's] Main Office has hired Ensign Navigator Orlov, who was with me for four years. I kept him occupied all the while he was with me, and he saw how I worked and therefore he could quickly become experienced. I recommend him: he is a good man, not without talent and potential, but he is still flighty, *aber das gibt sich* [though that will pass]. I would also like to recommend that you have careful meteorological observations made wherever possible with instruments which could be compared to permanent reliable ones in the [colonial] capital. I will try to have good thermometers and barometers sent to you, too.... Most of all, I beg you to make constant and detailed observations of the tides."[51]

Litke's fruitful and intense activity was interrupted by a completely unexpected assignment. The tsar placed him at the head of a detachment which was sent into the Atlantic Ocean with the officers of the first graduating officers' classes, with the senior class of naval cadets, and a naval training crew. With bitterness Litke wrote Wrangell: "In order to complete my work, of which, you can well imagine, I had accumulated a bottomless amount in three years, it was recommended that I be assigned to the hydrographer general and freed of any other duties. That is what I had wanted and I was beginning to work rather well; I carried on some experiments on the pendulum at the local observatory, I labored over calculations; and suddenly I hear that they are again sending me on a campaign ... a flattering commission, of course, but I was not in the least gladdened by it."[52]

But an order is an order. Under Litke's command fell the frigates *Anna* (Captain Second Rank Selivanov), and *Prints Oranskii* (Captain Second Rank Iur'ev) and the brig *Aiaks* (Captain Lieutenant Ivanov).

When Dr. Mertens, who had by this time been chosen as adjunct of the Academy of Sciences and transferred to the naval department, found out about the campaign, he immediately wished to take part in it. He managed to receive the post of chief detachment physician.

The voyage had little success. The crews had not once been at sea; the sailors did not know their duties. Litke even requested that several experienced sailors who had returned to Kronstadt with Geiden and Lazarev after the Battle of Navarino be assigned to each ship. We will not go into any detail about this voyage, which lasted from the end of April to the beginning of September.

In order to determine deviation, the detachment stopped at Revel, where the naval cadets made a practical survey of the roadstead. Litke flew his broad pennant on the *Anna*. While sailing on the Baltic Sea they held a course close to the shores so that the naval cadets could engage in nautical survey. On 2 June they arrived in Copenhagen, where the sailors were given a warm reception. Litke's old friend Tsartman organized an excursion through town, showing them the suburb and capital. Out of town, Litke taught front line maneuvers to "two sailor and artillery companies of the training crew while the local populace observed. Even though we had not had the chance to let our men practice for two months, their unison and precision in maneuvers and firing, and especially their military appearance aroused general surprise."[53]

The detachment went around Great Britain, reached the shores of Iceland and, without stopping in Reykjavik, continued on to Brest. On the way to France the ships had to face fierce storms, and arduous experiences fell to the lot of the inexperienced crew. In Brest, Litke transferred to the *Prints Oranskii*. At that time France had just had its July Revolution of 1830 which resulted in the fall of the Bourbon dynasty. It is only natural that the Russian detachment was not given the usual formal reception—after all, the French had enough things on their minds. "We came to Brest at an inopportune time," Litke wrote Wrangell, "with the terrible agitation going on, they had no time for us. The officials had been forewarned of our arrival, and were preparing to give us a grand reception, when suddenly the revolution broke out in Paris so that all the families went to their summer houses and we were deprived of our banquets."[54]

On the return trip, men on the *Prints Oranskii* became ill. Typhoid fever raged. By the time they arrived in Kronstadt, seventy men were afflicted with the disease. Ignoring the danger to his own life, Dr. Mertens fought the epidemic with all the means made available by Litke. They could do little. Moreover, the brave physician himself became infected aboard the frigate, but did not realize it until his return to St. Petersburg. Then his health worsened and after a two-week battle with the disease Mertens died in St. Petersburg on 17 September.[55]

The tsar expressed his patent discontent with the detachment's voyage, though Litke was awarded the Order of St. George Fourth Class that year for his eighteen naval campaigns. Litke thought he would now be left in peace, and returned to work on his notes and materials. However, new cares prevented him from pursuing his work. Until the end of that year, Litke had to take care of family business. He went to Vil'na [Vilnius] to get his recently widowed sister and her six-year-old daughter (Elizaveta Fedorovna Rozen). Returning from Vil'na, he stopped in Derpt (Tartu), where he became acquainted with astronomer Struve "and finally saw the world-famous observatory there."[56]

In St. Petersburg Litke rented the same apartment he and Wrangell had in the winter of 1824–1825. He liked this apartment because it was located on the ninth line, right opposite the Sul'menevs' apartment. During this period in his life, Litke again met his love, the mysterious Minna, about whom we know very little. At the moment when he renewed his acquaintance with her, she had already been married six years. The meeting stirred up old feelings and Litke admitted with sadness in a letter to Wrangell that: "I never loved anyone so much and of course, I could never love any other woman as much as M...It naturally follows that I am not meant to be happy." Litke did not yet know that very soon a new feeling would possess him and bring him happiness, a family happiness about which the sailor had dreamed so much and which he had always lacked.

On 5 May 1831 Litke presented his manuscript "Experiments on the Fixed Pendulum, Carried Out on the *Seniavin*" to the Hydrographic Depot. But soon he was again torn away from his scientific work.

The fact of the matter was that the Russian army in Poland was in a difficult situation at that moment. As a consequence of peasant revolts, its food supplies were interrupted. The government decided to buy supplies in East Prussia and to deliver part of them from St. Petersburg and Riga to Danzig and from there forward them via the Wisla River to the Polish frontier. The naval part of this operation fell to Litke, while the land portion was assigned to the Russian consul in Danzig. Lieutenants Bodisko (son of the admiral in Sveaborg) and Mofet, who had sailed on the *Moller*, helped Litke in this task.

In addition, A. S. Menshikov had assigned Litke a task. On 16 September 1831, he ordered Litke to find out the exact system of navigational safeguards on the southern shore of the Baltic Sea ("the exact name of the place where there is a lighthouse or other safety signal, its latitude and longitude"). On 24 October 1831, Litke reported the information he had been requested to gather.

At the beginning of 1832 Litke went with his calculations to Warsaw to Field Marshal Paskevich. Here he found his uncle, F. I. Engel, who had been assigned as chairman of the provisional government of the Polish realm, along with his cousin R. F. Furman, the former director of the finance commission. Litke spent three lighthearted weeks in their company and received the Order of St. Vladimir Third Class for "activity and good management displayed in the unloading of ships in Danzig and shipping of supplies via the Wisla to the active-duty army." He went to receptions and dinners at his uncle's, and often went to the theater where he admired the corps de ballet which was under the special patronage of the field marshal.

At the end of January Litke returned to St. Petersburg and soon after was assigned the post of aide-de-camp to the emperor. His happiness was mixed with great grief, however. Among the many victims of the cholera epidemic which broke out in St. Petersburg in the summer of 1831 were two men who had played an important role in Litke's life. V. M. Golovnin and G. A. Sarychev died. The former had taught him about sailing; the latter introduced him to science. Litke remembered these two teachers to the end of his days.

Litke again threw himself into his favorite activity. He completed his manuscripts, and insisted that they be published in parts. He himself supervised the printing. On 29 November he turned to A. S. Menshikov with a request also to publish the historical part of his voyage. "Our journal and art portfolio," he wrote, "contain many interesting materials, and it would be a great pity if one of the most successful voyages in recent times were not made known to the world. The death of my co-traveler, Dr. Mertens, and my assignment to service were the reasons for which I have taken no steps up to now to see this work published. I have now received the journals of the deceased from his heirs, I and another

134

co-traveler put in order the journals kept aboard the sloop, and we have selected the drawings. Nothing would now hinder us from publishing this work."[57] A sum of 20,000 rubles was allocated for the printing.

Litke rejoiced at seeing a reprint of his book on his voyages to Novaia Zemlia and he hoped soon to be holding the published materials of the *Seniavin* expedition. However, the printing was delayed. In November of 1832 Litke's life underwent an important change. He had sensed this change coming right after he returned from Poland, when he was made aide-de-camp to the emperor; after several conversations with the tsar and tsaritsa, to whom he had been presented on his promotion; after a voyage in the summer of 1832 on the steamer *Izhora,* when he accompanied the grand duchesses on a swimming excursion; after his invitations to the royal court multiplied. Now Litke was offered the post of tutor to Grand Duke Constantine, who upon reaching his majority would become head of the Russian navy. "I answered," Litke wrote, "that although I do not recognize in myself any sort of calling to such a position, have only dealt with naval matters in my twenty years of service, and do not possess the knowledge and abilities needed for such a task, His Majesty's rule is law and if your Highness wills it, it is my duty to obey."[58] What else could he have done?

However, before we begin to relate Litke's court life, it is necessary to summarize the scientific results of his expedition on the *Seniavin.* At the beginning of the account of his trip, Litke himself did this in a rather modest manner. The expedition, as we have seen, was assigned an exclusively important task: Staniukovich and Litke were to describe (and carry out many various observations in) the entire northern part of the Pacific Ocean, including the Aleutian Islands. They were also to describe the Carolines and Sandwich Islands in the central part of the Pacific. No other Russian expedition had ever been assigned such a task before this. The share of this work that fell on the shoulders of Litke and his coworkers was performed with excellence, although some of it remained incomplete. To jump ahead, we will say that Litke had performed much scientific work and research not foreseen in his immediate instructions.

Thus, in the northern part of the Pacific Ocean, in the Bering Sea, they "determined astronomically [the coordinates of] the most important points of the Kamchatkan coast from Avacha Bay to the north; measured the height of many volcanoes; described in detail the previously

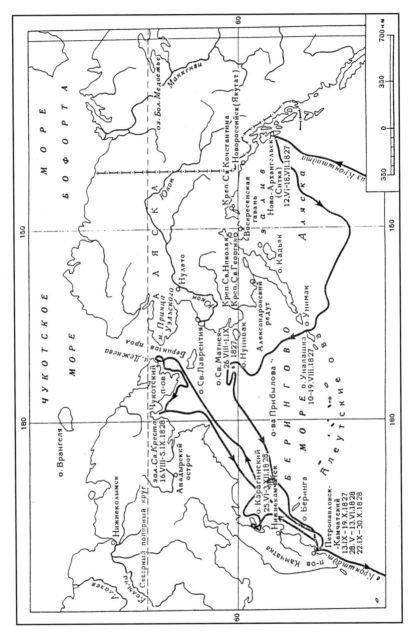

Route of the sloop Seniavin in the northern part of the Pacific Ocean.

unknown Karaginskii Islands along with St. Matthew Island and the coast of Chukotka from Vostochnyi Cape [East Cape] almost to the mouth of the Anadyr' River; and determined [the coordinates of] the Pribilof Islands and many others."[59]

During their hydrographic work, Litke and his officers (Semenov, Zavalishin, Aboleshev, Nozikov, Ratmanov, Glazenap, Orlov) did not limit themselves solely to nautical survey, which would have been sufficient to put the coast on a chart. They attempted, and not without success, to carry out complex research. Litke was one of the first naval officers during the period of hydrographic work who made hydrological observations, noting the magnitude of high and low tides and noting currents. Materials concerning the observations in Kresta Bay and St. Lawrence Bay, at Karaginskii Island, in Petropavlovsk Harbor, Sitka Sound, Three Saints Harbor, Pavlovsk Harbor, Etolin Harbor, and other places in the northern part of the ocean have been preserved. Litke also made accurate meteorological observations.

The combination of both types of observations with the descriptive materials represented a priceless physical geographical work which has not lost its historical geographical value to this day. Suffice it to say that the many charts drawn by Litke and his coworkers were used by navigators until the late 1930s, when Soviet hydrographers, under the leadership of L. A. Demin, repeated the hydrographic work from Karaginskii Island to Cape Dezhnev using new technology and a new scientific method. It was not in vain that Litke and the officers of the *Seniavin* labored if grateful mariners the world over used their findings for an entire century! The data concerning the tides in this part of the world laid the basis for an article by Academician E. Kh. Lents, which was published in the Bulletin of the Academy of Sciences.

It was not accidental that the Caroline Archipelago had been chosen for research. It had not been described or charted. Foreign navigators who sailed to this part of the world before Litke limited their activities to determination of the coordinates of discovered islands and to placement of those islands on the map. There had been no systematic nautical survey of all the islands, the geographic location of the known islands had to be refined, and it was highly possible that there were still some undiscovered islands in the Caroline Archipelago. The irreproachable hydrographic work by Litke allowed him to write that "the Caroline

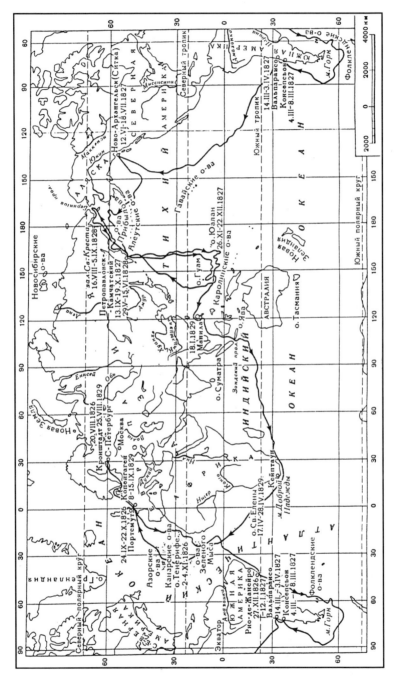

Chart of the sloop Seniavin's voyage under the command of F. P. Litke.

138

Archipelago region, which encompasses an area from Iualan [Kusae] Island to the Uliufyi [Ulithi] island group, has been researched; twelve island groups or individual islands were discovered and a total of twenty-six were described. The Caroline Archipelago, which up to now has been considered dangerous by navigators, will henceforth be as safe as the already known areas on the face of the earth."[60]

The results of the hydrographic work of the *Seniavin* expedition were reflected in the Navigational Atlas and an accompanying text dealing with sailing directions to the places visited. Both were an excellent guide for navigation in this region and in all the regions described. Here, too, it goes without saying, Litke did not limit himself to descriptive work alone. As in most of his work, hydrological and meteorological observations occupied an important place. Journals corresponding to these speak of such observations in the regions of the Caroline Islands, on Iualan Island, and also in the Bonin Sima [Bonin][61] Islands, which Litke found and described.

The results of the expedition's work are not limited to just these two major and laborious tasks. Of much greater importance are the observations of the fixed pendulum which were made at nine different places on the earth's surface:[62] St. Petersburg, Greenwich, Valparaiso, Novo-Arkhangel'sk, Petropavlovsk, Iualan, Guam, Port Lloyd (on Bonin Sima [Chichi-shima] Island), and on St. Helena Island. These remarkably increased our knowledge of the shape of the earth. Litke determined that the compression or flattening of the earth's spheroid was equal to 1/269 (based on his experiments) and taking into account other observations, it was equal to 1/288. For the sake of comparison, let us state that, according to present-day data, compression of the earth's spheroid is equal to 1/298.3 (the Krasovskii ellipsoid). Litke wrote a small but very interesting article on the compression of the earth's spheroid, which was reviewed by G. A. Sarychev and M. F. Reineke.[63] Many scientists used Litke's work with the gravimeter. During our time, A. E. Medunin has worked on the history of this question in great detail.[64]

The magnetic observations made by Litke in various parts of the world also have great significance for science and navigation. They were calculated and processed by Academician E. Kh. Lents.[65] This information was used by Ganstein in 1833 in his work on magnetic theory to produce a chart of isodynamic lines.

Title page of the atlas accompanying the historical section of Litke's books on the voyage of the Seniavin.

The years' meteorological observations by Litke and the officers of the *Seniavin* were a storehouse of information for climatologists and physical geographers. These were recorded in the tropical latitudes from 30° N to 30° S every half hour (observation of atmospheric pressure), while the air temperature was read every four hours. These observations were made with the help of two sympiesometers (barometers insensitive to sea motion), one barometer, and thermometers. These unique observations permitted Professor G. G. Gel'strem [Hällström][66] to draw certain conclusions about the prevailing temperatures and winds of these latitudes. It also allowed him to resolve certain questions about the prevailing winds in the tropics, about frequent changes in pressure, etc. In addition, daily readings of the water surface temperature were taken throughout the voyage.

Litke's observations during his round-the-world voyage on the *Seniavin* served as a cornerstone which, together with the results of the ocean voyages of other Russian navigators (beginning with O. E. Kotzebue on the brig *Riurik*), laid the foundation for oceanographic research and oceanographic science in Russia.

The *Seniavin* expedition also had great significance for the development of geographical science in Russia as well as for ethnography, geology, mineralogy, zoology, ornithology, and botany. In Litke's descriptions of his voyage, he noted many physical geographical characteristics of various regions where the *Seniavin* was anchored. These notes (on Russian America, the Aleutian Islands, Kamchatka, the Carolines, and elsewhere) often deal with subjects outside the geographical framework and give us a picture of the political and economic relationships existing at that time in those regions. Here we find a mass of ethnographic information which Litke used to compile a dictionary of the Caroline dialects. Of special interest are his "Remarks on the Chukchi" in which he dwells on their historical origins and gives characteristics of their social structure, customs, rituals, way of life, and family relations.

The third part of "Voyage Aboard the *Seniavin*," compiled by Postels and containing the work of the expedition's naturalists (Postels, Mertens, and Kittlitz), is of special interest. Some of the illustrations of the *Seniavin* expedition used in the present book were taken from the atlases of drawings by Postels and Kittlitz. The geological and mineralogical descriptions of Chile, Sitka [Baranof] Island, the islands of the Bering Sea, the coasts of Chukotka and Kamchatka, the Caroline Islands, the Bonin Sima [Bonin] Islands, and St. Helena Island occupy a special place in this third volume on the expedition. Sketches of examples of geological exposures and geomorphological formations were included in their description.

Kittlitz, who made a survey of the animal world, illustrated his descriptive work with a series of remarkable drawings in the above-mentioned atlas. Due to the untimely death of Mertens, who dealt mainly with the plant and animal worlds, that section of the volume is incomplete. It was partly compensated for by the publication in 1840 of a work by A. Postels and F. Ruprekht, "Drawings and Descriptions of Sea Plants ..." in Russian and Latin. This work was "aimed at clarifying the species of marine vegetation growing in the North Pacific Ocean along the shores of Russian possessions, which up to now have not been studied in great detail...."[67] In this work, many types of marine algae are described and illustrated on forty folios.

The naturalists turned over to the Academy of Sciences a collection of animals (more than 400), nearly 400 drawings of living organisms, collections of insects (nearly 700 species), 750 bird specimens, up to 2,400 plants (an herbarium), and nearly 330 rock specimens. They also brought back a rich collection of clothing, utensils, decorative artifacts and even several human skulls from the various tribes they visited.[68]

The work done by the naturalists and officers led by Litke in the field of natural sciences yielded valuable results which not only do Russian science proud, but which also were undoubtedly useful to all of humanity.

In commemoration of his scientific exploits, Litke was chosen as a corresponding member of the Academy of Sciences. He was quite proud of this honor and cherished it more than any other honorary title. For his published work on the *Seniavin* expedition, Litke was awarded the Demidov Prize by the Academy of Sciences. He learned of this happy event in his life in a letter from Academician P. N. Fus. In his reply (5 May 1836), Litke wrote: "In awarding me the Demidov Prize, the Imperial Academy of Sciences had honored my wish to be of service to our Fatherland and the Sciences with great honors. Your Honor has sent me news which I find flattering; please, relate to the Academy my thanks and readiness to dedicate to that same end what little free time I have."[69]

CITATIONS AND NOTES

1. F. F. Matiushkin and P. T. Koz'min took part in F. P. Wrangell's expedition. See F. P. Vrangel', *Puteshestvie po severnym beregam Sibiri i po Ledovitomu moriu, sovershennoe v 1820, 1821, 1822, 1823, i 1824 gg. ekspeditsiei pod nachal'stvom flote leitenanta F. P. Vrangelia* [F. P. Wrangell's travels to Northern Siberia and the Arctic Ocean in 1820, 1821, 1822, 1823, and 1824] (St. Petersburg, 1841).

2. M. M. Solev'ev, *Ber na Novoi Zemle* [Ber in Novaia Zemlia] (Leningrad, 1934); A. I. Aleksiejew, "August Cywolka-badacz Nowej Ziemi," *Czasopismo Geograficzne*, vol. 34, part 3, (Wroclaw, 1963).

3. TsGADA, f. Gosarkhiv, r. 30, d. 57, l. 181.

4. *Zapiski Gosudarstvennogo Admiralteiskogo departamenta*, part 10 (St. Petersburg, 1826), pp. xiii–xiv.

5. V. P. Bezobrazov, *Litke. Autobiography ...*, p. 110.

6. GIAE, f. 2057, op. 1, d. 452, l. 8–9.

7. From instructions to Captain Lieutenant M. N. Staniukovich, commander of the *Moller* and *Seniavin*, from the Admiralty Department (TsGADA, f. Gosarkhiv, r. 30, d. 59, ch. 2, l. 3).

8. Ibid., l. 41–43 ob.

9. TsGAVMF, f. 170, op. 1, d. 109, l. 1–2.

10. TsGADA, f. Gosarkhiv, r. 30, d. 59, ch. 2, l. 3.

11. Detailed instructions to Litke can be found in *Zapiski Gosudarstvennogo Admiralteiskogo departamenta*, part 11 (St. Petersburg, 1826), pp. xlix–liv.

12. TsGADA, f. Gosarkhiv, r. 30, d. 59, ch. 2, l. 19.

13. Ibid., l. 18–18 ob.

14. V. P. Bezobrazov, *Litke. Autobiography ...*, p. 111.

15. TsGADA, f. Gosarkhiv, r. 30, d. 59, ch. 2, l. 31 ob.–32.

16. F. P. Litke, *Puteshestvie vokrug sveta, sovershennoe po poveleniiu gosudaria imperatora Nikolaia I na voennom shliupe "Seniavine" v 1826, 1827, 1828 i 1829 godakh flota Kapitanom Fedorom Litke* [F. P. Litke's voyage on the *Seniavin* from 1826–1829], part 1 (St. Petersburg, 1834), p. 13 (hereafter, F. P. Litke, *Puteshestvie na "Seniavine."*)

17. After N. N. Nozikov, *Krugosvetnoe puteshestvie Litke na voennom shliupe Seniavin v 1826–1829 godakh* [The round-the-world voyage of Litke on the military sloop *Seniavin* in 1826–1829] (Moscow, 1933), p. 23. N. N. Nozikov is the grandson of G. Ia. Nozikov, who was a member of the expedition. He used his grandfather's memoirs and other materials, unknown to the author of the present book.

18. F. P. Litke, *Puteshestvie na "Seniavine"* ..., part 1, p. 15.

19. Ibid., p. 29.

20. Ibid., p. 31.

21. *Zapiski, izdavaemye Gosudarstvennym Admiralteiskim departamentom otnosiashchiiasia k moreplavaniiu, naukam i slovesnosti*, part 13 (St. Petersburg, 1827), pp. 1–9.

22. F. P. Litke, *Puteshestvie na "Seniavine"* ..., part 1, p. 37.

23. Ibid., p. 45.

24. Ibid., p. 77.

25. Ibid., p. 79.

26. Ibid., pp. 84–85.

27. TsGAVMF, f. 402, op. 1, d. 104, l. 20–24.

28. F. P. Litke, *Puteshestvie na "Seniavine"* ..., part 1, p. 180.

29. Ibid., p. 198.

30. TsGADA, f. Gosarkhiv, r. 30, d. 59, ch. 2, l. 121 ob., 129.

31. F. P. Litke, *Puteshestvie na "Seniavine"* ..., part 1, p. 233.

32. F. P. Litke, *Puteshestvie na "Seniavine"* ..., part 2, 1835, p. 2.

33. Ibid., p. 11.

34. Ibid., pp. 36–37.

35. Ibid., p. 39.

36. F. P. Litke, *Opyty nad postoiannym maiatnikom, proizvedennye v puteshestvie vokrug sveta na voennom shliupe "Seniavine" v 1826, 1827, i 1829 g. flota kapitanom F. Litke* [Pendulum experiments on the *Seniavin* by Litke 1826 to 1829] (St. Petersburg, 1833), p. 88.

37. TsGADA, f. Gosarkhiv, r. 30, d. 59, ch. 2, l. 135–135 ob.

38. F. P. Litke, *Puteshestvie na "Seniavine"* ..., part 2, p. 130.

39. Ibid., p. 131.

40. Ibid., p. 136.

41. Ibid., p. 144.

42. Ibid., p. 148.

43. Ibid., p. 161.

44. Ibid., pp. 181–182.

45. TsGADA, f. Gosarkhiv, r. 30, d. 59, ch. 2, l. 136–153.

46. GIAE, f. 2057, op. 1, d. 452, l. 27 ob.

47. TsGAVMF, f. 402, op. 1, d. 189, l. 1.

48. TsGAVMF, f. 402, op. 1, d. 215, l. 17.

49. V. P. Bezobrazov, *Litke. Autobiography* ..., pp. 117–118.

50. A. I. Alekseev, *G. A. Sarychev* (Moscow: Nauka, 1966), p. 145.

51. GIAE, f. 2057, op. 1, d. 452, l. 53–53 ob.

52. Ibid., l. 21.

53. TsGADA, f. Gosarkhiv, r. 30, d. 60, l. 15 ob.

54. GIAE, f. 2057, op. 1, d. 452, l. 49.

55. Karl-Heinrich Frantsevich Mertens (born in Bremen 17 May 1796, died in St. Petersburg 17 September 1830) wanted to take part first in Bellinsgauzen's expedition and then in that of Kotzebue; he finally took an active part in F. P. Litke's expedition on the *Seniavin.*

56. GIAE, f. 2057, op. 1, d. 452, l. 55 ob.

57. TsGAVMF, f. 402, op. 1, d. 458, l. 3, 9.

58. V. P. Bezobrazov, *Litke. Autobiography* ..., p. 133.

59. F. P. Litke, *Puteshestvie na "Seniavin"* ..., part 1, pp. 7–8.

60. Ibid., p. 8.

61. AAN, f. 34, op. 1, d. 10,12, 18.

62. *Opyty nad postoiannym maiatnikom, proizvedennye v puteshestvie vokrug sveta na voennom shliupe "Seniavine" v 1826, 1827, 1828 i 1829 godakh flota kapitanom F. Litke* (St. Petersburg, 1833).

63. TsGAMVF, f. 402, op. 1, d. 222, l. 1–6 ob.

64. A. E. Medunin, *Razvitie gravimetrii v Rossii* [Development of gravimetry in Russia] (Moscow: Nauka, 1967).

65. *Nabliudeniia nad nakloneniem i stepen'iu sily magnitnoi strelki, proizvedennye v puteshestvie vokrug sveta na shliupe "Seniavine" v 1826, 1827, 1828 i 1829 godakh flota kapitanom F. Litke, obrabotannye i vychislennye E. Lentsem* [Observations on the inclination and degree of force of the magnetic needle made aboard the *Seniavin* in 1826, 1827, 1828 and 1829 by F. Litke, processed and calculated by E. Lents], translated from German by Fleet Lieutenant B. Glazenap (St. Petersburg, 1836).

66. *Nabliudeniia barometricheskiia, simpiezometricheskiia i termometricheskiia, proizvedennyia v puteshestvie vokrug sveta kapitana Litke, vychislennyia professorom Gel'singforskago universiteta G. G. Gel'stremom* [Barometric, sympiesometric, and thermometric observations made on Litke's voyage around the world, calculated by professor of He'lsingfors University G. G. Hällström] (St. Petersburg, 1838).

67. *Izobrazheniia i opisaniia morskikh rastenii, sobrannykh v Severnom Tikhom okeane u beregov Rossiiskikh vladenii v Azii i Amerike v puteshestvie vokrug sveta, sovershennoe po poveleniiu gosudaria imperatora Nikolaia I na voennom shliupe "Seniavine" v 1826, 1827, 1828 i 1829 godakh pod kom. fl. kap. F. Litke* [Drawings and descriptions of marine plants gathered in the North Pacific Ocean near the shores of the Russian possessions in Asia and America ... on the *Seniavin* in 1826, 1827, 1828, and 1829], published by A. Postels and F. Ruprekht (St. Petersburg, 1840).

68. A. D. Dobrovol'skii, *Plavaniia F. P. Litke* [Voyages of F. P. Litke] (Moscow, 1948), p. 76.

69. AAN, f. 1, op. 2–1836, d. 221, l. 2.

* * *

a. Spelled "Baer" in his German publications.—Ed.

b. The Russian convention with England was concluded in 1825 and that with the United States in 1824.—Ed.

c. Dates follow the Julian calendar and thus are twelve days earlier than dates provided in the published French and English translations of the *Seniavin* voyage narrative.—Ed.

d. Razgruzhennykh i vooruzhennykh; likely a typographical error for *razoruzhennykh i vooruzhennykh,* unrigged and rigged.—Ed.

e. This caption is taken from the atlas accompanying the historical section of Litke's book on the voyage of the *Seniavin* (French edition, n.d.). It differs from the caption provided by author A. I. Alekseev in the work translated here.—Ed.

f. Don Jose Medinia Ipanado (V. M. Golovnin, *Around the World on the* Kamchatka, *1817–1819,* trans. and ed. E. L. Wiswell [Honolulu: Hawaiian Historical Society and University Press of Hawaii, 1979], p. 241, n. 5).—Ed.

INVOLUNTARY SERVICE
AND THE RUSSIAN GEOGRAPHICAL SOCIETY

The only thing left for Litke to do was to begin his unaccustomed career as tutor to the future admiral general who would one day stand at the head of the Russian navy. He took up his duty with his usual zeal. He quickly became acquainted with the course of things and within two years became his own man in the court and exerted a certain influence in many government matters. The most eminent nobles, dignitaries, and government officials began to take Litke's opinion into consideration.

In 1832 Grand Duke Constantine Nikolaevich was only five years old. Litke and other teachers had to remain constantly by his side until he got married. Litke worked out a program of studies for each year and sought out the appropriate textbooks. The teachers (among whom were the historian N. Shulygin, physicist E. Kh. Lents, historian A. F. Grimm, and poet V. A. Zhukovskii) who taught the heir to the throne changed, but Litke remained.

At the beginning of 1834 Litke wrote to Wrangell about his daily life during those years: "At nine in the morning, I take up my duties as tutor and continue in that capacity until nine in the evening when the grand duke retires. His old nanny spends the night with him, but this summer it seems that he will be entirely in my hands, and then I will begin spending the night, too, with him." Only after nine in the evening could he spend time with his siblings and on Wednesdays they would gather in his quarters at the Winter Palace. "And these are my 365 days a year, without change," he concluded, not without irony.

Despite such a strict regimen and extraordinary duty, Litke was not left on the sidelines of scientific interests in the capital. All his thoughts where occupied with the publication of the descriptions of the *Seniavin* voyage. In his rare spare moments, he would run to various establishments, go to the printer, attend meetings of various scientific organizations, and often drop by the Smirdin bookstore which Litke praised very highly: "Smirdin's *Biblioteka dlia chteniia* [Library for Reading] is truly a literary phenomenon in two respects: first because of its merits and then because it has 4,000 subscribers."[1]

Litke also visited the inventor of the electromagnetic telegraph, P. L. Shilling, who first demonstrated his experiments in transmission by wireless telegraph as early as 1832. Litke had a friendly relationship with him and wrote to Wrangell about this visit: "Another remarkable project of Baron Shilling (if not the greatest of people, then at least the fattest), is the development of a telegraph which can cover any distance, across land or water, and can be used to communicate at any time, at night and in fog, and the time interval in transmission of signals equals zero! What do you think of that?"[2]

The first project that Litke had mentioned [in his letter to Wrangell] was the forthcoming voyage of the Russian-American Company's ship *Amerika,* which had already sailed to Russian America under the command of V. S. Khromchenko, and now was under I. I. Shants. Incidentally, from this letter we can determine Litke's relationship to this navigator and toward the Baltic Germans in general: "I don't know how these Shkantses, or Shantses, or Shvantses prove themselves on Kekura (Litke has the islands in mind—A. A.), but I can admit to you that on land I don't particularly like them. He is ... an adjutant to the Headquarters Chief: this is his only asset."[3]

Science was not the only thing which troubled Litke. The time had come for a deep and serious feeling. He had seen her for the first time in 1832 when he accompanied the grand duchesses on the steamer *Izhora* on a swimming excursion to Revel. His acquaintance with Julia Browne, the daughter of an English officer and governess to Grand Duchess Alexandra Nikolaevna, gradually became a strong, intense feeling. "When I least expected it," he wrote to his bosom friend Wrangell, "a wonderful being entered my world and gently gave me her hand and promised to support me in my life and bear all my hardships with me ... She is a poor orphan with a good heart, educated mind, and pleasant spirits—I cannot tell you any more at this time because, although the first step has been taken, the door has not yet opened before me and I need to put all my house in order before I can approach her."[4]

At this time, Litke's duties increased. When Constantine turned seven, he was separated from his nanny and Litke took on his twenty-four-hour watch of the child. He slept in the same room and took care of his every need. In a letter to Wrangell (15 March 1835), he complained about his life: "With the Admiral General turning seven, the little nanny was sent away and now, he is completely in the care of his little uncle, who from morning till evening stays close to him and from evening till morning sleeps with him. That is, I am on twenty-four-hour watch, seven days a week. To that you can add domestic duty and thousands of little fusses which by day's end seem enormous, and sprinkle that with responsibility, anxiety, and sometimes for a change, with unpleasant-ness, and you will get a small understanding of the essence of my present duties."[5]

In 1835 Litke took his pupil to sea for the first time. They sailed from Kronstadt to Danzig and back on the steamer *Gercules.* And every year after, Litke, commanding a detachment of ships, would sail about the Baltic Sea and later abroad as well. In 1836 he commanded a detachment consisting of the frigate *Bellona,* the corvette *Kniaz' Varshavskii,* the brig *Patrokl,* the schooner *Dozhd'* and the tender *Lebed',* which com-pleted passage from Kronstadt to Sveaborg and back.

Under such conditions, it was hard for him to set up a private life. However, Litke cleaned house and decisively put an order to things which had prevented his and Julia's happiness. On 17 December 1835 their wedding took place, which was honored by the presence of the imperial family, teachers, tutors, close friends, and family members. V. A. Zhukovskii, who attended the wedding, sincerely congratulated the young couple. Litke adored his chosen one and loved her passionately and everyone who knew and saw Julia Vasil'evna (this was the Russian appellation they gave Litke's wife) spoke flatteringly of her beauty and outstanding spiritual qualities.

Litke awaited the Wrangells' return from North America with great impatience. In one of his letters inviting the Wrangells, who had already arrived in St. Petersburg, to visit him in Peterhof soon, he wrote that he yearned to show Ferdinand and [his wife] Elizaveta Vasil'evna his "old lady sent to me by Providence—an angel of comfort." This meeting occurred in September. The wives were pleased with one another and their feelings matched those of the two friends.

In 1837 Litke and his pupil sailed on the *Avrora* to Holland, accom-panied by other ships. In 1838 the *Avrora* and the *Pallada* sailed on a route that took them from Kronstadt to Borgholm, Libava [Liepaja], the Aland Islands, and back to Kronstadt. By the way, this was the very same *Pallada* whose first commander was the valiant P. S. Nakhimov and on which the famous researcher of the [Russian] Far East, G. I. Nevel'skoi, served and which was sunk in 1855 at Imperatorskii Harbor (now Sovietskii Harbor). Litke sailed with Constantine on those same ships to Kiel in 1840, to Holland in 1841, to the Gulf of Bothnia, and from there to the Sound [Øresund] in 1842, and in 1843 they sailed about the Gulf of Bothnia again. In this manner, Litke had the means to keep his naval duties and navigation skills fresh in his mind.

On 25 August 1837 a son, Konstantin Petr (in honor of Litke's pupil and grandfather), was born to the Litke family. The child's godparents were Grand Duke Constantine Nikolaevich, his sister Grand Duchess Alexandra Nikolaevna, and of course Ivan Sul'menev and Litke's wife's sister, Anna Browne. On 7 September Litke wrote from Tsarskoe Selo to V. A. Zhukovskii: "It is nice and peaceful in our pleasant Tsarskoe! Here I can find a few minutes, just a few, to rest with my wife and little boy."

At the end of the year the Litke family moved to quarters in the Shepelevskii Court. Now they lived where Litke worked. In a letter to Zhukovskii at the beginning of 1839, Litke wrote that the tsar "made my duties somewhat easier by allowing me to leave the Grand Duke in Ozerov's care (Captain Lieutenant Aleksandr Ozerov had been assigned to assist Litke—A. A.) from evening to morning. This gives me at least a little time to rest my body and mind." Litke had been working on a history of the Russian navy and had reached the section on the Peace of Nystadt. During this time Litke managed to get a pardon for the Decembrist F. S. Lutkovskii who, upon his return to St. Petersburg, even became a tutor to the grand dukes. It was with enthusiasm that Litke wrote articles on the Battles of Gangut [Hangö] and Grengam for Pliushar's encyclopedia.

I would like to call the reader's attention to the following circumstance. In none of Litke's letters, which this author had to read by the hundred, nor in his diary, was there ever any mention of A. S. Pushkin, and there is not even any comment on his death. There are frequent mentions of Griboedov and his *Gore ot Uma* [Woe from Wit]. Litke repeatedly quotes Chatskii,[a] which indicates the great popularity of Griboedov's comedy even in those days.

There was no way he could not have known Pushkin. There could have been meetings at the Olenins, at Engel's, with Matiushkin at a friendly carousal, or at Smirdin's bookstore. Probably, Pushkin himself

152

wanted to meet the famous traveler, since the poet had once dreamed of going to Russian America.

Perhaps this can be explained in that Litke, because of his close relations with Bulgarin, Polevoi, and Gnedich, abstained from speaking his mind about the freedom-loving poet. Litke, who had became intimate friends with Zhukovskii and knew better than others about the true relationship of the tsar's family toward Pushkin, preferred not to emphasize his opinions on the matter, at least not in writing.

We can also suggest another reason which might have prevented Litke from keeping a careful diary. His wife was often seriously ill for long periods. It was natural that Litke was troubled by her health and therefore had no time for detailed notes. But all of this is just conjecture.

In 1839 Litke took his first and only vacation. He and his wife traveled to Devonshire, England, where he left Julia in her relatives' care while he, on 12 June, left for the Rhine to take a cure at Ems, Baden-Baden. On the way he stopped at the Hague, and on the way back to England he stopped at Dieppe on the coast. All this time he carried on a wide correspondence with his relatives. Twelve-year-old Constantine wrote to him, bored without his knowledgeable "uncle." On 14 August Julia gave birth to a second son, Nikolai. Litke rejoiced, although his wife was sick.

After returning to St. Petersburg, Litke threw himself into his service and his favorite scientific studies. Thanks to the publication of his books, scientific work and atlases, his fame grew considerably in the scientific world. Many scholarly societies, universities, and academies made him an honorary member. Litke was promoted several times. On 24 June 1835 he became rear admiral; in 1840 he was awarded the Order of St. Anna First Class; in 1842 he was promoted to adjutant general.

In 1841, as we have already mentioned, Litke, commanding the frigate *Avrora*, corvette *Kniaz' Varshavskii*, and brig *Kazarskii,* took Constantine to Holland. The detachment left on 3 June and sailed into Copenhagen within ten days. The mariners looked over the city with interest. Litke himself told about its major sights, the Frederiksburg Castle and the Admiralty. They also visited the Historical Cartography Archives, where they looked over collections of nautical charts, including quite a few ancient Russian charts.

On 26 June they crossed to Holland and arrived at the Hague. Here they were received by the king, who awarded Litke the Order of the Lion for his work in the sciences. Then the mariners traveled throughout the country and visited Amsterdam and a site dear to every Russian, the small house where Peter I, the tsar-carpenter, had stayed in Saardam [Zaandam]. In Leiden they "became acquainted with Mr. [F. F. von] Siebold, a pleasant, scholarly and intelligent man, famous for his travels in Japan." On 23 July they returned to Kronstadt.

From here Litke sent Wrangell a letter in which he recommended Gavrilov, an ensign in the Corps of Fleet Navigators who had served on the *Avrora*, for service in the Russian-American Company.[b] Later, in 1846, Aleksandr Mikhailovich Gavrilov, commander of the brig *Konstantin*, was sent by Wrangell to study the estuary of the Amur River and thus became the immediate predecessor to G. I. Nevel'skoi, who subsequently studied the [Russian] Far East. "I can," Litke wrote, "recommend Gavrilov both as an excellent navigator and as an orderly and good man. The Company will not regret taking him into its service." It must be said that G. I. Nevel'skoi did not part with Litke either, from 1836, when he completed officers' school and first came under the ten-year-old admiral general and thus Litke, until 1846. In 1846 he [Nevel'skoi] was sent on a long-yearned-for round-the-world trip to study the estuary of the Amur and Sakhalin Island. This was made possible through Litke's intercession and protection.

Litke was awaited in Peterhof by his sick wife, who, in his words, no longer considered heart trouble and shortness of breath to be an illness, "even though it makes any movement impossible for her. She cannot walk from one room to another without losing her breath. God only knows what the outcome of this will be." But winter came and Litke again spent all his time at court with his pupil, who had become quite attached to him. If Litke were absent for any reason, Constantine would often write to him, confess all his "sins," and give an account of his every action. On 2 November 1841, he wrote to Litke: "I now have three fathers, the omnipresent Heavenly Father, Papa who is also my Lord and Tsar, and you, who are always concerned with my happiness. How can I not be happy with such a family !!!"

But such love did not make it any easier on Litke. In a letter to Zhukovskii (6/18 March 1842) he expressed himself ironically concerning the hopelessness of his situation. "This steam engine under the shingle 'Tutorial Duties' continues to work from morning to evening, today, as yesterday, and as it will be tomorrow. The only variation is that now this gear has to be tightened, now another has to be loosened, depending on the situation; but meanwhile *all* (emphasis Litke's—A. A.) my time is taken up. And if you were to ask me what I have accomplished, I would not know what to answer. One must wait about ten years for an answer."[6]

The year 1843 brought sadness to him. He did not foresee anything special. Litke left with the same squadron on a voyage around the Gulf of Bothina. When he returned, his wife gave premature birth to a daughter. It was with great pain that Litke wrote to Wrangell on 30 August: "It is sad to bury a being who has not yet set eyes on the world."

His wife's condition remained serious. Litke remained by her bedside. In fulfilling his duties at court, F. S. Lutkovskii wrote in his report to the tsar on 5 September that "Fedor Petrovich cannot write to your Majesty personally because of his wife's serious illness."

Julia Vasil'evna's condition worsened. The shock to her weak body was overwhelming and on 8 September she passed away. Litke took his loss hard. He spent whole days with his children, without going out or writing to anyone. Only after several days did he ask Wrangell to visit him. "The numbing of the first terrible minutes has passed, but I feel the need to speak about her and pour out my grief to a friend. This will ease my aching soul."

At the very beginning Natal'ia Petrovna, his sister, took care of Litke's children. Soon after, he enrolled them at the Morits boarding school and often sent them to Elizaveta Vasil'evna Wrangell, where they spent their time with her children. But as a rule, in the winter Litke took the children home.

On 6 December 1843, Litke was promoted to vice admiral. His service at court became calmer. Ozerov spent more time with Constantine, especially at night. Litke now had more free time to go out and meet with friends and relatives. They, too, visited him more often after Julia's death. In March his brother Aleksandr and wife came from Warsaw to visit him. Litke also met with his cousin Teofil Pankrat'ev, whom he had not seen since 1821 when Litke left for Novaia Zemlia. In all probability the conversations at these meetings dealt with the death of Litke's wife and the children's education. Once alone, still under their influence, he wrote in his diary: "I will weep for her as long as I am alive and a reunion with my friend is the final goal of all my wishes and prayers."

It would be a long time before he could get over the loss of his beloved wife and loyal friend. In his diary, kept throughout his life, Litke recalled Julia's memory often. He remained faithful to her until the end—he never remarried. On 12 March 1844, while pondering his lot, he wrote the following lines in his diary: "Eleven and a half years have passed since that time (since the beginning of his court service—A. A.) and what years! Only God and the one who is no longer with me to share my grief and happiness know that."

But service did not recognize sentiments. Litke again threw himself into his work at court. Besides the usual occupations, he looked over papers submitted through him to Constantine and went on trips and excursions. Together with Constantine, he visited the Izhor factories, Main Headquarters, and the Mint, and was present at the emplacement of mines. He spent quite a bit of time satisfying the requests of his many relatives who exploited his closeness to the court. Thus, he placed one nephew (Rostislav Pankrat'ev) in the Page Corps, one niece in the Ekaterina School for Women, and obtained some aid, pensions, etc., for others.

With the coming of spring, Litke began preparations for a trip around Scandinavia. This was the first major cruise abroad for the grand duke. It was proposed that it would begin in Arkhangel'sk and would end in Kronstadt. There was a fair amount of preparation, but Litke did find time for his own affairs. He often met with friends and scientists and their conversations usually focused on the creation in Russia of a center for geographic sciences. During these meetings, various thoughts and wishes were expressed.

On 14 April Litke and all the inhabitants of the capital were shocked by the disappearance of the Isaakiev bridge. It turned out that the ice on the Neva had gone out during the night and broken the great bridge, which in those days connected Isaakiev Square with the Academy of Arts, and had carried it out into the bay. Remains of the bridge were found as far away as Kronstadt.

On 24 April the naval officers sincerely and warmly celebrated the fifty-year jubilee of the naval service of Admiral Petr Ivanovich Rikord, the famous navigator and companion of V. M. Golovnin on the *Diana*. After official toasts, Nikolai Polevoi read a biographical sketch. Following that Faddei Bulgarin read his verses. Litke was present at this celebration.

At the end of April, Litke sent his children to his sister's. With the coming of warm weather, he wanted her to take them to Wrangell's in the country. And on 13 May he and Constantine were already on the road to Arkhangel'sk, so familiar to Litke. On the way there, they stopped at Shlisselburg, where the grand duke visited the fortress where ten secret prisoners were being held at that time. They also visited a monastery on the island of Konevets and the historic Lodeinoe Field. On 23 May they arrived in Arkhangel'sk.

Here the ship *Ingermanland* and the frigate *Konstantin* had already been lowered into the water. The former was built by engineer Lieutenant Colonel Zaguliaev. For those days, this was an excellent and large ship, with a length of over fifty meters. The water displacement of the *Ingermanland* was 1,371 tons. The vessels were quite well armed. The ship had seventy-four cannon and the frigate twenty-two. The crew of the ship consisted of 745 sailors and noncommissioned officers and 30 officers, while the frigate had 330 men of lower ranks and 15 officers. The *Ingermanland* was commanded by one of Litke's old friends, Captain Second Rank Mofet, and the frigate by Lieutenant Shatilov. The grand duke stood an independent watch in the rank of lieutenant.

These were towed out of Arkhangel'sk on 5 June, but got beyond the bar and under sail only nineteen days later. A headwind in the White Sea interfered with the ships' movements and there was frequent fog. They spent three days in getting to the Barents Sea, where the weather improved. Litke, who knew each cape and small bay in these areas, told Constantine and his officers about them. They quickly passed the Murmansk coast and on 1 July the ships sailed by the northernmost tip of Europe. Driven by a fresh tailwind, they quickly sailed south. On 10 August they were already sailing into the Copenhagen Roads.

The receptions and visits did not last very long. On 14 August the *Konstantin* and *Ingermanland* weighed anchor and reached Kronstadt in nine days.

Litke and Constantine returned to Tsarskoe Selo. The place no longer seemed so pleasant to Litke. As before, he missed his favorite person. On 5 August, when the ships were sailing to Great Britain, Litke wrote in his diary: "Today my little son Konstantin turned eight. His incomparable mother did not live to see her firstborn enter adolescence. Oh how the wound in my heart opens at such moments! The emptiness around me becomes unbearable. I do not even find joy in embracing my children."

The winter of 1844–1845 promised Litke the end of his court service. He would spend more time with his children. They had already returned from the Wrangells' able to speak German, and were again placed under the care of Natal'ia Petrovna.

The great fabulist Ivan Andreevich Krylov, whom Litke knew very well, died on 9/21 November. In his diary, Litke expressed his grief in the following lines: "A veteran of our literature, Krylov, has died. At least he lived to be seventy-eight years old. One more person who reminded me of my childhood and youth has died. He, among others, was very intimately acquainted with my late uncle, F. I. E[ngel], and dined at his house every week, until a certain relationship drove away all his best friends (the relationship between Engel and A. K. Adamovich—A. A.). I also met Krylov at Olenin's, rarely of late, but always as an old friend. Before dying, he had the touching idea to order that all his friends be sent a copy of his fables with an invitation to his funeral. This was just like him."[7]

Following his mentor V. M. Golovnin's example, Litke paid particular attention to the officers who served with him and whom he trusted. Navigator Dmitrii Ivanovich Orlov, who had sailed with Litke on the *Seniavin*, had gotten into trouble, had been broken in rank, and was left in Siberia in exile. Litke fought for him and managed to find service for him in the Russian-American Company. As a consequence of Litke's efforts, Orlov's rank as an officer was reinstated. Litke wrote to the Irkutsk authorities concerning this matter and in February of 1845 received the following answer: "Your Honor wishes to take a hand in the fate of Dmitrii Orlov, former lieutenant in the Corps of Fleet Navigators who was serving in the Okhotsk flotilla. You have written to me about this once. My turn has come to intercede on his behalf. With the present mail I am sending a paper about him (No. 194) to Prince A. S. Menshikov. The fate of the unfortunate Orlov will depend also on Your Honor's solicitation to His Highness Prince Aleksandr Sergeevich."[8] Soon after, Orlov, reinstated in his rights, became one of the most active participants in the Amur expedition of 1850 to 1855, which, under the leadership of G. I. Nevel'skoi, made great inroads in the research of the Far Eastern regions of our country.

It was at this time that the first steps were taken to organize the Russian Geographical Society. There was a vital and growing need to coordinate all the scientific geographical efforts in Russia. Geographical societies already existed in England and France. The idea of creating such an organization in Russia had long excited the scientific minds in the capital. F. P. Litke, F. P. Wrangell, K. M. Ber, K. I. Arsen'ev, V. I. Dal', and others were the most active in the practical realization of this idea. From Litke's letters to Wrangell, and from Ber's letters to Litke, it appears that Litke was the main activist, the organizing pivot, around which all matters pertaining to organization of a geographical society turned. It was he who had the initial idea to form such an organization in Russia.

As early as 1838 Litke had sent Wrangell a short note in which he invited him to talk about geographical affairs in Russia: "This evening (15 January—A. A.)," he wrote, "several who have been to Novaia Zemlia—Ber, Tsivol'ka and others—are coming to my place. People who have been to Kolyma are countrymen of those who have been to Novaia Zemlia, so won't you also join the circle of superfighters?" There are many such notes in Litke's and Wrangell's archives. In some of them, there are not only hints of forming a society but also thoughts of publishing a geographical journal or almanac. In the winter of 1842–1843, Litke invited Wrangell to an evening with "Ber and Gel'mersen to talk about our almanac over a cigar. Will today's frost cool the geographical ardor of many?"

The reader has probably noticed that no date appears on this letter. Wrangell and Litke corresponded so often (every day or two) that they did not need any dates. Now we can surmise the approximate time they were written only from certain hints in them. The main indicator is the almost obligatory postscript with news concerning his wife's health. Based on this indicator, we can divide the letters into those written before the fall of 1843 and those written during the winter of 1843–1844. In one of these letters, written in the spring/summer of 1843, Litke related to Wrangell that the usual "circle was very small—Savel'ev, Hagemeister, Miliutin (Colonel), Prince Golitsyn, Savvich and Golovnin." Ber was sick and was not present. Litke wrote that they discussed things for a long time and met until midnight.

In general, beginning in 1843, Litke became rather active in trying to organize a society. From the extensive correspondence, it is clear that the question had already been prepared in detail. The future cofounders would either meet at Litke's apartment in the Anichkovyi Court or at his wife's apartment in Shepelevskii Court. There is no doubt that the idea of such an organization came up in the winter of 1843–1844. One cannot doubt that the death of Litke's wife on 8 September delayed the founding of the organization with Litke as the principal initiator.

From Litke's letter to Wrangell it is quite clear that P. P. Semenov-Tian-Shanskii was undoubtedly closer to the truth than L. S. Berg when he wrote: "The conversations and meetings about establishing a Russian Geographical Society took place during 1844." L. S. Berg affirmed that "the first exchange of opinions on the desirability of founding a Russian Geographical Society" took place immediately after 20 March 1845, when there was talk of it at a dinner in honor of A. F. Middendorf, who had just returned from his voyage to northern and eastern Siberia.

It is quite clear that by the spring of 1845, after Litke had overcome the loss of his wife to a certain extent, he again enthusiastically took up the matter, and the groundwork for the creation of such a society was laid. Such a project came about mainly thanks to Litke's efforts, connections, and suggestions to the grand duke and other members of the imperial family. During the dinner mentioned by L. S. Berg, it was apparently decided to take practical steps toward creating such a society.

Litke was assigned the task of producing a draft of the society's charter and of seeking a means of turning it into a government body. Of course, in making his decisions, Litke took into account his companions' opinions, especially those of Wrangell and Ber. In order to give the reader a sense of the times, we are including several excerpts from Litke's letters.

During one of those ardent days (Litke was in a hurry because at the onset of the navigation season he was supposed to go to sea), he wrote to Wrangell: "My dear Ferdinand, I am sending for your preliminary perusal these drafts, which I hurriedly put to paper and which will be presented at a meeting of the founders. Look at them, please. Make your comments and return them to me today, as soon as possible, so that I can get them to Berg and Ber."[9] When the draft was ready he again asked Wrangell: "I don't know, my dear Ferdinand, whether you spoke to Rikord about our project. I don't plan to send the draft to him directly for his signature. Instead, I would like to ask you to do so. Then, you can send it to Chikhachev for his signature and for the signatures of Murav'ev and Odoevskii, whom he invited."[10]

It becomes clear that the draft was being readied by Litke with Wrangell's and Ber's approval and then was sent for perusal and signature to those whom Litke, Wrangell, and Ber invited to participate as founders in organization of the society. The founders included: F. P. Litke, F. P. Wrangell, K. M. Ber, K. I. Arsen'ev, V. I. Dal', I. F. Kruzenshtern, P. I. Rikord, V. Ia. Struve, G. P. Gel'mersen, P. I. Keppen, Pl. A. Chikhachev. A. I. Levshin, F. F. Berg, M. P. Vronchenko, M. N. Murav'ev, V. F. Odoevskii, and V. A. Perovskii.

V. I. Dal' served as secretary to the Minister of Internal Affairs, L. A. Perovskii, the brother of the Orenburg governor, V. A. Perovskii. It was thus decided that it would be best to ask the tsar's permission for organization of the society through him, rather than through Minister of Education Uvarov. Litke's letter to Wrangell forwarding Dal's letter is typical (Dal', considering that statistics were a matter for the Minister of Internal Affairs, recommended that Litke change the organization's name to the Geographical-Statistical Society): "I am sure in advance that the esteemed cofounders will be in agreement," Litke wrote, "and I have authorized Dal' to use Geographical Statistical Society throughout my drafts wherever needed and to accept Perovskii's suggestion. I hope you will approve of this."[11]

We were unable to document active participation in the society's creation by K. I. Arsen'ev, although P. P. Semenov-Tian-Shanskii mentions his name along with Litke's. Of course, such a supposition is fully possible, since Arsen'ev and Litke met daily for many years, talked together repeatedly, and could have discussed such ideas often.

K. M. Ber actively participated in working out the program documents of the society. On 25 April 1845, he invited Litke and Wrangell to his house to discuss several practical questions. We do not know if such a meeting took place, but on 30 April in a letter to Litke, Ber concretely laid out his views on the future society's structure. If he had formerly considered having the following four departments: physical-mathematical, geographical (topographical), statistical, and ethnographic, now he changed, or rather, refined his views and suggested the following departments: physical-mathematical, naturalistic (which included geology, geography, botany, and animal habitat), geographical-statistical or topographical-statistical, and ethnographic.

On 1 May, when everything was ready and right before his trip south, Litke went to see L. A. Perovskii at the founding members' request and handed him a report they had all signed concerning the desirability of creating a Russian Geographical Society, the main function of which would be "the gathering and dissemination, both in Russia and abroad, of information on our fatherland that is as complete and reliable as possible." Having given this report to Perovskii, who received it favorably with the promise that he would give it to the tsar, Litke departed on his travels.

On 6 August, in Litke's absence, the tsar approved organization of the society, confirmed its charter, and allotted 10,000 rubles yearly for its needs. On 15 August, the *Senatskie vedomosti* published the following notice: "Due to the solicitations of Adjutant General Litke and several other persons concerning the establishment of a Russian Geographical-Statistical Society under the Ministry of Internal Affairs, under whose authority the statistics of the government belong, he, the Minister of Internal Affairs, presented it in the Committee of Ministers, on whose recommendation the Emperor, on 6 August, approved the founders' solicitations. The society, the aim of which is to deal with questions of national geography, statistics, and ethnography, is called the Geographical Society. At the same time his Majesty confirmed the charter submitted by the founders and allotted the society 10,000 silver rubles yearly from the National Treasury."[12] Litke's pupil, Grand Duke Constantine, who had to a considerable degree been prepared for this role by Litke himself, was appointed chairman of this society. On 19 September, eight of the seventeen founders gathered at V. I. Dal's apartment. They discussed those things concerning documentation and chose Litke as vice chairman and L. A. Perovskii as honorary first member. Fifty-one active members were chosen during the society's first meeting.

Litke himself made plans for a new voyage. Constantine turned seventeen and Litke, seeing that he would be the future leader of the Russian navy, applied all his knowledge and efforts so that the grand duke would turn out to be a competent and knowledgeable naval officer. Jumping ahead, one can say that though Litke had not himself experienced a good upbringing, he was completely successful in raising the grand duke.

On 11 May Constantine and Litke, accompanied by a large retinue, left St. Petersburg. Their itinerary took them through Rezhitsy, Polotsk, and Vitebsk. In this city Litke wrote his impressions of the first three days of his trip. "What amazed us most during the last three days," he remarked, "was the poverty which affected the two provinces through which we traveled. The people out here could not remember such famine. The livestock has died and the fields are unsown. There is nothing to sow them with. The winter crops have perished. There is nothing to eat. People are literally dying of famine. In Liutsin, an unimportant little settlement in the province of Vitebsk, two hundred people have died. The measures usually taken in such circumstances have been taken. Senators have been sent, grain has been ordered, but meanwhile, people are dying and trudging north in droves to the Promised Land, St. Petersburg. At every step of the way, we met unfortunate people, on their knees, praying to God to deliver them from a hungry death."[13]

From Vitebsk they drove through Orsha, Gomel', Chernigov, Kiev, Belaia Tserkov', Uman', and Elisavetgrad on their way to Nikolaev. In his diary Litke wrote more and more of his impressions. Literally everything interested him—the price of products, the working of factories, the life of city dwellers, and of course, nature. Outside of Kiev he admired the fertile Ukrainian soil. He was amazed at "the richness of the soil, abundance of water, beautiful broken terrain, the mountains and valleys, the forests and groves ... Oh, if only a small portion of the labor and millions absorbed by the swamps of Ingermanlandiia were diverted to this area. How great this place would be!"[14]

In Nikolaev, the travelers were the guests of Admiral M. P. Lazarev. They became acquainted with the astronomical observatory and visited the Hydrographic Depot, where they looked over all the latest cartographic novelties of the Black Sea. They were also aboard the steamers *Gromonosets* and *Bessarabiia,* in which they were to sail to the Bosporus. The artist I. K. Aivazovskii joined Constantine's retinue here.

From Nikolaev they sailed on the *Bessarabiia* on 31 May to Odessa, where M. S. Vorontsov greeted them warmly. The travelers spent two days in this city, visiting the lyceum, the Museum of Antiquities, the Botanical Gardens, and the Institute for Noblewomen. In Sevastopol' the admiral general was greeted by the entire Black Sea fleet—eleven ships, five frigates, three corvettes, and ten assist-vessels ceremoniously lined up in the roadstead. The exalted guests transferred from the *Bessarabiia* to the ship *12 Apostolov,* where drills took place, then races in gigs and a ceremonial dinner.

In Sevastopol' a special squadron was being readied for sailing into the Mediterranean under Litke's command. The squadron consisted of the frigate *Flora*, the corvette *Andromakha*, the brig *Persei* and the schooner *Drotik*. The corvette *Menelai* (the future *Olivutsa,* sent to the waters of the [Russian] Far East for a cruise in 1851) joined the squadron in the Mediterranean.

After sailing out of Sevastopol', Litke made the following note: "If the shores surrounding Sevastopol' Bay had retained only a part of the vegetation which used to cover them before the Russians took possession of them, this area would be one of the most wonderful and amazing places on earth. Unfortunately, nowhere has our passion left such definite traces as here. Everything is barren, scorched by the sun, covered with dust and waterless, while fifty years ago everything used to be covered with dense forest."[15] Litke's heart protested against man's barbaric attitude toward nature.

After safe passage on the Black Sea, the *Bessarabiia* anchored on 6 June in the Bosporus, in Büyükdere across from the Russian ambassador's house. Turkish General Rifat-pasha and Captain Akhmet-bei greeted Constantine upon his arrival.

The Russian sailors were impressed for a long time by their passage through the Bosporus. "To say that everyone was enraptured," Litke wrote, "would be one of those inadmissible banalities. In order to express such subjective feelings, one needs more time and more skill than I have ... Wonders! Only a poet can talk about such things."[16] After two weeks he wrote to Wrangell "... not to write at least a few lines from Tsargrad [Constantinople] would be unforgivable. To see this entrancing place for the first time must be an 'epoch' in the life of any thinking man. Your head spins from the numerous impressions."[17]

Litke disliked the reception at the Turkish sultan's palace in Beylerbeyi. It was a stiff and strained affair. The twenty-two-year-old Sultan Abdul-Mejid, who had come to the throne in 1839 and declared war against Russia in 1853, did not deign to rise and scarcely spoke at all. "The sultan received everyone silently," Litke noted, "only when artist Aivazovskii's name was called out did the sultan grinningly approve of our having brought along an artist."[18]

Litke and the others looked over the Naval School, the Admiralty, the Medical School, and the famous Eyüp Mosque where in the olden days the newly crowned sultan would be girded with his saber. As a sailor,

Litke was more interested in the Turkish navy. This is what he noted: "The Turkish navy exists only in appearance and within a few years it will perhaps not even be here. It isn't a sin that they do not build more ships. It is better that they use their money for acquiring steamers, which are more useful to them than sailing ships."[19] In this last phrase Litke summed up his generally correct understanding of the role of the growing steam-powered fleet.

The travelers visited the sultan's famous harem, passed through the Golden Gates, were present at a meeting of the government council, and visited the picturesque Princes Islands [Kizil Adalar] in the Sea of Marmara. They traveled throughout the country for a while, visiting Izmir [Izmit?] and Bursa. From there they sailed through the Dardanelles to the Archipelago. On 27 June they viewed the ruins of Troy. In Smyrna [Izmir] they transferred to the *Menelai* and their voyage on the Mediterranean Sea commenced.

The travelers stopped on the islands of Mitiken [Mytilene (Lesbos)?] and Khios where they visited a famous monastery. On 7 July they made an excursion to the grape-rich island of Samos and then through several Greek islands, arriving at Rodhos. It was with special interest that Litke became acquainted with a small and secluded Russian monastery near the Afon [Athos] Monastery. In his diary he told in detail about this visit and about meetings with the Russian hermits.

On their return trip to Russia, they again visited Constantinople. On 22 July the travelers returned to Odessa on the *Bessarabiia* and on 9 September they were already in Sevastopol'.

Great news awaited Litke on his return. Perovskii informed him of the favorable decision with regard to the Geographical Society. Litke wrote the following long letter to Wrangell:

> After arriving here yesterday, I was gladdened by the official news from Perovskii concerning the happy results of our endeavors, which we apparently began at an opportune time. It was a good idea to let Perovskii handle matters. I doubt that Uvarov would have been as successful and expedient. I don't understand, however, why Grand Duke Constantine was chosen as chairman. As a pro-rector or trustee, that would have been all right, but as chairman—an important and responsible post?

However, everything will become clearer with time; we cannot stop halfway now, *hat man A gesagt, muß man auch B sagen* (whoever said A, must also say B). Well, this B consists in opening the society ceremoniously by the time of the chairman's arrival in St. Petersburg in October.

This moment will be memorable for him and the members and important for the society. Therefore, dear Ferdinand, try to make all the necessary preparations (advertise in the papers, etc., and get as many members as you can to open the society) by our return at the beginning of October.

Litke would make sure that Constantine's introductory remarks would be favorable to the society. It was with that goal that he assigned the speech writing to Academician P. N. Fus ("the one you least expect has the greatest practice"), adding that the speech must correspond with Constantine's age. The letter ended with the following words: "These are my thoughts. The founders will see and decide to what degree they can implement them."[20]

At the end of September Constantine and his retinue returned safely to Tsarskoe Selo after a tiring and rainy trip from Nikolaev to St. Petersburg. As soon as he returned, Litke began to take an interest in the society's affairs. Things were going well. Everything was being prepared for a great event in the scientific life of the country. Litke was in a hurry to open the society; he was again sailing soon. For unknown reasons, the grand duke could not attend the society's opening ceremonies. Litke chaired the ceremonial meeting which took place on 7 October 1845 in the great conference hall of the Academy of Sciences.

In his short but thorough speech, Litke laid out the goals and tasks of the society, including its position within the framework of other scientific organizations in Russia. Calling the attention of those present to the fact that the geographical societies of other countries had aims to study general geography while relegating their own countries' geography to a secondary role, Litke pointed out that the vastness of Russia's boundaries "indicate that the chief subject of the Russian Geographical Society must be the geography of Russia, approaching geography in the broadest sense of the term."[21]

Further, Litke noted that this did not mean that they would not pay attention to general geography. This subject would also occupy an important place in the society's activities. In order to carry out the tasks of the Geographical Society, Litke noted these basic means: the gathering of data by means of expeditions; the processing of data already gathered; and finally, the publication of all the data. The Geographical Society was in direct contact with the Topographic Depot, the Hydrographic Department, and the Academy of Sciences.

Litke dwelt especially on the society's relations with the latter, since up to that time, geography had been one of the Academy's major activities. Answering the inevitable question of why a geographical society was then needed, Litke stated: "Geography belongs mainly to the category of natural sciences and in part to historical sciences. Both of these branches of human knowledge are pursued by the Academy, but only in certain respects, and for that reason it is impossible to research all the lateral branches with the same level of results. Limited in means and number of workers, and by its obligation to pursue all other branches of science simultaneously, the Academy did not have the possibility to do everything that could be done for geography—more could have been done—and that is the aim of the Russian Geographical Society, which finds considerable support in the generosity of the monarch and in the large number of its cofounders. Thus, from a scientific point of view, the Geographical Society, an independent organization, is like an extension of the Academy, but with a special aim."[22]

At the meeting, the names of the various department chairmen and the society's council were announced. The department of general geography was headed by F. P. Wrangell; the department of Russian geography by Academician V. Ia. Struve; the department of ethnography by Academician K. M. Ber; and the department of statistics by Academician P. I. Keppen. The following were chosen as members of the society's council: K. I. Arsen'ev, F. F. Berg, M. P. Vronchenko, Academician G. P. Gel'mersen, V. I. Dal', A. I. Levshin, Academician E. Kh. Lents, and M. N. Murav'ev.

On the day following the meeting, Litke wrote a curious note in his diary which disclosed a "secret of the creators" of the geographical society: "I don't know how I became one of the mainsprings of this useful and important undertaking. The idea of the need to found such a geographical society had been in my mind for a long time. It became especially clear after the banquet which we gave in honor of Middendorf. One evening I talked about it with Ber and Wrangell, who were visiting, and we decided to try the idea out. We invited F. F. Berg, Struve and about five other persons. They asked me to come up with the draft charter. Later they brought in about ten other members. With all of this I had to go to the Ministry of Internal Affairs (since one of our subjects was the statistics of Russia). This was before my departure south. In Sevastopol' I received official news from L. A. Perovskii that the society had been approved, and with a subsidy of 10,000 silver rubles and with Constantine Nikolaevich as chairman. Upon my return to St. Petersburg, I found out that I had been selected as assistant chairman. Well, you can't back out once you've begun. Despite the lack of time and other troubles, we had to open the society and we did it on 7 October."[23]

With troubled thoughts, Litke left for a voyage around Europe. He was leaving the newly organized society for a long period of time. Of course, he rejoiced at the fact that his court service would soon end. A fiancée had already been found for the grand duke. She was a German princess named Alexandrine. To a certain extent the upcoming voyage looked like a bride-show. On 10 October Litke and Constantine sailed out of Kronstadt, commanding a detachment consisting of the *Ingermanland* and the corvettes *Kniaz' Varshavskii* and *Menelai*. Litke knew the way to London well. Although he had sailed farther, he had not stopped at various ports. That is why this voyage was of interest to him.

On 1 November the detachment arrived in London and, without stopping at any port, crossed to Gibraltar and entered the Mediterranean Sea. In Palermo, Constantine met his fiancée. During his voyage in the Mediterranean, Litke regularly received letters from A. V. Golovnin, the son of the famous navigator, who had been recommended by Litke for the post of secretary of the Geographical Society. "News about the Geographical Society is of special interest to me," he wrote Wrangell from Rome. "Our punctual secretary sends me entire notebooks about it, for which I am quite grateful to him. I read them to our president (Constantine—A. A.), who is quite interested in them."[24]

Golovnin wrote that soon after Litke's departure, he had spent some time with the Minister of Internal Affairs, and upon returning to St. Petersburg, he had taken up his responsibilities as secretary at the end of the year. P. I. Keppen "set things in motion for me." The society now consisted of ninety-nine actual members, six founding members and four honorary members. For the time being, the society's activities took place as before in the hall of the Academy of Sciences. At the end of January at the fifth session of the council it, among other things, reviewed a proposal from Litke on organizing an expedition "for geographic and ethnographic research to the Bering Sea and the Aleutian and Kuril islands, as areas about which little is known but which are remarkable in many ways."[25] After studying the proposal, the council assigned the department of general geography to come up with "a draft of the expedition, spelling out its aims and defining what means it will need and what things are expected of it."[26] Litke, for his part, also wrote to Wrangell about organizing such an expedition, and shared his thoughts on what help the Russian-American Company could give it. "The Company could be of great help, not just moneywise, but by furnishing transportation from place to place, workers, and a thousand small services which do not cost much money but are much more important than money for attaining success. The Academy would help with instruments. It would be up to the society to find a couple of men to head it."[27]

In another letter (7 February 1846) the secretary of the Geographical Society told Litke about an interesting controversy between P. I. Keppen and M. N. Murav'ev concerning the reliability of statistical data, with which Keppen had dealt all his life. Murav'ev was supported by P. N. Fus, and Keppen by K. I. Arsen'ev. "Senator Murav'ev," Golovnin wrote, "although recognizing the use of statistical data, those which have been gathered rationally, finds that everything which has been gathered and published on this topic is worthless because it is extremely unreliable, written at random, and besides, the original information comes from the ranks of the police, i.e., from people who have no understanding of statistics." Keppen and Arsen'ev were insulted, having taken Murav'ev's attack personally. Then the latter had to respond that he was "not at all referring to P. I. Keppen's works, but that, having been governor in three provinces, he is well aware how statistical information is gathered." Therefore, in the opinion of the Minister of Internal Affairs and in the opinion of Murav'ev himself, the society should not use such information but "must do something new for science and find new means of gathering more satisfactory and reliable information."[28]

Golovnin also related that in March they had begun to compile their first booklet *Zapiski Obshchestva* [Notes of the Society]. "It is definite that the *Zapiski* [Notes] of the Russian Geographical Society will come out in Russian," he noted, "but for foreigners special care will be taken in printing in the original those articles which were sent to us in a foreign language, and to translate into French or German those Russian articles which might be of interest abroad."[29]

Litke answered Golovnin regularly. However, as before, he wrote most often to Wrangell. In one of those letters, he related Golovnin's letter and criticized Keppen, who demanded that the society pay editors for their work and also print the books at its own expense and then give them all to the author. Litke angrily remarked that such behavior goes "against both the customs of a scholarly society and common sense." Litke did not forget to take down his impressions of Italy where for the most part he lived in the villa Olivutsa, in honor of which the corvette *Menelai* was renamed. Litke did not find Rome pleasant, but was ecstatic about Naples and Vesuvius. In Alexandria he was notified that he had been appointed chairman of the Naval Scientific Committee. On learning of this, he immediately wrote to Wrangell, asking him to find out how the committee functioned and "to think and advise me of ways to instill life into that lethargic body."

Above all, Litke was worried about the Geographical Society members' unity of action. After finding out that at the April meeting controversies had arisen between D. A. and N. A. Miliutin and the society's council and that the session had been disorganized and unproductive, Litke wrote Wrangell a long letter from Toulon (21 April 1846). In it he laid out his point of view on the way the society was working: "What I have heard concerning the meeting of 9 April does not please me at all. If the spirit or, let us say, if the habit of controversy takes root in the way it manifested itself at that session, the development of scholarly aims will be crushed and we will be left with various factions (the Minister of Internal Affairs had warned Litke of this possibility when he agreed to the formation of such a society—A. A.). Steps have to be taken so that the May session does not get noisy, I mean fruitless noise, and that it does not turn into debates which should not occur in general session. It is necessary that those with good intentions close their ranks behind the president and support him. At the April sessions, there was hardly anyone present on whom he could have relied, neither you, nor Fus, nor Ber, nor Struve. It will be a shame for us if our child (as we can call the Geographical Society) dies at its birth because of dissension."[30]

In this same letter Litke shared with Wrangell his apprehensive and happy feelings about his upcoming liberation [from tutoring]. However, he was worried about returning to his previous occupations. This showed how accustomed he had become to tutoring. "It would be better to start with a clean slate," he wrote, "but that too has its unpleasant side. What will be, will be, and whatever happens, is God's will," he concluded thoughtfully.[31]

Litke returned from his voyage on 29 June 1846. On the return trip, he stopped in Toulon, Algiers, Cadiz, Lisbon, Portsmouth, and Copenhagen. He also traveled to Weimar, Berlin, the Hague, Breslau, and Warsaw. In Lisbon he was present at a reception given by the Queen of Brazil. He devoted particular attention to his visit to London, where he tried to strengthen ties with the president of the Royal Geographical Society, R. I. Murchison. It is not by accident that the temporary statutes of the Russian Geographical Society seem to be an adaptation of the English statutes. Extensive and detailed information concerning Litke's meetings with Murchison and their conversations can be found in the files in Litke's archive.[32]

There were many impressions from the trip, but all in all, Litke plainly was sick of it. It was with joy that he threw himself back into life in St. Petersburg. He accepted his new post as chairman of the Naval Scientific Committee. He energetically introduced improvements into the rotted and rusty so-called scientific apparatus of the navy. On his initiative (which went into effect on 27 November 1847), the committee was transformed. Henceforth, its functions would be the dissemination of necessary and useful nautical information to the navy and to naval circles in general, and the review of projects dealing with new inventions and various proposals concerning naval affairs. Litke succeeded in establishing the periodical *Morskoi sbornik* [Naval anthology], which is still published today. In his presentation dealing with this matter, he wrote "The articles which the Naval Scientific Committee became responsible for publishing when it was established should contain mainly the fruits of its own activity, that is, articles which include important data dealing with all facets of nautical science."[33] Litke developed the format of this naval journal. In his opinion,

> it will be constituted of the following types of articles:
> 1. A brief review of the most noted inventions and experiments in all branches of nautical science.
> 2. News about naval affairs in Russia, about the voyages of vessels and squadrons, and notes on military ports, etc.
> 3. News concerning the present condition of foreign military fleets and ports.
> 4. News about nautical expeditions that are notable in a military, scientific, or commercial respect.
> 5. Events dealing with past naval feats, short historical articles, biographies, and obituaries.
> 6. News about unusual occurrences on the seas, wrecks, etc.
> 7. Literary articles dealing with nautical affairs, stories, anecdotes, etc.
> 8. Bibliography. Brief reviews of the most notable works dealing with the nautical.
> 9. Miscellany. Any kind of observation, news, facts, phenomena, questions, answers, opinions, etc.[34]

Thus, Litke can rightly be considered the founder of *Morskoi sbornik*. He succeeded in obtaining an annual subsidy from the government, a sum of 2,000 rubles. Captain First Rank B. A. Glazenap, who had sailed with Litke on the *Seniavin*, became the first editor of *Morskoi sbornik*. The first number came out on 15 March 1848.

Of course, Litke persisted in his activities with the Geographical Society, where there were still many important things to be done. Statutes acceptable to all the members still had to be worked out. Litke himself labored over this problem and often turned to the members of the council. However, dissension concerning individual questions were so considerable that the acceptance of the statutes was constantly postponed.

But the society was hard at work. In its second year of existence, it managed to organize several expeditions, one of which was a geological-geographical expedition to the northern Urals under the leadership of an active member, E. K. Gofman, and also an astronomical expedition to the province of Vladimir, under the leadership of A. N. Drashusov. The society also took part in compiling an atlas of the Tver province. In conjunction with the Academy of Sciences, it organized an expedition for Master Tsenkovskii to southern Egypt and commissioned him to obtain a geographical description of the Nile from its sources to its mouth, and an ethnographic description of the inhabitants of its banks.[35] In cooperation with the Russian-American Company, which was sending mining engineer Doroshin to do geological research in Alaska,[36] the society commissioned him to make meteorological and barometric observations.

On 29 November 1846, Litke read a summary report at the first annual meeting of the Geographical Society.[37] He turned the members' attention to the fact that, despite its preoccupation with internal affairs, the society had managed to make itself known to a certain extent in the scholarly community. The number of active members had grown to 128, and founding members to 12. After characterizing the departments' activities, he concluded his account with a speech dedicated to the memory of one of the society's founders, one of the first round-the-world navigators, Ivan Fedorovich Kruzenshtern, who had died on 12 August 1846. Establishment of the highest award of the Geographical Society—the Konstantin [Constantine] medal—was announced at this meeting.

Meanwhile, Litke's service responsibilities had to be carried out. He again began preparations for a trip to Europe with his now adult pupil. In the offing was the official betrothal between Constantine and Alexandrine. The retinue being sent was large and consisted mainly of teachers and tutors: F. S. Lutkovskii, A. F. Grimm, A. F. Berg, Baron Brunnov, Count Orlov, and others. They left St. Petersburg on 1 April by a route that went from Luga to Ostrov to Dinaburg to Kovno to Warsaw. In Dresden they visited the famous picture gallery and then moved on to Leipzig. They arrived in Altenburg on 10 April and remained there two weeks.

On the return trip, they stopped at Magdeburg, Hannover, Berlin, Amsterdam, and the Hague. From Rotterdam they crossed to London by steamer. Here they traveled throughout the country, met scholars, and conversed with Murchison at the Royal Society. Litke visited old friends at the Greenwich Observatory, and visited the British Museum, mines, and blast furnaces. On 29 July the entire delegation moved aboard the frigate *Pallada* and the corvette *Olivusta*, which were in the Spithead Roads and on 12 August arrived in Kronstadt. Eleven days later Litke was already in St. Petersburg at his sister's, where he could embrace his boys. "Kostia is a little thick-headed, but diligent. Niksa shows potential, but lacks spirit and tires quickly,"[38] he wrote in his diary.

Litke did not remain at home very long. Soon he was to accompany the tsar's family south. The trip lasted from September of 1847 to the spring of 1848. As with any job to which one has dedicated so much of one's life, it was hard to give up. Whenever Litke thought about the end of his service as tutor and future career, he felt uncomfortable. By a decree of 26 November 1847, Litke was no longer considered a tutor but a guardian of Constantine. He seriously thought about retiring and even decided to acquire an estate.

On 30 August 1848 Constantine was married. Litke's feelings and anxieties, which overwhelmed him at this time, are clearly expressed in his letter to V. A. Zhukovskii. On 17 September 1848, he wrote: "My odyssey is in its twenty-fourth autumn which I spend as chairman of the Naval Scientific Committee and I yearn for nothing better. The work I am doing now is enough to fill up the few years that I have left, but it also leaves enough leisure time to care for and bring up my children. God grant that I see them established in life. My position is not completely established and I hope they will not offend me in comparison with my predecessors."[39] They did not offend Litke. They safeguarded his former salary and gave him a fifty-year contract for 4,000 silver rubles. He remained chairman of the Naval Scientific Committee, directed the affairs of the Geographical Society, and was influential in the Academy of Sciences. Finally, but belatedly, he obtained what he had aimed for all his life: peace, children, carefreeness, and his favorite activity.

But the urge to return to his former life was stronger. A little later, he again shared his somewhat disturbed feelings with Zhukovskii. In his letter of 27 October 1848, Litke expressed an unusual feeling of loss. "Finally, I have separated myself from the world where I lived for sixteen years," he wrote Zhukovskii. "Although I never felt completely at home in that world, which was neither made for me nor I for it, a man's habits are so strong a force that in my new situation, I again feel awkward. But I will grow accustomed to this much more quickly than I grew accustomed to my previous change. I hope only that it all works out."[40]

The thought of buying an estate occurred to Litke as early as the beginning of 1847. F. P. Wrangell willingly helped his friend in this serious venture. He informed Litke that he had his eye on the estate Avandus, not far (17 versts) from Wrangell's own estate, Ruil'.[41] On 28 March 1847, Litke answered that he would be glad to become Wrangell's neighbor and asked him to find out all the details and fine print concerning the purchase. An intense correspondence on this topic lasted throughout 1848. In one of his letters Wrangell expressed doubt and suggested that Litke buy the estate Spoka, to which Litke replied (22 January 1848): "Due to my complete ignorance of country dealings in general and Estliandiia [northern Estonia] in particular, I am unable to tell you anything definite and can really say nothing. The only thing that is certain, and I hope you understood me, is that I wish to leave the Avandus matter in your hands."[42]

On 10 December 1848, sorrow struck Litke. After serious illnesses, his dear sister Natal'ia Petrovna, who had been like a mother to him, died. Not long before this, his other sister, Elizaveta Petrovna, had also died. His brother Aleksandr was seriously ill and Admiral Ivan Savvich Sul'menev was already seventy-eight years old. Litke understood that he was now responsible for his nieces and nephews who had become orphans so early. He still had fresh memories of the days of his own unhappy childhood. Negotiations over the purchase of Avandus were closed successfully. On 27 December Litke became master of this estate and an Estliandiia landowner.

During this time, important events occurred at the Geographical Society. At the founding of the society temporary statutes had been accepted. As already mentioned, these were the Russian adaptation of the statutes of the Royal Society (England). Therefore, in February of 1848 Litke chaired a commission assigned by the society's council to work out permanent statutes. The commission was to be composed of K. M. Ber, G. P. Gel'mersen, P. N. Musin-Pushkin and P. N. Fus from the council, and E. K. Meiendorf, N. A. and D. A. Miliutin, and M. N. Murav'ev from the society. The latter refused to participate and was replaced by V. S. Poroshin. Essential differences arose between the basic group of the commission and an opposition consisting of N. A. and D. A. Miliutin and V. S. Poroshin. Litke and his supporters were adherents to the statutes of the Royal Society. Litke, clearly under the influence of his English colleagues and the personal charm of Sir R. Murchison, defended conservatism in this question with a special zeal. The opposition was in favor of revising the various articles of the statutes and was largely successful in its goal. This was especially shown in the revision of the articles dealing with the society's aims. As a result, the department of general geography was abolished and instead, departments of mathematical and physical geography were created. The opposition also succeeded in electing those who would head the departments and their assistants at a general meeting of the society (according to the temporary statutes, these positions were assigned by the council). They did not succeed in resolving the method of choosing the vice chairman and secretary. They also could not agree on the mutual relationships between the council and the society. The Miliutins and Poroshin were for full democratization of the society and for subjugation of the council to the society. Litke favored a conservative platform.

These differences found expression in the Miliutins' and Litke's personal opinions.[43] A draft of the statutes was sent to many members of the society, was revised several times for greater precision, and was then examined by Constantine, who personally established the method of choosing the vice chairman and assistant (they would be chosen at a general assembly from among three candidates proposed by the council). In all probability it was Litke who turned the grand duke's particular attention to this point. Up to then Litke had been subject to the majority who wanted to have the right for direct election of the vice chairman of the society. The statutes were confirmed on 29 December 1849. The society was renamed the Imperial Russian Geographical Society.

In the first paragraph of the statutes it stated: "The aim of the Imperial Russian Geographical Society is to gather, process and disseminate geographical, ethnographic and statistical information in general and specifically about Russia, and to disseminate reliable information about Russia to other countries."[44] According to the statutes, the department chairmen were chosen by the members of each department; the council consisted of fifteen members: a vice chairman, his assistant, four department chairmen, eight members chosen by the society, and a secretary. The society received its basic code which was mainly worked out by Litke and was in effect until 1931.

During this period Litke spent much time with his children. They were being raised along with the children of Pastor Morits and spent the summer together in the country village of Ovtsyno. At the beginning of 1849 the elder son, Konstantin, began to attend a Lutheran church school. Litke's cares turned more and more to his estate. He wanted to establish a home for his family as soon as possible so that he could spend his leisure time in peace. In his letters dating from this period he even rushed Wrangell: "Can I hope to see the plan of the whole estate soon? I have to understand what I possess," he wrote on 10 January 1849. Litke sent furniture to the estate himself and began looking for an architect.

At the same time Litke gladly commented on all useful undertakings of the Naval Scientific Committee, attended as many of the sessions and meetings of the Academy of Sciences as possible, had friends over, and zealously visited the Symphonic Society of which he had long been a member. Besides these activities, he was appointed commander-in-chief of the Revel Naval Port. Litke agreed to accept the post, thinking that this would bring him closer to Avandus and his friends, the Wrangells.

After sending his children to his summer home, Litke left for Revel at the beginning of June of 1849 in order to become acquainted with his future place of service. Soon after, he returned to St. Petersburg. After taking leave of absence, he left for Avandus. Subsequently this estate played a large role in his life: the older Litke became, the more time he spent at Avandus.

He spent the winter of 1849–1850 in St. Petersburg. From Revel he received news that the commander of the port of Revel, Count L. P. Geiden, was in poor health. At the same time, he was caught up in all the affairs of St. Petersburg. In his letters to Wrangell he would regularly relate the latest news. In particular, in a letter dated 9 December 1849, Litke expressed his indignation concerning M. F. Reineke's promotion to major general when he should have been promoted to rear admiral: "Shouldn't a captain with fifteen years at sea be at least promoted to rear admiral! Of course, none of it surprised us after what we have seen and experienced. But poor Mikhail Frantsevich [Reineke] is quite upset and I fear that it may adversely affect his health, which was already shaky prior to this news."[45] Informing Wrangell about the new appointment of

V. S. Zavoiko (the future hero of the Petropavlovsk defense and married to Egor Petrovich Wrangell's daughter, Iuliia Egorovna), Litke remarked "Zavoiko is up for a much more pleasant change. They say that he is being appointed military governor of Kamchatka, upon the recommendation of Murav'ev, whose trip to Kamchatka will, it appears, result in important reforms for that region. Okhotsk is being done away with, the port is being transferred to Petropavlovsk, supplying will be from here, etc." Litke's suppositions were realized.[46]

In this same letter he told his friend of a curious fact: "Yesterday there was an experiment in lighting St. Petersburg from the Admiralty tower using a galvanic-electrical light. They expected it to be so strong the Police Gazette warned the public to protect their eyes, and not to let the horses get frightened...The Foundry [*Liteinyi*] lighting experiment using alcohol-gas was more successful."[47]

CITATIONS AND NOTES

1. GIAE, f. 2057, op. 1, d. 452, l. 85 ob.–86.

2. Ibid., l. 85.

3. Ibid., l. 84.

4. Ibid., l. 92–92 ob.

5. Ibid., l. 91.

6. Manuscript Department of the Institute of Russian Literature AN SSSR (hereafter, PD). F. P. Litke's letters to V. A. Zhukovskii 28,122/CCII b. 29, l. 9.

7. AAN, f. 34, op. 1, d. 2, l. 15 ob.

8. TsGADA, f. Gosarkhiv, r. 30, d. 33, l. 3.

9. GIAE, f. 2057, op. 1, d. 454, l. 121.

10. Ibid., l. 205.

11. Ibid., l. 66.

12. P. P. Semenov-Tian-Shanskii, *Istoriia poluvekovoi deiatel'nosti Imperatorskogo Russkogo geograficheskogo obshchestva (1845–1895)*, part 1 (St. Petersburg, 1896), p. 5.

13. L. S. Berg, "Puteshestvie admirala F. P. Litke iz Peterburga v Konstantinopol' v 1845 g." [Admiral Litke's trip from St. Petersburg to Contantinople in 1845], *Trudy II Vsesoiuznogo geograficheskogo s"ezda* vol. 3 (Moscow, 1949), p. 263. (Hereafter, L. S. Berg, "Puteshestvie admirala Litke ...")

14. Ibid., p. 264.

15. Ibid., pp. 264–265.

16. Ibid., p. 265.

17. GIAE, f. 2057, op. 1, d. 453, l. 50.

18. AAN, f. 34, op. 1, d. 2, l. 73.

19. L. S. Berg, "Puteshestvie admirala Litke ...," p. 266.

20. GIAE, f. 2057, op. 1, d. 453, l. 42–43.

21. *Zapiski Imperatorskogo Russkogo Geograficheskogo obshchestva*, books 1 and 2, izd. 2 (St. Petersburg, 1849), p. 13.

22. Ibid., pp. 15–16.

23. AAN, f. 34, op. 1, d. 4, l. 2–2 ob.

24. GIAE, f. 2057, op. 1, d. 455, l. 1 ob.

25. *Zap. Imp. Russ. geograf. ob-va,* books 1 and 2, izd. 2, p. 21.

26. TsGADA, f. Gosarkhiv, p. 30, d. 35, l. 69.

27. GIAE, f. 2057, op. 1, d. 455, l. 16.

28. TsGADA, f. Gosarkhiv, r. 30, d. 35, l. 69 ob.–70.

29. Ibid., l. 78 ob.

30. GIAE, f. 2057, op. 1, d. 455, l. 6 ob.–7 ob.

31. Ibid.

32. TsGADA, f. Gosarkhiv, r. 30, d. 26.

33. Ibid., d. 63, l. 1.

34. TsGADA, f. Gosarkhiv, r. 30, d. 63, l. 9–10.

35. *Zap. Imp. Russk. geograf. ob-va,* book 3, izd. 2. (St. Petersburg, 1849), p. 10.

36. Mining engineer Doroshin was the first to point out gold deposits in Alaska. Unfortunately, no one listened to him at that time.

37. From here on we shall not deal in detail with Litke's activities in the daily life of the Russian Geographical Society due to the fact that this was done previously by P. P. Semenov in *Istoriia poluvekovoi deiatel'nosti Imp. Russkogo Geograficheskogo obshchestva*; in the collection *Dvatsatipiatiletie Imp. Russkogo Geograficheskogo obshchestva* [Twenty-five years of the Russian Geographical Society] (St. Petersburg, 1872); and in L. S. Berg's work *Vsesoiuznoe Geograficheskoe obshchestvo za sto let* [The All-Union Geographical Society after one hundred years] (Moscow: AN SSSR, 1946). The theme of "Litke and the Geographical Society" is so broad and interesting that it undoubtedly deserves a separate monograph.

38. AAN, f. 34, op. 1, d. 7, l. 16 ob.

39. PD, Litke's letters to V. A. Zhukovskii, l. 21–21 ob.

40. Ibid., l. 23–23 ob.

41. According to information from GIAE, No. 4, 8 January 1968, Avandus belonged to the Simun (Simonis) Parish, Vezenberg (Virumaa) District, on the bank of the Ped'ia River. This is now administratively in the Rakveresskii region of the Estonian SSR, 40 kilometers from the city of Rakvere and 14 kilometers from the railroad station of Rakke.

42. GIAE, f. 2057, op. 1, d. 456, l. 5.

43. P. P. Semenov-Tian-Shanskii, *Istoriia poluvekovoi deiatel'nosti Imperatorskogo Russkogo geograficheskogo obshchestva (1845–1895)*, part 3, supplements 2 and 3 (St. Petersburg, 1896), pp. 1320–1322.

44. Manuscript Dept., M. E. Saltykov-Shchedrin Public Library, f. N. I. Vtorov (63), no. 68, l. 4.

45. GIAE, f. 2057, op. 1, d. 456, l. 116.

46. For details see: G. I. Nevel'skoi, *Podvigi Russkikh morskikh ofitserov na krainem vostoke Rossii* [Exploits of Russian naval officers in the Russian Far East] (St. Petersburg, 1878); and A. I. Alekseev, *Okhotsk—kolybel' Russkogo Tikhookeanskogo flota* [Okhotsk-the cradle of the Russian Pacific Fleet] (Khabarovsk, 1958).

47. GIAE, f. 2057, op. 1, d. 456, l. 116 ob.

* * *

a. A character in *Woe from Wit.*—Ed.

b. By this time Wrangell was on the Russian-American Company's board of directors in St. Petersburg.—Ed.

MILITARY FIGURE AND STATESMAN

Litke celebrated the new year of 1850 with the Sul'menev family. The holidays passed and he returned to his usual everyday life connected with science, service, and preparations for his final move to Revel to his new post.

In the evenings Litke's house turned into a peculiar geographical club. Well-known travelers and geography scholars often gathered there. This was an interesting period in the world of geography. Great discoveries were taking place in eastern Russia, Central Asia, and in the South Seas. It was at that time that G. I. Nevel'skoi, a friend of Litke from their joint voyage under the flag of Grand Duke Constantine, arrived in St. Petersburg. He brought sensational news concerning the navigability of the Amur River and about the possibility of entering the river's mouth both from the north and south in seagoing vessels. This meant that Sakhalin was an island. At the same time there arrived in the capital A. I. Butakov, who had surveyed the Aral Sea, and M. P. Manganari, who had researched the Sea of Marmara. In a letter to Wrangell (3 February 1850) Litke wrote, among other things: "I beseeched him (Manganari—A. A.) that he not follow his brother's example and that he furnish us with *nautical charts* prepared according to *English* and *Danish* models [emphasis Litke's], and not picture-book etchings. Butakov's charts will probably decay hidden in the archives if they aren't published through some back door."[1] The last lines are quite remarkable and refer to the fact that Butakov was in disfavor because of his support for the disgraced poet T. G. Shevchenko who had been sent into military service.

In another letter (10 February) Litke again touched upon the so-called Asiatic question—the creation of an Amur expedition under the command of G. I. Nevel'skoi for further and detailed research of Primor'e, Priamur'e, and Sakhalin. "Last night," he wrote Wrangell, "our Asian travelers Nevel'skoi and Butakov, plus your brother Wilhelm, Reineke, Chikhachov and others got together at my house and discussed matters

F. P. Litke

very pleasantly until midnight. Right now the Asiatic question is, as it were, being stirred up. I hope to God that the asphyxiating gas from the Asian Department does not extinguish this spark at its inception."[2] At that time Nevel'skoi had just been assigned to the command of the Governor General of Eastern Siberia, N. N. Murav'ev, and an Amur expedition was formed which took place during 1850–1855.

That winter Litke experienced hardships due to certain events. The Russian Geographical Society had received a new charter. It seemed that it was to have expanded the scientific work under Litke's leadership, but again he reacted in the conservative manner that had already been displayed when working out the society's basic document. On 16 February 1850 the first annual meeting of the society was taking place, along with the selection of those who headed the divisions in accord with the new charter. At this time the Geographical Society, especially at the top, was run by outstanding scholars of German ancestry or in any case, men with German surnames. The Miliutin brothers, the Khanykov brothers, and K. D. Kavelin were behind the Russian group. The opposition decided to attack.

"Possessing an unusual liveliness and conviviality, N. A. Miliutin very quickly managed to unite around him the young members of Russian science. These young Russian men thirsted not only for a rapprochement with the Russian people and study of their way of life, but also wanted to see an end to serfdom."[3] Of course, the young Russian scientists passionately wanted to go their own "pure Russian" way and not copy the English example. To them, it seemed, the leading figures of geographical science in Russia did not adequately reflect the power of Russian patriotism and weakly emphasized the Russian national character of geographical science in Russia. This explained the fact that by 1850 the department chairmen of ethnography, statistics, and physical geography were replaced (in particular, F. P. Wrangell had left his post in 1847) and an opposition was growing against Litke.

"F. P. Litke, having put all his soul into the creation of the Russian Geographical Society," wrote P. P. Semenov-Tian-Shanskii, "involuntarily looked at it as an experienced and intelligent captain would his well-supplied and beloved ship in a storm at sea. He, of course, treated the scientific knowledge of his lieutenants, the department heads, with deep respect, and often submitted to their views. In his eyes, however, those chosen from the younger generation did not have enough authority, and despite his own high feeling of patriotism, he was skeptical of the national sympathies of the comparatively young people of the society who had been elected. On the other hand, these young representatives, fully conscious of their rapidly growing strength, aimed at broadening their power by taking up the multifaceted study of their fatherland, and especially of the Russian people, to facilitate development of its national independence."[4]

These relationships became rather acute at the society's annual meeting on 16 February 1850. Litke was sure that he would be elected. Three candidates were nominated: F. P. Litke, M. N. Murav'ev, and M. N. Musin-Pushkin. After the voting Litke had two more votes than Murav'ev, while Musin-Pushkin received several votes. A second round of votes was called and Musin-Pushkin withdrew his candidacy. As a result, Murav'ev received one more vote than Litke.

"Those who were at the meeting will not forget the great figure of the chairman, a gray-haired old man, rising from his seat and addressing the society with a firm, yet deeply moved voice in the following words: 'I hope from the bottom of my heart that the successor you have chosen today will better carry out the wishes and aims of this rapidly expanding society and bring it success. On my part, I can say only that I did not spare any effort within my reach to promote the development and enlightenment of this society, which is dear to me. Be assured that even now that I turn over my duties to someone you find more trustworthy than me, and leave my coworkers in the council with grief, I, of course, will preserve my loyalty to the interests of the Russian Geographical Society and will try with all my power, even outside active participation in your activities, to be of use to the society.'"[5]

As a result of the elections only four men with non-Russian surnames remained among the sixteen members of the council (F. F. Berg, E. K. Meiendorf, P. N. Fus, V. Ia. Struve); the chairmen of the departments were V. Ia. Struve, A. D. Ozerskii, N. I. Nadezhdin, and A. P. Zabolotskii-Desiatovskii. A. K. Girs, Litke's nephew, remained the secretary.

Despite his self-control and even bravado, Litke took his defeat hard. He thought that without his leadership, the society would cease to exist. Of course, he was wrong. In connection with this it is interesting to note excerpts from his letter to Wrangell (24 February) and from his diary which testify to his genuine feelings. "M. N. Murav'ev has been chosen vice chairman," he wrote Wrangell. "The result was very pleasant for me personally. It freed me from work which was beginning to bore me and from which I could not otherwise rid myself. But as a manifestation promising the society an unhappy future, it cannot but grieve those who wish success for the Geographical Society, which from this moment will cease to be geographical or scholarly. What will become of it? And the abominations to which this well-known party resorted to obtain this result shame the society to the point that it is almost humiliating to be a member of it. What a pity!"[6]

This last exclamation expresses Litke's true reaction to the situation. These same notes of grief, indignation, and even a certain lack of understanding of the fact of his nonelection (how could there be a society without him, Litke?) run throughout his diary. An entry addressed to Wrangell reads:

> Now I must tell you about another happening which is much less serious but no less interesting. You know that the first annual meeting of the Russian Geographical Society since confirmation of a new charter was called

for last month, during which the election of certain responsible positions, including that of the vice chairman, was held. My insignificant person was among the candidates for the post and, based on all considerations which it would be superfluous to enumerate to you, that person had the greatest assurances of being chosen. I also thought that I should have been chosen, but it was not to be so. Well, what? After the first balloting, I lacked one vote for an absolute majority. After the second balloting, M. N. Murav'ev was chosen.

On the following day, everything became quite clear to me. This was a manifestation on the part of that party against which I had fought so much during the revision of the charter. It was not their particular intention to get rid of me. It will not be easy to replace such a drone as I. They only wanted to shine with the force of a minority to prove their weight and importance in the society and to protest against the ultra-conservative beginnings which I defended and which were upheld in the charter, they supposed (and not without basis), through influence upon the chairman. They did not think that another party would join them against me for totally different reasons—the party of ultra-patriots which cannot stand the German spirit...If I were to add to that all the intrigues used to reach that result, then my conviction, that by removing me these gentlemen have rendered me a true service (on my own, I never could have freed myself), will not seem like an affectation. Thus, I am happy for myself, but I fear for the future of the society. I am afraid that it will soon cease to be either geographical or scientific. And what will it be? Only Apollo knows![7]

And so, senator M. N. Murav'ev, director of the Surveyors' Corps, became the vice chairman of the Geographical Society. It goes without saying that Litke was wrong in writing that the society would perish and cease to be active without him. In the 1850s the Geographical Society greatly supported the Amur expedition of G. I. Nevel'skoi, and showed great zeal in helping N. A. Ivashintsov organize the famous hydrographic expedition that described the Caspian Sea. In 1851 the Caucasus and Eastern Siberian divisions of the society were established with a yearly subsidy of 2,000 rubles each. The Geographical Society organized a Siberian astronomical and geographical expedition under the leadership of L. E. Shvarts and F. B. Shmidt, an expedition headed by R. K. Maak, and an expedition by P. P. Semenov to Tian-Shan in 1856–1857. The first ethnographic map of European Russia (1851) was compiled by P. I. Keppen and published. An expedition was organized under the leadership of K. M. Ber and N. Ia. Danilevskii to research fishing in the Caspian Sea, and much other work was done. Forty volumes of various works were published, coming to a total of 1,260 printed pages.[8] So, as we can see, the society existed and flourished.

After calming down somewhat, Litke took up domestic chores and prepared for his departure to Revel which, according to him, "played an important role in my life and which had a decisive influence on me. In 1832 when I was assigned to accompany the grand duchesses to Revel, where they partook of bathing in the sea that year, it was done with the purpose, it is now clear, of getting to know more intimately the person who was predestined to be 'uncle' to the admiral general [Grand Duke Constantine]."[9]

Litke still considered himself the mentor of the grand duke and felt relatively free. He spent that summer in St. Petersburg, in Ovtsyno at Morits's, where his children were, and at Avandus. As usual, Litke related all the news to Wrangell, who had set up permanent residence at his estate in Estliandiia. On 28 February 1850, he wrote him that Andrei Freigang had been assigned to Kamchatka as assistant governor and captain of the port and because of that had hurriedly, within a week, married Madame Kop'eva, a real grenadier, "a head taller and almost twice as old as her husband." We can say that this Madame Kop'eva became infamous in Kamchatka for her despotism and vulgar behavior.

During that summer Litke took his children from Avandus to Revel. He again returned to St. Petersburg where Nadia Bykova, Sul'menev's daughter, died on 30 June, and his own brother Aleksandr was gravely ill. Litke took upon himself the responsibility for his brother's children and also took care of the now aged Ivan Savvich [Sul'menev].

In November of 1850 Litke was invited to occupy the post of commander-in-chief as well as military governor of Revel. On 6 December 1850, he received his official orders. He remained Constantine's mentor and advisor, playing a role in all affairs dealing with naval forces in Russia. Officially his mission as such was supposed to end in the fall of 1852 when Constantine turned twenty-five, but in actuality the grand duke used Litke's invaluable services for many more years.

On Saturday, 20 January 1851, mariners headed by P. I. Rikord organized a farewell dinner for Litke, during which N. I. Grech read a speech in verse. Another dinner was held on 27 January. This time scholars and academicians, Ber, Gel'mersen, Struve, Fus, Lents, Gofman, Berg, Postels, and others were bidding him farewell. Within a day Litke was saying goodbye to the imperial family.

Litke arrived in Revel at the beginning of February and took up his new responsibilities. Naturally, the first thing he did was to acquaint himself with the port, ships, city, and naval officers. Litke observed the low standard of discipline among a good portion of the officer corps who spent their time mainly in establishments of questionable reputation. In Litke's opinion, one of the reasons for this was that Revel, a large maritime trade and military port on the Baltic, lacked a naval club and naval library. Litke wrote a report to Prince A. S. Menshikov: "Of all the Russian ports, Revel alone has no officers' club. This circumstance is partly the reason for the disturbances which have often occurred among the officers in the port of Revel. Coming here only for the winter, they have not had time to become acquainted with society, which, for its part, has shunned them, nourishing prejudice against them, exaggerated, of course, but with some basis. Left thus to their own devices, the officers have been forced to seek entertainment in vulgar German clubs or to carouse among themselves; all of this could easily go beyond the bounds of propriety. This situation could be eliminated if they had a permanent place where they could gather and which would be a source of pleasure, but where they would have to maintain a proper decorum."[10] Remarking that an officers' club would be the nucleus of a naval officer society, Litke wrote further: "There will be no exclusiveness in the matter. Instead our club will be opened to the best elements of Revel's society, and the goal of the establishment will be attained when the club becomes the meeting place of all strata of society in Revel."[11]

On 16 August Litke received permission from the tsar to open a naval officers' club in Revel. The official opening took place on 9 September. The Revel naval club and its large library rallied various segments of town society. Local officials, especially the younger ones, often visited the club and library. They served as places where people of varied specialties met. A commissioned portrait of Litke in all his regalia was hung in the naval club.

Being governor, Litke devoted much attention to the public amenities of the city. Many of the streets, including Narvskaia, were covered with cobblestones, and the main streets were lighted with lanterns. The city officials had strict rules concerning the cleanliness and order of its streets.

As we have already mentioned, Litke played a very important role in directing the Russian military naval forces. In particular, at Litke's initiative, Constantine, who had officially taken over the naval ministry, worked out and adopted a new naval statute and also a decision concerning a series of basic reforms connected with the transition from sailing ships to steamships and ironclad ships. By the end of the nineteenth century Russia already had a large and modern armored fleet.

It was a rare working day when Litke did not receive a voluminous package containing a request-order from Constantine to render his conclusions on one or another document or simply to work out some complicated matter. And Litke conscientiously and meticulously studied the fine details and carried out his pupil's will. We will tell more about this below.

How did Litke feel about his new and unaccustomed post? "Having gotten used to living in a large room," he once wrote in his diary, "it will seem stuffy in a small one, until you begin to feel at home; these were my first feelings when I arrived in Revel." He arranged for his son Kostia to live at Dr. Plate's boarding school (Domschule Plate). Kostia made his father happy with the results of his preliminary exams. "At first that little jester Niksa feared for his brother, then rejoiced, of course, more than he will rejoice for himself in the same situation. He has a good little heart, that small being."

Initially everything was going well. But with the coming of spring Litke began to receive unpleasant and troubling news concerning family and naval matters which deeply touched him. He was informed of the death of his brother Aleksandr (26 March 1851), with whom he had sailed on the *Novaia Zemlia*. Grieving, Litke wrote Wrangell: "Out of the six brothers, only I remain, the one who was orphaned younger than the rest." Expressing his condolences to Litke, Feopempt Stepanovich

Lutkovskii wrote: "I am deeply sorry for the death of our kind and good-hearted Aleksandr Petrovich, but those who saw him lately say that the poor soul was in so much pain that he himself wished for his end."

On 28 April Litke received news of Admiral M. P. Lazarev's death. According to Litke, the admiral had regained consciousness before dying and asked to be buried in Sevastopol'. It was at approximately this same time that Litke's cousin, Furman, died and F. F. Bellinsgauzen was feeling quite ill. But the saddest event took place on 22 May: while moving to a new apartment, Ivan Savvich Sul'menev died. It was also sad that Litke could not go to St. Petersburg for his funeral because he had received news that Grand Duke Constantine was heading to Revel with a squadron. Litke wrote to his nieces Natasha and Katia Sul'menev, inviting them to move in with him in Revel.

A squadron of seven vessels and the flagship, the frigate *Pallada*, arrived in Revel in the beginning of June. Litke and Constantine often talked alone, discussing questions concerning the transformation of the Russian navy. But above all, they spoke about the draft of the naval statute, each section of which was sent by a special commission to the leading figures in the navy. In 1851 the "Committee, established by the emperor, to examine Naval statutes" was created. The committee was headed by A. V. Golovnin who later became Minister of Education (1862–1864). The draft of the statute was sent in its entirety to admirals and officers, including Khrushchov, Berens, Villamov, Anzhu, Vasil'ev, Zavoiko, Nevel'skoi, and others.

Litke regularly received information about St. Petersburg life from A. V. Golovnin, who was part of Constantine's retinue. On 27 March 1851, he wrote Litke: "As far as I can judge, your response to M. P. Lazarev's proposal concerning signals has changed the grand duke's view on the matter because his Highness, after conceding to two of the navy's major authorities, no longer defends the new system."[12] It was in this spirit that Golovnin almost constantly related Constantine's reactions to Litke's remarks on the papers sent for his comment or implementation.

A. K. Girs and A. V. Golovnin kept Litke informed about the Geographical Society's situation. Thanks to this, Litke was kept current with the activities of that organization. From his correspondents he found out that A. Humboldt's work *Kosmos* had been translated into Russian by Lieutenant N. G. Frolov.

During these years Litke kept up a correspondence with many society and scientific figures. L. L. Geiden was among them. With him, Litke corresponded in French. In one of his letters (29 May) Geiden promised to help Litke come to St. Petersburg in order to "assist in securing your nieces' future."

Such an opportunity arose that fall. Judging from Litke's letters, he was already in St. Petersburg at the beginning of October. He stayed at his relatives'. There began days of visits. Litke met with P. I. Rikord, P. F. Anzhu, and A. V. Golovnin, and visited the Geographical Society, spending several hours in the company of friends and academicians. He was quite glad that his niece Natasha Sul'menev had recovered from her illness. Litke did not forget his other nieces, whose affairs were settled. He returned to Revel in the middle of October and again threw himself into his official work.

During this period Litke was preoccupied with organizing the officers' leisure time. He even attempted to organize musical evenings in his own home, as he had regularly done in St. Petersburg.

As usual, he corresponded extensively with friends, scholars, and sailors. The letters dealing with this period speak of his care and anxieties for those close to him. At the end of his New Year greetings to Wrangell and his wife, he wrote: "My wish was, is, and will be, to have them (nieces and nephews—A. A.) at my house, but all will depend on Natasha's health." Getting ahead of the story, we shall remark that Litke took on the entire responsibility of caring for his nieces and nephews, and that his favorite niece, Natasha Sul'menev, lived in his house until his death. It was mainly she who took care of Litke in the last few hard years of his life when he was almost blind and could not move about.

The year 1852 passed in work and cares. The world situation was becoming complicated. New tasks arose for the navy in the Black Sea and the [Russian] Far East. There were also new tasks for the Baltic fleet, and consequently for the port of Revel which, along with Sveaborg, protected access to the Gulf of Finland and to the main naval fortress, Kronstadt.

Litke took all sorts of measures to fortify the defense lines, as he felt the approach of war. As early as 1850 the old discord between the Catholic and Orthodox clergies intensified over a question concerning the right of possession of Christian holy relics in Palestine. This strife about "holy places" was artificially exaggerated by Napoleon III and carried over into the diplomatic conflict between Russia and France which led to the war (1853–1856) between Russia and the coalition of England, France, Turkey, and Sardinia [the Crimean War]. The real reason for the war, however, was a conflict of the political and economic interests of these countries in the Near East. It is for that reason that the war mainly took place in Crimea and on the Black Sea, although it also encompassed the seas of the [Russian] Far East and the Baltic Sea.[13]

It is true that at the beginning of 1852 no one spoke of war aloud, but in high circles they were getting ready for a possible military conflict and Litke was well informed about that. He mainly fortified the shore defenses because the forces of the Baltic fleet were undoubtedly weaker than the English.

In addition to that, Litke remained Constantine's closest adviser, and his duties as governor also took up much of his time. He was also anxious about his family. He wanted his elder son Kostia to become a sailor without fail. It was with this goal in mind that he thought of sending him on the frigate *Pallada* which was sailing to the [Russian] Far East along with the schooner *Vostok* in order to reinforce the Pacific fleet. In this connection, it is interesting to read Golovnin's letter to Litke (30 June 1852) which clearly describes the situation of that period in the capital. "You probably already have detailed information about the *Pallada*'s assignment," Golovnin wrote. "Here we are still being secretive, while the English openly speak about it. For the latest news, it's best to address oneself to the English consul in Kronstadt, who openly declares that the *Pallada* is sailing for Japan. Yesterday Putiatin[14] arrived from England and is returning there at the end of the month. The *Pallada* will pick him up in September and then sail to the Eastern Ocean; we will keep confirming that the ship is in the Mediterranean Sea, so that Europe does not know."[15] Golovnin also informed him that Kostia Litke did not get on the *Pallada*, and that Constantine promised to send him on the next voyage. Misha Lazarev, the son of M. P. Lazarev, had been assigned to the *Pallada*.

As already mentioned, Litke constantly concerned himself with the Sul'menev family. His care had increased especially after Ivan Sul'menev's death. Litke petitioned for a full pension for the family of the honored admiral. At first he corresponded about this matter through Golovnin, but the latter asked that Litke make an official request. On 5

September 1852, Golovnin informed Litke that the Sul'menevs "would be allotted a yearly lump sum of 715 silver rubles from the government treasury," that is, more than the legal pension.

From 12 July to 10 August Litke rested with his children at Avandus. The Wrangell family was also there. Litke's son Kostia had just returned from a trip with his teacher to Finland. He entertained them with the story of his trip and told of his wish to become a sailor and how his teacher, Berg, "exhausted" everyone by constantly dragging them through Finnish cities and "showing them the nature of this northern, but wonderfully beautiful region."

On 7 September Litke received a letter from Grand Duke Constantine from Pavlovsk. I think it is necessary to include it in its entirety. On the one hand it shows that Litke had brought up the grand duke well by making him a real leader, and not merely a formal leader, of the navy. On the other hand, it obviously shows what influence Litke had on Constantine and consequently on Russian naval affairs.[16]

"Dearest Fedor Petrovich!

"In two days I shall turn twenty-five and in conjunction with this your tutelage will come to an end. In this manner our twenty-year relationship will officially be over. I say officially because I am sure that you have no doubt that it does not affect our private heartfelt and spiritual relationship in the least. You will always remain for me my old Fedor Petrovich, with whom I spent sixteen uninterrupted years and if God allows me to be of any use to the navy in my present position that will mean that you have been the main reason. So, accept from me my final, most sincere, and heartfelt thanks for everything that you did and sacrificed for me and I finally ask your forgiveness for all the grief which I willingly or unwillingly caused you at that time and believe me that my gratitude, deeply imbedded in my heart, will never be effaced."[17] Along with the letter came an official announcement bestowing the award of the Order of St. Aleksandr Nevskii on Litke, for having tutored Constantine, and for his excellent service.

There was also unpleasant news. On 20 April his old friend and comrade, F. S. Lutkovskii, died. In the spring of that same year, V. A. Zhukovskii died in Baden. And Litke's sister Emiliia was seriously ill.

Not far off was the year 1853, the year of the beginning of the war. Changes were occurring in the navy. Ships were readied for war, the frigate *Avrora* was readied for a trip to the [Russian] Far East, new ships were launched, and there were new assignments.

On 15 October 1852, Litke wrote to Wrangell from Revel that in Nikolaev they launched the 120-cannon *Velikii Kniaz' Konstantin* [*Grand Duke Constantine*] and that the keel had been laid for the 120-cannon screw steamship *Bosfor*. In relating the news of V. A. Kornilov's promotion to vice admiral, he directly hinted that Kornilov was being readied to take the late M. P. Lazarev's place as commander-in-chief of the Black Sea fleet. "Kornilov's leap has been colossal, he passed over ten men and was only a rear admiral for four years. Apparently everything is going his way."

Meanwhile, E. V. Putiatin left for England. Russia tried at all costs to come to an agreement with England and thus to isolate France. The English, however, did not come to any agreement, and in February of 1853 Nicholas I sent an extraordinary mission to Constantinople, headed by Prince A. S. Menshikov who arrogantly demanded that Turkey restore the privileges of the Orthodox clergy in Palestine and recognize the right of the Russian tsar to protect the Orthodox subjects of the sultan—Serbs, Bulgarians, Greeks, and others. The English and French diplomats did everything they could to undermine Menshikov's mission. Unsuccessful in his endeavors, the latter declared that diplomatic relations between Russia and Turkey had been broken, and on 9 May 1853 left Constantinople. Whetting the appetites of England and France, Turkey had sent its squadrons to the Dardanelles as early as February. In answer to that move, Nicholas I sent Russian troops into Wallachia and Moldavia on 14 June. Turkey, feeling the support of England and France, made no concession. The Turkish government demanded that Russia withdraw its troops from its principalities, but this did not take place. On 4 October 1853, Turkey declared war on Russia. On 15 and 16 March 1854, France and England allied themselves with Turkey, thus declaring war against Russia as well. The Eastern or Crimean War of 1853–1856 had begun.

On 26 February 1853, when war did not yet seem so close, Constantine had asked Litke "to secretly inform [him] about the improvements which you consider most useful in matters under your direction." Litke answered that mainly "they consist in various types of construction, both new construction and repairs" (sheds for safeguarding rowboats,

193

and compass, lighting, artillery, and other workshops). It was also necessary to restore and repair all the shore artillery emplacements and to construct barracks for the lower ranks. He requested that he be sent a dredger, a water-supply ship for watering vessels in the roads, and cast-iron pipes for water piping, that he be allotted a permanent steamer for the port, etc.

As usual, Litke actively participated in the review of documents and projects sent to him by Constantine, who was directing the Naval Ministry. Thus, in March of 1853 he made detailed comments on the draft "Charter of a society for saving the perishing and the seemingly dead," and "Draft regulations concerning the Kamenno-Ostrovskii Invalid Home." In April he looked over the "Dictionary of Nautical Vocabulary and Expressions" written by Schultz, which Litke did not particularly like. On 2 April Constantine wrote to Litke: "I am sending you a backlog of proposals on naval affairs, and I ask you to read them slowly and to make your remarks either in the margin or on separate sheets of paper."

Many of the drafts sent dealt with a reorganization of hydrographic matters. We shall deal with this topic in the concluding chapter of this book. We shall remark now that Litke advised that Kronstadt remain a rear base ("as a repair arsenal for ships and as a steamship station") and that all warships, all the naval forces of the Baltic fleet, be transferred to Revel and Sveaborg. He wrote Constantine: "Before thinking of any other improvements, it is important to establish a balance between the aims and the means. We must either increase our means based on the extensiveness of our goal, or proportion the goal to the means. Without this balance between the aim and the means there can be particular attempts to improve this and that, but a complete revamping of an important branch of the government is not possible. It is no use to blind oneself to this reality."[18]

In these lines one can sense a major government action; it is mainly this kind of action that Litke had taught Constantine. In April Litke reviewed the drafts "Rules governing crew life" and "Instructions for establishing a guild of free sailors in Kronstadt." In his answer to Constantine he wrote these remarkable words: "The life of each individual sailor must be as dear to the government as the life of the guild."

As soon as the break in Russian-Turkish relations became known, Golovnin hurried to inform Litke about the mood in the capital. On 18

July 1853 he wrote: "News from the south (i.e., from the Black Sea— A. A.) is very reassuring. It can be said with certainty that there will be no war and that everything will be settled peacefully." In addition to other news, Golovnin wrote that Constantine "has less and less to do with the Geographical Society, where his Highness does not much care for Murav'ev."

Litke was officially invited to write a history of the Russian navy, but he declined, although as we shall see later, he wrote several serious works on the history of the navy. This task then "was assigned to Viskovatov, Sokolov, and Veselago, each of whom was to work on this topic separately. It was ordered that the archives be opened to them and that they be given clerks, and it was promised that if the Scientific Committee approved of their work, their manuscripts would be published at the treasury's expense."[19] Thus the works of these scholars on the history of the Russian navy appeared.

In August of 1853 Litke's elder son, Konstantin, was assigned as a cadet on the *Avrora*, which was sailing to the [Russian] Far East. The frigate *Diana* also soon sailed for there, to replace the frigate *Pallada*.[20] Litke was agitated at having to part from his son, but outwardly he did not show his emotions.

On 21 November 1853, when the war was already being waged in the south, Constantine ordered Litke to "submit his considerations" in case war were to break out in the Baltic Sea in 1854. At that time Litke, who had received a new assignment (on 4 November he became commander-in-chief of Kronstadt port and military governor of Kronstadt), was still in Revel, where he was to be replaced by Ivan Petrovich Epanchin. He answered Constantine's request in detail, underlining two important facets of this question: "(1) Arming of the northern section of the military harbor with artillery and (2) supply of the port with provisions and materials for repairing ships."

When the world found out about the brilliant victory of P. S. Nakhimov's squadron at Sinope and about the routing of the Turkish fleet, it became evident that France and England would enter the war without delay and would take naval action not only in the Black Sea. It was because of this development that Litke was transferred to Kronstadt, which was considered the main base of the Baltic fleet. Soon Kronstadt was connected to the St. Petersburg Admiralty by telegraph. In addition to that, it was decided to establish daily mail. In answer to Constantine's analogous inquiry in case of possible naval action in the Baltic in 1854, Litke wrote: "If the enemy appears in the Baltic Sea in the spring, he will come, of course, in such force, that it will be impossible for us to go into open battle against him." He thought that it would be necessary to carry on a defensive war, to concentrate all three divisions (twenty-four new and seven old sailing vessels of the line, ten steampowered frigates and twenty-six oar-powered cannoneer boats) at Sveaborg. In this, he took into consideration the fact that out of this, at first glance, remarkable number of ships, only eleven could be used in squadron formation. "In order to wage a successful defensive war," Litke continued, "it is necessary to concentrate our forces so as to paralyze the action of the enemy and have the possibility, if the situation arises, to inflict more or less painful blows." Developing his thought, he affirmed that our men were very good, but that the captains were inexperienced. "No one will doubt their fearlessness," Litke underscored, "but scorn of death alone is not enough for coolness and presence of mind in battle; one needs to be sure of oneself, and that comes only from experience."[21]

Litke turned out to be correct. In the spring of 1854 the English squadron of Admiral Napier sailed into the Baltic Sea, greatly surpassing the forces of the Baltic fleet both in the quality of the ships and in the number of contemporary fighting units. Having arrived in Kronstadt overland, with a detour to the capital, where there was only talk of the recent battle at Sinope ("I found St. Petersburg ecstatic about our sailors' exploits," he wrote in his diary), Litke immediately took measures to defend the base and to organize the forts, reinforce them with artillery and provisions, and lay mines in the channel. On 20 April 1854 the first emergency drill took place. On 13 May all crews were shown the English military flag (from the *Tiger*, taken at Odessa) and two Turkish flags taken at the battle of Sinope.

It became known at the beginning of June that fifty enemy units had approached Sveaborg: fourteen screw steamships, fifteen sailing ships, two screw steam frigates, four sailing frigates, and fifteen steamships. But the enemy, as is well known, never reached Kronstadt. It took a long time and heavy losses before the English could take possession of the small island fortress of Bomarzund in the Aland Islands. Then the actions of Napier's detachment were directed against the city of Abo [now Turku] and the Sveaborg fort, but could not do any more than bombard the area. Later, the enemy carried on a piratical blockade at the entrance to the Gulf of Finland and the Gulf of Bothnia, sailed into the Gulf of Riga and attacked the mouth of the western Dvina, Libava [Liepaja], the island of Nargen [Naisaar], Pärnu, and other coastal areas. The same thing was repeated in 1855 when Admiral Dundas's squadron bombarded Sveaborg. The war ended with the signing of an armistice on 2 March 1856; on 18 March a peace accord was signed in Paris.

In addition to his military concerns about the defense of the Gulf of Finland and especially of Kronstadt and its forts, Litke carried out Constantine's various tasks, concerned himself with the welfare of Kronstadt, and took part in hundreds of small and large matters which could be resolved by his authority. In April, Litke actively corresponded with Nobel in conjunction with placing mines in the northern Kronstadt channel. Litke also decided important fiscal questions and was busy with the publication of *Morskoi sbornik*. He worked a great deal on a critique of the *Code of Naval Decrees*, worked on a draft of new regulations concerning the Naval Scientific Committee, looked over a draft of the charter of the Archaeological Society, wrote "Certain remarks about Kronstadt Port," and expressed his views on Constantine's proposals about organizing squadrons of frigates and steamships in 1855 to repel possible enemy attacks. He also did a careful study of the personal matter of the commander of the transport *Neman*, Captain Lieutenant Shkot, concerning the wreck of his vessel. Litke saved the commander from severe punishment. The matter ended with Shkot's retirement with the right to be reinstated at the lowest officer rank. Finally, Litke made a careful study of measures to fight scurvy in Kronstadt and made a series of practical suggestions which were implemented (beds instead of plank-beds, warm clothing—overcoats, better food rations, and physical exercise in fresh air, etc.).

Despite his zealous service, Litke was not a born naval leader or military admiral. One can even say that this kind of combat service burdened him. And of all the cities and ports, Litke disliked Kronstadt most of all. He probably wrote and spoke to Constantine about this more than once. On 27 March 1855, Litke was promoted to full admiral and continued his Kronstadt duties nearly all of that year.

Much water passed under the bridge. Wrangell's relative, Rear Admiral V. S. Zavoiko, brilliantly repulsed an attack by the enemy Anglo-French squadron on Petropavlovsk-Kamchatskii, and early in the spring of 1855, after sawing a channel in the ice, he led the entire garrison out of Petropavlovsk aboard semi-military ships to Chikhachev (De Kastri) Bay, literally under the nose of the enemy cruising at the entrance to Avacha Bay. From Chikhachev the squadron (with the exception of the frigate *Pallada*) was taken to the mouth of the Amur River to Nikolaevsk-on-Amur, which had been founded by G. I. Nevel'skoi's expedition to the region.

Litke was glad to receive a letter from I. N. Izyl'met'ev, commander of the frigate *Avrora*. On 4 September 1854 he wrote to Litke about Kostia, who during his voyage "earned the respect of all the officers for his moral behavior, enthusiasm toward service, and his personal qualities; and he has been helpful to me in dealing with foreigners because of his knowledge of foreign languages. On the twentieth and twenty-ninth during an attack and bombardment of Petropavlovsk by the Anglo-French squadron, your son was attached to the military governor, and under heavy fire, carried out all orders clearly and firmly. His display of bravery promises a future sailor and hero to the benefit of the fatherland."[22]

At this time the heroic defense of Sevastopol' continued. The names of heroes who defended the port rang everywhere. The names of P. S. Nakhimov, V. A. Kornilov, V. I. Istomin, E. Totleben, sailor Petr Koshka, and many others were on everyone's lips. The heroic defense of the city lasted eleven months, during which Nakhimov and Kornilov, two outstanding naval leaders, died. The ineptness of the high command finally caused the city to surrender. Somewhat earlier the commander-in-chief A. S. Menshikov had been removed from his post. Litke made an interesting observation in his diary concerning the matter. He tells in detail about Menshikov's suspension from all his duties as commander-in-chief, head of naval headquarters and governor general of Finland. Litke underscores that he remained only an adjutant general and a member of the Government Council. "What a terrible disgrace!" Litke wrote. "We shall see if he can bear this fall with the same Christian humility that his great-grandfather displayed when he was exiled. I doubt it, knowing Menshikov's personality and his relations with people. It is possible to be happy in disgrace, if you leave the field with a clear conscience and the sympathies of honest people accompany you. This source of solace does not exist for Menshikov. He has nothing in his soul besides boiling bile. His whole life is nothing but negation of the spirit—*ein verneinen der Geist.* In his adversity he will find one happiness—malicious words. Unhappy man!"[23]

However, it was in vain that Litke felt pity for Menshikov. With the ascension of Alexander II to the throne, Menshikov was again appointed commander-in-chief of the land and naval forces, while E. V. Putiatin became chief of naval headquarters. Litke, who was promoted to admiral and was receiving a mass of congratulations because of it, continued his varied functions. In the winter of 1854–1855, he worked out the regulations for junior flagmen and wrote a report "about abridging correspondence in the division, brigade, and crew staffs"; he also made his comments on a memorandum concerning children's admission to the naval corps. In matters relating to this subject, Litke believed the main thing was that "none of the graduates from the Naval Corps should be unfit for sea duty either physically or mentally." In addition to this, Litke looked over Academician B. S. Iakobi's reports, which dealt with placing a barrier of galvanic mines in the southern Kronstadt channel.

Litke's letter to A. V. Golovnin dated 28 March 1855, dealing with a collection of sayings and proverbs by V. I. Dal', is simply unique. Litke carefully read the collection and concluded the following. "Dal's proverbs are herewith being returned. It is an enormous work. It would be a pity if it went to naught. But in order to publish this collection, it is my opinion that it needs a major revision. First, it needs to be cleaned up. Much can and should be excluded. Much of it is superfluous. It includes things that can be called neither sayings nor proverbs. There are things that are simply passages from Scripture. Others are awkward or improper for publication. Second, the sayings which are now arranged by categories should be put in alphabetical order. Without this, the collection would be difficult to use and one of its main goals—to be as complete as possible—will not be attained. For example, I recall several interesting proverbs that I do not find in the collection. How can I be sure that they really are not included? One cannot read through two thick volumes for that. The example I cite is not a figment of my imagination, but a fact. I wrote out in pencil two or three proverbs which I was sure (or at least thought) were not in the collection. I have several more sound ones [proverbs] in reserve, but how do you know whether they are in the collection? Finally, the third thing and the hardest—each proverb which has no apparent or generally understood meaning must be explained. Without this, the collection will lose its chief interest. No one can correct all of these things except Dal' himself, or at least someone under his immediate supervision. This undertaking is worthy of the grand duke's patronage. It is properly a matter for the Geographical Society."[24]

Meanwhile, Litke's prayers to be "freed from Kronstadt prison" were heard. On 23 October 1855, he was appointed a member of the Government Council, while Vice Admiral P. M. Novosil'skii replaced him in Kronstadt. Litke retained his salary as governor general of Kronstadt and was awarded a house on Angliiskaia [English] Quay (now the Red Navy Quay).

Novosil'skii arrived in Kronstadt in November. With pleasure, Litke gave him the reins of government and with still greater pleasure returned to his beloved St. Petersburg.

On the eve of 1856, the permanent secretary of the Academy of Sciences, A. F. Middendorf, informed Litke that he had been selected as an honorary member of the Academy on 28 December 1855. An interesting detail is that instead of gratefully accepting this well-earned and respected title, Litke asked if he could still consider himself a corresponding member. Only when he was, as an exception, allowed to retain both titles, did he agree to accept the diploma of honorary member. That is how much he cherished his real affiliation with the Academy.

The war was coming to an end. It seemed that now Litke would be free to pursue his scientific endeavors. But Constantine still considered him his first and foremost counselor. Apparently trying to draw lessons from the still unfinished war, on 7 January he asked Litke's opinion concerning "what significance and what meaning and composition our Baltic fleet ought to have in view of Russia's particular political situation in connection with other governments and after the revolutionary changes in the navies of all nations due to the introduction of the screw steam engine."[25] Litke replied quite candidly that given the complicated circumstances and in the short term "Russia cannot have a navy which could compete with the English on the high seas," and that this was "a clear fact that needs no proof." In his opinion the government and the head of the navy must first concern themselves with strengthening coastal defenses (in proportion to the forces of Sweden and Denmark). "But in order for the Baltic fleet fully to carry out its mission," Litke wrote, "it is necessary for its ships to exist not only on paper, but as real entities, ready and equipped for war at any time; and that these ships be equal to those of other nations in their strength, equipment, and qualities, and also in the skill of their officers and crews."[26]

Up to 1864 Litke actually directed the activities of the naval ministry, although, as already mentioned, he had no particular liking for military matters. In his capacity, Litke touched all matters concerning the navy. He criticized the projected organization of the naval ministry, and Constantine agreed with his criticism; he approved the draft port regulations, and Constantine confirmed them; he decided budgetary matters dealing with the naval ministry. On 30 April 1856 Litke wrote a report to Constantine "On the aim and purpose of the Russian Navy." In the report he foresaw a yearly increase in allocations to the navy. He was interested in the activities of the officers' classes and justifiably asked: Why is it that these officers' classes cannot be called academies? Litke was proposing the formation of a Russian Naval Academy, which was later organized on the basis of the officers' classes. He advised the desirability that the officers be taught physical geography and suggested L. I. Shrenk for that purpose—"a scholar who completed a voyage on the frigate *Avrora* and is therefore qualified to present the topic in a manner concordant with naval officers' needs and level of understanding." Soon after, the officers were able to attend the wonderful lectures of Academician Shrenk, which were later published.

In a word, Litke spent these years at the rudder of Russia's naval forces. However, when, in 1857, he was offered the post of Chief of the Main Naval Headquarters, he refused. It is hard to explain this refusal. At that time Litke was going on sixty-one and he could still continue working for the good of the navy. The clue, apparently, lies in his love of and devotion to science, and his scientific designs, which again took hold of him after he was unanimously elected vice president at the annual meeting of the Geographical Society in January of 1857. This did not mean, of course, that Litke was freed "of military duties." As before, he reviewed a large number of diverse projects which Constantine sent to him for advice or simply for implementation. Hydrographic questions are allotted much space in these papers.

In his fundamental work, P. P. Semenov-Tian-Shanskii tells in detail of Litke's exceptionally fruitful activity in the Geographical Society. For that reason, we shall not deal in detail with that aspect of his life. We shall simply mention that all of Litke's energies during those years were directed toward the study of Priamur'e, Primor'e, and Sakhalin, which had initially been studied by G. I. Nevel'skoi and the officers who had accompanied him on the Amur expedition. Litke was sincerely happy with the successes of the naturalists sent to that area: F. B. Shmidt, P. P. Glen, A. D. Brylkin, P. Maak, and G. I. Radde. In one of his letters to P. I. Keppen, he calls Radde "our fine fellow."

Even though he had not freed himself completely from his military duties (how could he and remain in the navy!), he slowly moved away from them. True, from time to time, he was assigned to various military committees or commissions. But gradually Litke, as a commonly accepted scholar, honorary academician and vice president of the Geographical Society, began to occupy himself more often with questions dealing with the organization of science in Russia and began personally to work in the scientific field. He worked fruitfully in the area of hydrography of the sea, and wrote reviews of the scientific significance of the books and manuscripts submitted in competition for the Demidov Prize.

In this connection, it is curious that Litke gave a sharply negative review (1855) of P. M. Novosil'skii's book on the voyage of F. F. Bellinsgauzen and M. P. Lazarev to Antarctica. In 1862 he gave a favorable review of P. A. Tikhmenev's book *History of the Formation of the Russian-American Company,* for which the author received the full Demidov Prize. Litke reacted to the book in the following way: "The work is well grounded and conscientious, and satisfies all the demands of a historian and political economist; it truthfully portrays the activities of an important commercial and at the same time governmental establishment; it uses facts to refute passionate and one-sided views of the Company."[27]

Litke considered that Novosil'skii's book was presented in diary form and was without scientific conclusions, comparisons or inferences. Consequently, the author did not work with a scientific goal and therefore, did not deserve any special award, aside from those already received for completing the voyage itself. Tikhmenev's book was the result of many years of historical archival research; it was full of conclusions, inferences, and analyses which gave a full picture of the many years of activity of the Russian-American Company. This meant that the author had proved himself as a scholar who had handled a huge task excellently and deserved to be awarded the Demidov Prize.

In 1859 Litke was appointed a member of a commission of the Academy of Sciences to examine the draft statutes of the Main Nikolaev Astronomical Observatory and was also chosen to serve on the commission which would annually review the observatory's activities (together with V. Ia. Buniakovskii, B. S. Iakobi, A. N. Savich, D. M. Perevoshchikov, and S. I. Zelenyi). But his main occupation was work in the Geographical Society. Here he actively worked with the scholarly secretary, his future biographer, V. P. Bezobrazov, and from 1862 he worked closely with Fedor Romanovich Osten-Saken, who for ten years served as secretary of the society. At first, however, Osten-Saken wrote Litke that he was not capable or worthy of these duties and asked to fill this post only temporarily. In his later letters, such pessimism vanished. This can be attributed to Litke's influence. In 1867 Osten-Saken went on an expedition to Turkestan and was late in returning to St. Petersburg. Afraid that he might be replaced, he even wrote and asked Litke not to do it. "I cherish my post as secretary," he wrote.

In July of 1859, while serving on the Government Council, Litke was assigned "to an office in the Department of Laws." He actively participated in the commission which was preparing reforms dealing with liberation of the serfs and he received a gold medal on an Alexandrov ribbon, "to be worn in the buttonhole in memory of the liberation of manorial serfs."

As before, awards rained down upon Litke as from a horn of plenty. In 1858 he was awarded the diamond clusters of the Order of St. Aleksandr Nevskii. On 26 September 1863, Litke had served fifty years in officer rank. In honor of this event, he was given the tsar's letter of commendation, which mentioned Litke's services in the navy, the government, and scientific fields. He was awarded the Order of Vladimir First Class with a large cross. Litke was congratulated by the Academy of Sciences, the Geographical Society, and other scholarly organizations. At a general meeting of 5 October 1863 the Geographical Society "unanimously decided to decorate the society's hall with a portrait of Litke and to commission the council to convey to him those feelings of gratitude and respect for his work which had inspired the society."[28] The portrait by artist Tiutriumov still hangs in the Geographical Society today. The council of the society, in informing Litke of the news, wrote: "Our present expression of the society's recognition is without doubt too small a gift for your work in the field of geography which brought you universal fame in the scientific world, and for your many years of work dedicated to the establishment and development of the Russian Geographical Society, for whose conception you alone are responsible."[29] This announcement was signed by P. P. Semenov-Tian-Shanskii, E. P. Kovalevskii, E. I. Lamanskii, S. I. Zelenyi, and others.

At this time, Litke was an honorary member of the following societies and establishments: honorary professor of Khar'kov, Kazan', Petersburg, and Derpt [Dorpat] universities; honorary member of the Free Economic Society, Naval Academy, Imperial Academy of Sciences, Royal Geographical Society in London, the Copenhagen Institute of Antiquities, the Brazilian Institute of History and Geography, the Austrian Geographical Society, and the Berlin Geographical Society; and associate member of the French Academy of Sciences in the sections of geography and navigation. In 1875 he was awarded the honorary diploma of the International Geographical Congress.

In concluding this chapter on Litke's military and government activities, we would like to quote one phrase from a speech by F. F. Wrangell in 1897 on the hundredth anniversary of the birth of Fedor Petrovich Litke: "Having been called to participate in the higher echelons of government affairs, F. P. Litke carried out his responsibilities with his usual hard work and conscientiousness, but did not take an active or outstanding part in them, with the exception of the reorganization of the Naval Department which was undertaken on the initiative of the young admiral general [Constantine]."[30] This exerpt is clearly erroneous. The materials show that, willingly or unwillingly, Litke participated quite actively in Russia's governmental affairs, mainly directing the activities of admiral general Constantine in leading the country's naval military forces. And he was the one who initiated the navy's reorganization.

CITATIONS AND NOTES

1. GIAE, f. 2057, op. 1, d. 457, l. 6.

2. Ibid., l. 10. For G. I. Nevel'skoi's activities see his book, cited above, and A. I. Alekseev's *Spodvizhniki G. I. Nevel'skogo* [Associates of G. I. Nevel'skoi] (Iuzhno-Sakhalinsk, 1967).

3. P. P. Semenov-Tian-Shanskii, "Epokha osvobozhdeniia krest'ian v Rossii (1857–1861)" [The period of emancipation in Russia (1857–1861)], *Memuary*, vol. 3 (Petrograd, 1915), p. 13.

4. P. P. Semenov-Tian-Shanskii, *Istoriia poluvekovoi deiatel'nosti Imperatorskogo geograficheskogo obshchestva (1845–1895)*, part 1 (St. Petersburg, 1896), p. 58.

5. Ibid., p. 59.

6. GIAE, f. 2057, op. 1, d. 457, l. 16.

7. AAN, f. 34, op. 1, d. 4, l. 94–96.

8. *Poluvekovoi iubilei Imperatorskogo Russkogo geograficheskogo ob-va* [Fiftieth anniversary of the Imperial Russian Geographical Society], *Zemlevedenie*, vol. 2 (Moscow, 1895), pp. 140–141.

9. AAN, f. 34, op. 1, d. 7, l. 73 ob.

10. V. V. Ivanov, "K biografii F. P. Litke" [Toward a biography of F. P. Litke], *Morskoi sbornik*, vol. 55, no. 9, 1861, p. 60.

11. TsGAOR, f. 722, op. 1, d. 177, l. 14.

12. TsGADA, f. Gosarkhiv, r. 30, d. 35, l. 86.

13. For a more detailed account of the war, see E. V. Tarle, *Krymskaia voina* [The Crimean War], vols. 1 and 2 (Moscow, Leningrad: AN SSSR, 1950).

14. Evfimii Vasil'evich Putiatin, vice admiral, and head of the expedition on the frigate *Pallada*, was a diplomat who led talks with Japan and China, and concluded the Tientsin Sino-Russian Treaty in 1858 which was a supplement to the Aigun Treaty. The Peking agreement of 1860 finally secured the borders between China and Russia in the Priamur'e and Primor'e regions.

15. TsGADA, f. Gosarkhiv, r. 30, d. 35, l. 144 ob.

16. In this connection, it is interesting to remember L. S. Berg's characterization of Constantine: "The first chairman of the Geographical Society, Grand Duke Constantine Nikolaevich (1827–1892), the second son of Nicholas I, belonged to the intelligentsia of the [18]60s, and took an active part in the peasant reforms. After being relieved of all his government duties by Alexander III, he spent his last years as a private citizen, in disgrace. Besides being the chairman of the Geographical Society, he was also the chairman of the Archaeological and the Musical Society." (L. S. Berg, *Vsesoiuznoe geograficheskoe obshchestvo za sto let*, Moscow, Leningrad: AN SSSR, 1946, pp. 35–36.) It must be added that documents show that he was not formally the chairman of the Geographical Society, but that he took an active and direct part in securing various advantages for it. The naval officers were delighted with him. Of course, this was due to Litke. The letter cited speaks of this.

17. TsGADA, f. Gosarkhiv, r. 30, d. 12, l. 26.

18. Ibid., d. 13, 1. 62.

19. Ibid., d. 35, 1. 159 ob.

20. The fate of the *Pallada* was the following: In 1855 it could not enter the Amur estuary and be brought to Nikolaevsk; it was therefore left to winter in Imperatorskaia (now Sovetskaia) Harbor. Afraid that the frigate would be discovered by the French and English in the summer of 1856 (news of the armistice had not yet reached the Far East), V. S. Zavoiko ordered it to be sunk, and that its armaments be brought ashore to strengthen the Konstantinovskii post (this order was carried out by Midshipman G. D. Razgradskii, a member of the Amur expedition under G. I. Nevel'skoi). It is impossible to raise it from the sea bottom. A memorial has been placed on the shores of the bay.

21. TsGADA, f. Gosarkhiv, r. 30, d. 14, 1. 13–16 ob.

22. TsGAVMF, f. 15, op. 1, d. 24, 1. 8–8 ob.

23. AAN, f. 34. op. 1, d. 8, 1. 39 ob.

24. PD, A memo from Litke to Golovnin, No. 27473/CXCVI/b/5.

25. TsGADA, f. Gosarkhiv, r. 30, d. 16, 1. 3.

26. Ibid., 1. 7–7 ob.

27. *Tridtsat' pervoe prisuzhdenie uchrezhdennykh P. N. Demidovym nagrad 25 maia 1862 goda* [The thirty-first awarding of the P. N. Demidov Prize, 25 May 1862] (St. Petersburg, 1862), p. 90.

28. AVGO, f. 1–1863, op. 1, d. 18, 1. 17.

29. TsGAVMF, f. 15, op. 1, d. 4, 1. 16 ob.

30. *Izvestiia Imperatorskogo Russkogo geograficheskogo obshchestva*, vol. 33, vyp. 4 (St. Petersburg, 1897), p. 342.

TO THE ACADEMY OF SCIENCES

Because of his great authority in scientific circles, recognition of his scholarly merits throughout the world, and absolute confidence shown in him by the imperial court, Litke was chosen to the highest scientific post in the country—President of the Academy of Sciences. The appointment took place on 24 February 1864. Grown wise with years and life experiences, gray-haired Litke nevertheless spoke with great nervousness to his academic colleagues when presented to them in his new position:

> It is not without confusion and not without great doubt in my own strength that I take my place among you in such a post ... When I think of the remarkable predecessors who held this post, I ask myself: to what do I owe this honor? I, a simple sailor, prepared for this high post neither by initial education nor by subsequent public activity? I find only one answer to this question. Without doubt, I owe it to none other than my love and respect for science which nourished me throughout my life and which moved me to bring my mite, my widow's mite, to the altar of science. But is this condition sufficient to warrant me the right to preside over a circle of such remarkable representatives of science? This is not for me to judge. But it [this condition] was sufficient for the Academy to turn its attention to me, when thirty-five years ago it made me one of its corresponding members; it was sufficient to build a foundation for a long and more or less close relationship between me and many, the majority, of you, dear sirs. Thus, I am not a complete stranger among you and you will find in me the same respect for science and the same zeal to serve it which I felt when I was young and which has not left me in my

old age …On my part, I will use all the strength I have
left to reach, with your help, this goal which now
becomes my own goal in life.[1]

During these happy days Litke received many congratulations. Navy
friends, numerous groups of scholars, the grand duke, the Minister of
Education (Golovnin), all his relatives and many acquaintances came to
express their feelings of respect. If we were briefly to summarize Litke's
activities as president of the Academy of Sciences, we must say that an
organizational element prevailed in them. All of Litke's scientific
interests were tied mainly to the Geographical Society.

However, at that time the activities of the Geographical Society were
perceived as joint activities with the Academy of Sciences. It is not
accidental that in the heyday of the Geographical Society, which was
organizing a whole series of outstanding geographical, ethnographic,
hydrographic, statistical, and other expeditions, the range of geographical research carried out by the Academy of Sciences per se was not great.
It is not necessary to criticize the Academy of Sciences or Litke for this
because, as vice president of the Geographical Society, he organized
these expeditions. Actually, geographical science was relinquished by
the Academy of Sciences to the Geographical Society and the former did
not consider it its right to deal with geography. Suffice it to say that later,
on 1 February 1892, there were no geographer-academicians in the
Academy of Sciences. In the three departments of the academy—
physico-mathematical, Russian language and literature, and historico-
philosophical—there were the following academicians: in astronomy,
O. A. Baklund and F. A. Bredikhin; in mineralogy, N. I. Koksharov; in
geognosy and paleontology, F. B. Shmidt; and in geology, A. P.
Karpinskii. Out of the seventeen scientific establishments which came
under the Academy of Sciences, none dealt especially with questions of
geography. Separate disciplines of geography were run by the Mineralogical Office, Zoological Museum, Botanical Museum, the Museum of
Ethnography and Anthropology, the Main Physics Observatory, and the
Magnetic and Meteorological Observatory. The Geographical Society
filled the role of the geography branch of the Academy of Sciences.

Litke's exceptionally fruitful and useful activity in the Geographical
Society continued until 1873, twenty-five years after its inception, when
Litke refused the post of vice president and recommended P. P. Semenov-

Tian-Shanskii for the post. Accepting this position on 17 January 1873, Semenov-Tian-Shanskii stated:

"It is the last time that F. P. Litke appears before us in the position he has held for twenty years. There was a time when, filled with youthful vigor, a love for geography, and a thirst to discover unknown countries, Fedor Litke sailed his ship for the first time into the unfriendly polar seas and, four times cutting through those icy regions, opened and conquered for science the cold shores of that land which had the right to be called Novaia Zemlia [New Land] only until his explorations there. A few years later we see our brave navigator in charge of a Russian round-the-world expedition. He crosses the equator twice and on the way makes geographical discoveries, but he turns to his beloved north, into the cold, foggy and icy seas where the two continents of the Old and New Worlds almost touch. Fedor Petrovich's geographical research and discoveries in the Bering Sea, Aleutian chain, the shores of Kamchatka, Chukotka and America are well known to us; they brought him acclaim in the scholarly world."[2]

Besides the society's departments of Eastern Siberia and the Caucasus, opened in the administration of M. N. Murav'ev, the Northwestern (in Vilnius) and Orenburg departments also began to function. In 1858 gold and silver medals (besides the Konstantin medal) were established, and in 1873 the gold F. P. Litke medal was established. From 1871, the society began to receive from the government treasury an annual sum of 15,000 rubles instead of its original 10,000.

We, of course, shall not enumerate everything that Litke did to bring about the success of the society; neither shall we elaborate on the society's activities instigated by Litke. This would necessitate a special book. We shall only mention the major expeditions of that period.

It was marked by a continuation of the Great Siberian expedition led by F. B. Shmidt, with the participation of P. P. Glen, G. B. Shebunin and A. D. Brylkin. In this connection, we wish to cite an unpublished letter by Litke to P. P. Semenov-Tian-Shanskii, who had just been selected as chairman of the physical geography department. On 31 January 1860, congratulating him on his new post, Litke wrote: "Most respected Petr Petrovich, I have just found out that at yesterday's meeting the physical geography department unanimously chose you as its chairman. I congratulate the department and am glad for the society's council. Like a wild animal running to the hunter, you are faced with a question which must be resolved. This deals with choosing a new assistant for our geologist Shmidt, to replace Maidel', who will not be able to take part in the expedition because of an illness. We have Glen in mind. G. P. Gel'mersen, whom you will, of course, see, will inform you of all the details of this affair which must be resolved as quickly as possible. I am sincerely happy that I shall become more closely involved with you. Please, accept and be assured of my sincere respect."[3] This letter well demonstrates Litke's leadership style and underscores his affection and personal feelings for the energetic and talented Semenov-Tian-Shanskii.

Also dating to this period are the travels of R. K. Maak to the Ussuri River basin; the first trips of the young N. M. Przhevalskii, the first geological investigations of Sakhalin Island, carried out by I. A. Lopatin, and the outfitting of the Vitim expedition (I. A. Lopatin), the Turukhan expedition (I. A. Lopatin), the Olekma expedition (P. A. Kropotkin, I. S. Poliakov), and the Chukotka expedition (G. G. Maidel'). Litke attracted Polish exiles (the revolt of 1863) to work in the Eastern Siberian department of the society—I. D. Cherskii, V. I. Dybovskii, V. Godlevskii, and A. I. Chekanovskii—and then obtained amnesty for them. At the same time, a series of expeditions were taking place in Manchuria and Mongolia (P. A. Kropotkin, A. F. Usol'tsev, Matusovskii, Radlov) and in Tian-Shan (Golubev, K. V. Struve, N. A. Severtsov and Kaul'bars). An important enterprise was the outfitting of an expedition to Khorasan (northern Iran) in which Khanykov, A. A. Bunge, E. Kh. Lents and a group of geologists took part. With Litke's immediate and active participation, an expedition to New Guinea led by N. N. Miklukho-Maklai was organized. During its flourishing period, the society published numerous works. Large-scale maps (forty versts to the inch) were printed of European Russia, the Caucasus, the southern part of Central Asia, and Eastern Siberia; several volumes of *Meteorologicheskii sbornik* [Meteorological anthology] came out; several works on historical geography were published; and the publication of the *Geographical-Statistical Dictionary of the Russian Empire* was begun under the editorship of P. P. Semenov-Tian-Shanskii. During this period a total of eighty-two volumes of various publications came out in print in the society's name. The Ethnographic Museum was founded during the years of Litke's active participation in the Russian Geographical Society.

We must mention that Litke personally gave much consideration to statistics and ethnography. In a letter to P. I. Keppen (12 March 1862) he turns his attention to "a subject which has recently very much interested our society, namely, that of the migration of the Bolgars from Turkey to Crimea. The origin and language of that people are still unclear to us, as readily attested, for example, by the few lines which Lezhan dedicates to the Bolgar tribe in his ethnography of Turkey. You would be doing a great service to the society if, on your trips around Crimea, you should manage to get some information about these new migrants, their language, manners, and customs."[4] We know from Keppen's work how closely he took Litke's advice and what a contribution that scholar made in Russian statistics and demography.

While one is far from enumerating everything done for the society by Litke as vice president, it is necessary to note his work for the Academy of Sciences itself, of which the Russian Geographical Society was part. However, the Academy of Sciences, independently and together with the Geographical Society, also organized a series of expeditions, mostly on Litke's initiative. For a little more than twenty years (1860–1881) Academician G. P. Gel'mersen and assistants made trips through the Moscow, Tula, Kaluga, Simbirsk, Samara, Tver, and Riazan' provinces and through the Baltic region [Pribaltika], the Donbass, the Urals, and Poland. The aim of all these expeditions was to study the geology of these territories, especially those areas rich in coal deposits. In these instances the main task of Gel'mersen was to determine the surface area and richness of the coal deposits. From 1865 to 1868 Academicians A. N. Savich and P. E. Lents undertook an expedition to conduct gravimetric observations along the line of the measured arc of a meridian to determine the force of gravity at various points between Torneo and the Danube. In 1867 Academician L. M. Kemts carried out magnetic observations in the western provinces of Russia and in part abroad. As already mentioned, the well-known zoologist and geographer of the Academy of Sciences, I. S. Poliakov, traveled throughout Russia, Siberia, and the [Russian] Far East in the 1860s and 1870s. In 1868 Academician A. F. Middendorf traveled through Western Siberia and described the Barabinskaia Steppe. In his remarkable work *Baraba*,[5] Middendorf was the first to describe in detail one of the most interesting regions of Western Siberia. In 1878 Middendorf, engineer V. Perru, and botanist S. M. Smirnov undertook a trip to Central Asia, where they made detailed observations of the Fergana Basin. As a result of their trip, they published a detailed description entitled *Sketches of the Fergana Basin.*[6] In this work they presented a general picture of the possible long-term development of the productive forces of the Fergana. I. D. Cherskii traveled from 1871 to 1881 on the initiative of the Geographical Society, but his expeditions were financed by the Academy of Sciences and he carried out separate missions for it. In 1879 the tireless A. F. Middendorf, while sailing on the corvette *Variag* in the White and Barents seas, schematically traced the flow of the Gulf Stream east of Nordkapp where this current had practically not been studied. The materials of the oceanographic observations carried out on the corvette *Vitiaz'* were turned over to the Academy of Sciences by S. O. Makarov and later published.[7]

In the introduction to this chapter we briefly mentioned the style of Litke's leadership within the Academy. He was businesslike and strict. He furthered in every possible way the development of scientific societies and institutions. It was during his years as president that the activity of the Pulkovskaia Observatory was significantly broadened. He carried on an extensive correspondence with G. Vil'd and M. A. Rykachev, in which they discussed various questions dealing with the work of the Main Physics Observatory, gave much consideration to the question of the organization of an International Geophysical Bureau, etc. In 1874, on behalf of the Academy of Sciences and the Pulkovskaia Observatory, O. V. Struve organized observations at various points in Russia (L. E. Shvarts in Nerchinsk, F. A. Bredikhin in Saratov, M. L. Onatsevich and others in Vladivostok) to follow the path of Venus across the sun. Litke took an active part in organizing the expedition of I. V. Mushketov to choose the route for the Central Asian railroad and to determine the navigability of the Amu-Dar'ia River and the possibility of diverting it back to the Caspian Sea by way of an ancient channel.

The older Litke became, the longer he remained at Avandus, especially in the summer. There he regularly received reports from the permanent secretary of the Academy of Sciences, K. S. Veselovskii. As an example, we would like to refer to a letter sent by Veselovskii on 27 June 1878. In it he informed Litke about Middendorf's arrival in St. Petersburg from his trip to the Fergana. Middendorf was very satisfied "with the observations made there, which will serve to resolve some very curious questions." Further on in the letter, he related that "there arrived at the Zoological Museum through A. F. Filippeus bones of the Steller sea cow, found on the shores of the Bering Sea: nine skulls, one of which is larger than the one we already had, and many other bones besides, which, however, do not constitute an entire skeleton."[8]

At different times, Litke's way of running the Academy of Sciences was judged differently. For us, only one thing remains important and without question: Litke loved science and by using his authority, connections, and power, he tried to influence its improvement and its future development in Russia.

In addition to periodicals (*Zapiski Akademii nauk* [Notes of the Academy of Sciences] and others), during Litke's presidency nearly five hundred separate works were printed (works by I. Veniaminov, K. I. Maksimovich, A. F. Middendorf, P. L. Chebyshev, L. I. Shrenk and others). In addition, the following publications by the Archaeographical Commission continued to come out: *Polnoe sobranie russkikh letopisei* [Complete collection of Russian chronicles], *Akty Arkheograficheskoi ekspeditsii* [Documents of the archaeographical expedition], *Akty istoricheskie* [Historical documents], *Dopolneniia k Aktam istoricheskim* [Supplement to historical documents], and others. To these we can add a no less extensive list of books published in foreign languages. *Memoires* of various series were regularly published, of which nearly eight hundred came out.

It is no coincidence that in 1880, Litke, in the decline of his life, rightfully reported to the government on the work the Academy of Sciences had done the past twenty-five years: "Observatories in Pulkovo and Petersburg were allocated new buildings; a model for Europe was created in our building the Meteorological Observatory in Pavlovsk; a network of stations has been organized throughout the empire for the purpose of studying the climate; a special laboratory has been equipped for chemical research, so important in our time; academic museums, which have an educational significance for society, have acquired many collections, so necessary for knowledge of the natural resources of one's own country; finally, the Lomonosov and other prizes have been established to encourage scholarly literary work, and in general, the material means of the Academy have been strengthened."[9]

In regard to Litke's methods of operating and his personal feelings during his years as president, none expressed them better than F. F. Wrangell in his previously mentioned speech on Litke's hundredth anniversary. He noted that in the Academy at that time, as well as in the Geographical Society, there was an influx of new faces, but for the moment, it was still "dominated by *ostzeitsy* [Baltic Germans]" before whose authority he was accustomed to bend, "and we can say with assurance, that the president's sympathies were on the side of old traditions. With two passionate camps, a diplomatic and firm hand would have been needed to maneuver his ship through the turbulent sea of political passions and intrigues into the serene waters of scientific work, for which he was equipped and predestined. With the years, however, the pilot's strength weakened; the ranks of heroes who constituted the glory and strength of the earlier Academy were getting thinner; and new faces, foreign to Litke, replaced them; his task to stand against the tide was in vain and thankless. Those close to Count Litke knew how he suffered from all this dissension and how bitter it was for him to see the unfair appraisal of his efforts which had always been directed toward the good of his dear Academy."[10]

Let us introduce Academician O. V. Struve's comments concerning Litke's activities in the Academy of Sciences: "We all remember clearly the sense of duty which governed all his activities and how zealously he tried to improve the scientific means of the Academy; how he responded to its tasks with all his heart; with what enthusiasm he greeted every new step toward expansion of human knowledge; how high and firmly he held the banner of serious science as long as he had the strength."[11]

"For his long, zealous, and useful service, which won him fame in the European scholarly community for rendering special and important services," F. P. Litke was awarded the title of count on 28 October 1866. In 1870 he was again called to court service, after being assigned "in plurality" as tutor to Grand Duke Nicholas Konstantinovich. Soon after, he was awarded the Order of St. Andrew the Apostle along with its diamond clusters. On 28 January 1877, Litke became an honorary member of the Naval Academy, which he had helped organize firsthand.

But Litke's strength gradually left him. He turned eighty years old. By 1881, he hardly went out of his house. His hearing and sight worsened. During these years his favorite niece, Natasha Sul'menev, stayed by his side.

When Litke could still see and write, he wrote his own will in a broad hand. The basic body of the will follows: "My sons Konstantin and Nikolai are sole heirs to my properties which consist of several [stock] shares and other papers worth 20,000 rubles and kept at G. M. Anderson and Company, along with a small personal sum listed to my credit with the same company. My sons shall divide this inconsequential inheritance like friends and brothers. They will also divide all movables, with the following limitations: the eldest male should inherit the portraits of

*F. P. Litke in the
last years of his life.*

my father and mother (the latter is a small silhouette profile, hanging under my wife's portrait), the portraits of my deceased wife, and the portraits of grandfather and grandmother Engel. My deeds, diplomas, patents, letters from the tsar, letters from high-ranking persons, and documents dealing with my service years should also not be divided. All this constitutes family property."[12]

Until 1880 Litke spent almost all his summers at Avandus with the family of his younger son Nikolai, who had retired with the rank of captain lieutenant and was busy developing a gold mining enterprise. Beginning in 1880, however, Litke no longer left St. Petersburg. It was initially thought that he would have to undergo eye surgery. His elder son, Konstantin, who was still serving in the navy, wrote to his godfather, Grand Duke Constantine, on 27 June 1881: "The question of the eye operation is becoming extremely doubtful. In the left eye, it appears that a part of the vitreous humor is beginning to turn to liquid, and if part of this liquid is lost during an operation, it is nearly unavoidable that the wished-for success will not be attained and his sight will not be restored anyway. The right eye is still so far from blind that it is doubtful father will live that long."[13]

During that period, Litke still went on his daily walks in the company of either his sons or Natasha, who, when he could still hear somewhat, read him letters, newspapers and journals. But on 9/21 February 1882, Konstantin wrote to the grand duke: "Last summer father still thought about the operation and lived with the hope of having his sight restored, but since then his strength has fallen and is falling so rapidly that in general his physical ailments, such as his blindness, deafness and stomach spasms, have taken a back seat; now we are most concerned with his mental well-being. He has become absent-minded, recognizes no one, and is beginning to talk nonsense."[14]

All this time, while there was still hope for his recovery, Litke remained president of the Academy of Sciences. But now it was becoming obvious that his days were numbered. On 25 April he was freed from the post of president. On 8 August he died. We also learn of Litke's death from his son Konstantin's letter to his godfather: "Father spent his last days in a state of unconsciousness, so that he could not recognize me or my brother. He took no food; the beef extract we tried to feed him would remain unswallowed in his mouth and his excretory functions stopped. The only sign of life was his breathing, sometimes very strong, sometimes so weak that we expected the end. On 8 August, finally, at 12:30 he let out a great moan, then gasped twice and died. More than a month before his death he could no longer express his thoughts clearly and at the end we could no longer understand him."[15]

Litke's funeral took place at the Volkov cemetery on 12 August. The Lutheran church of St. Anna on Furshtadtskaia overflowed with wreaths made of fresh roses and was decorated in black cloth. Litke's coffin was covered with an admiral's flag. Many grand dukes and duchesses, members of the Academy of Sciences and the Geographical Society, officers and admirals were present . The funeral procession was joined by a large crowd of people. Under a sailors' salute, his coffin was lowered into a grave next to that of his parents and his beloved wife.

Many newspapers and almost all the scientific journals in Russia and abroad wrote obituaries, praising the famous mariner and scholar. They all noted Litke's great accomplishments in organizing Russia's scientific community and his personal merits in developing the nautical and geographical sciences. At a memorial gathering of the Academy of Sciences, on 29 December 1882, Academician O. V. Struve read a "Speech on Count F. P. Litke's scholarly accomplishments." A similar speech was read by F. F. Veselago on 26 January 1883, at a meeting of the Geographical Society.

In concluding his speech on Litke, Struve said:

> This highly respected gathering has, without a doubt, every right to expect from me several remarks on Count Litke's merits as president of the Academy of Sciences for eighteen years. Forgive me if I only respond to this expectation in a limited manner. Having just lost him, our minds are not free enough from our emotions to judge him clearly. Like the works of every socially active person serving in a prominent, responsible post, his activities were subject to gossip, depending on the point of view from which they were judged. More than once they encountered unwarranted reproach. Impartial history will be the judge, free from personal impressions; and it will assess the difficulties Litke had to overcome, and will turn in a more reliable verdict. It will show him in his academic service to be the same as he continues to live in our grateful hearts. Remember, dear friends, his tireless work for the Academy and the personal well-being of each and every one of us. Remember that warm greeting, that encouragement which every new step of science found in him. Look at the rich means and activities of the Main Physics Observatory, and the model meteorological and magnetic observatories in Pavlovsk. Compare the number of prizes now given out for scientific and literary works with the limited number in previous times. Compare the present-day quality of our museums, collections, and other scholarly tools with those that existed before. And in all probability, you will testify to the world how very fruitful Litke's administration was for the Academy. But above all, we shall remember him for his tireless effort to resurrect and preserve among us the spirit of pure and serious science, the conscientious service of which is our main task and duty to our nation.[16]

CITATIONS AND NOTES

1. AAN, f. 34, op. 1, d. 9, l. 33–33 ob.

2. L. S. Berg, *Vsesoiuznoe geograficheskoe obshchestvo za sto let* (Moscow, Leningrad: AN SSSR, 1946), pp. 24–25.

3. PD, M. I. Semevskii archive, f. 274, op. 3, d. 196.

4. AAN, f. 30, op. 3, d. 158, l. 20 ob.

5. A. F. Middendorf, *Baraba, Zapiski Akademii nauk*, vol. 19 (St. Petersburg, 1871), suppl. 2.

6. A. F. Middendorf, *Ocherki Ferganskoi doliny* [Sketches of the Fergana Basin] (St. Petersburg, 1882).

7. S. O. Makarov, *Vitiaz' i Tikhii okean* [The *Vitiaz* and the Pacific Ocean] (St. Petersburg, 1894).

8. TsGADA. f. Gosarkhiv, r. 30, d. 13, l. 24 ob.–25.

9. Ibid., l. 61 ob. Published in *Pravitel'stvennyi vestnik*, no. 53, 1880.

10. *Izvestiia Imp. russk. geogr. ob-va*, vol. 33, vyp. 4 (St. Petersburg, 1897), pp. 344–345.

11. V. P. Bezobrazov, *F. P. Litke* (St. Petersburg, 1888), p. 183.

12. TsGAVMF, f. 15, op. 1, d. 2, l. 9–9 ob. Of all the portraits mentioned, only that of Litke's wife has been found.

13. TsGAVMF, f. 224, op. 2, d. 52, l. 1 ob.

14. Ibid., l. 4 ob.

15. Ibid., l. 6 ob.

16. V. P. Bezobrazov, *F. P. Litke* (St. Petersburg, 1888), pp. 152–153.

LITKE AND RUSSIAN MARINE HYDROGRAPHY

No matter what positions Litke held in his long life or where he had to serve, he remained, above all, a scientist—a sailor-hydrographer. It is for this reason that we deem it necessary to have a separate chapter about his contributions to marine hydrography and his work and merits in this field.

Litke's activities in the area of marine hydrography, like all his scientific activity, can be sharply divided into two periods. The first period was one of direct scientific research, the production of vast hydrographic works during his voyages, and subsequent summarization of his research in charts, atlases, individual articles, and books. The second period was one of organizational activities, when he was deprived of the means to do direct hydrographic research, but still attentively followed its development in Russia and directed its course, first through M. F. Reineke, and then as vice president of the Geographical Society and president of the Academy of Sciences.

While sailing on the *Kamchatka*, under the command of the experienced mariner and hydrographer V. M. Golovnin, young Litke recommended himself as a mariner knowing his craft and showing great potential as a hydrographer. The charts Litke made at that time (some of which have been presented in [the Russian edition of] this book) demonstrate the outstanding abilities of the young officer and the necessary qualities of a scientific researcher: accuracy and industry. Litke took a most active part in the description of the Aleutian Islands and his charts were subsequently published by the Hydrographic Department. Another priceless quality Litke possessed was his capacity for detailed observations, which he demonstrated in his early years as a mariner and hydrographer. His diary, kept aboard the *Kamchatka* and from which we have quoted repeatedly, is one such example. If his diary had been published in its time, it would have been an immense help to navigators who had occasion to sail into the ports, bays and harbors where the *Kamchatka* had been. But Litke's diary lay in the archives for a century and a half and now has only historical and geographical value.

Pendulum apparatus used by Litke to measure gravitational variation.[a]

An objective and strict Golovnin understood quite well the abilities of the young lieutenant and boldly recommended him as head of the hydrographic expedition to Novaia Zemlia. During the four years spent in hydrographic work under the harsh conditions of the Far North, Litke displayed his talent as a scientist hydrographer in the broadest possible sense. He not only took up the task of charting Novaia Zemlia, which had scarcely been studied prior to his investigations, but on his own initiative, supported by G. A. Sarychev and I. F. Kruzenshtern, he mapped out the entire coast of the Murmansk Peninsula to the Norwegian frontier. Litke and the officers of the brig *Novaia Zemlia* compiled very detailed charts of literally every area of the Murmansk coast which might be used by sailors for anchorage, and described each of these areas. After his second voyage to the shores of Novaia Zemlia, Litke was unofficially (after his third voyage, officially) the

Detail of
pendulum apparatus
used by Litke.

Detail of pendulum apparatus used by Litke.

head of the first special hydrographic expedition to the Arctic Ocean, which included not only the expedition of the brig *Novaia Zemlia* per se but also the western and eastern detachments of the Pechora expedition (I. A. Berezhnykh and I. N. Ivanov) as well as the expedition on the brig *Ketti*, which was charged with the description of the White Sea.

During those four years the following work was accomplished: 370 miles of the Murmansk coast, 650 miles of the Novaia Zemlia coast, and 60 miles of Vaigach and Kolguev islands were described and eighteen general and detail charts were produced. At the beginning of the nineteenth century the Murmansk coast had only two astronomical points; Novaia Zemlia had none. The charts made by Litke's expedition were based on twenty-four astronomical observations. From 1821 to 1824 the declination of the compass was determined at forty-six points, on the basis of which one could have a rather complete image of magnetic declination in the Barents Sea. A constant current was discovered flowing north along the western shore of Novaia Zemlia; it was later named after Litke. Currents inconstant in strength and direction were discovered along the Murmansk coast. Litke noted the definite conformities of ice formations of the Barents and Kara seas.

We have already quoted from Litke's letter to Ber in June of 1825, which displayed Litke's modesty. He sincerely believed that his expedition had yielded almost nothing except for a few contributions to hydrography. The fact that his remarks are more than modest can be seen in the exceptionally important data of his expedition found in his fundamental work. Reading this work, it becomes quite clear that his serious hydrographic work was supplemented with detailed research of the climatic and hydrological peculiarities of the White, Barents and, in part, the Kara seas. This work also contained a valuable and fully scientific review of the research in these seas.

Response to Litke's work was most favorable. We have quoted from F. F. Shubert, G. A. Sarychev, and V. K. Vishnevskii. After the publication of Litke's book, it was translated into German. In the introduction to the translation, the well-known German physicist and traveler A. P. Erman wrote that "with the survey and description of all the points of the Arctic Ocean he reached, he so surpassed all his predecessors in his scientific zeal and objective judgment that this work cannot be passed over in silence either in the history of navigation or in the history of geography."[1]

V. P. Bezobrazov, who knew Litke intimately, noted that his voyage "brought an entirely new light to geographical science relating to this whole region of northern Europe and [Russia]."[2]

Academician O. V. Struve responded to this work in the following manner: "Without limiting himself to a dry account of hydrographic and geographic facts, which by themselves would have been a valuable contribution to science, [Litke] embellished his book every step of the way with deep analysis of geographical and navigational questions dealing with the arctic seas. In his introduction he added a detailed historical survey of previous, but mostly unsuccessful, expeditions to Novaia Zemlia and its neighboring seas and countries. This introduction is not only important in a historical respect, but as a guide for each navigator in the Arctic Ocean."[3]

F. F. Veselago remarked on Litke's most important contribution to the exploration of the White, Barents, and Kara seas at a meeting of the Geographical Society on 26 January 1883. He said that Litke's research "exerted a positive influence on the further development of our hydrographic work." Litke's hydrographic work was the first of its kind, and was followed by the activity of another remarkable hydrographer, M. F. Reineke, one of the closest friends of Admiral P. S. Nakhimov. Reineke was assigned to that research at Litke's entreaties and he performed his tasks with excellence, charting the White Sea and describing sailing directions for the Murmansk coast.

Throughout his activities in the north Reineke was directed by Litke's instructions and consultation. It is sufficient to look through the correspondence between these two outstanding hydrographers to understand that from 1825 to 1831 Litke continued to provide scientific guidance for all hydrographic work in the White and Barents seas and that he continued to do this even when he was on a round-the-world voyage aboard the *Seniavin.*

It is interesting to note the end of the instructions directed to Reineke by Litke upon his return on the *Seniavin* in 1830. In them, Litke points out that a hydrographer's efforts cannot bring about the desired results if they are not brought to a conclusive end, if they are not worked out and presented in the form of final conclusions. In particular he wrote: "An observer has done his duty in every way if, first, he has not missed any of the smallest details on which the veracity of the experiments depend, and then if he has laid out all his data and has not changed a single reading and has explained all the details of his work. But without these conditions, his work will remain in vain because it will yield no truth."[4]

Characterizing Litke's book on his work in the north, F. F. Veselago noted that "In this work, as in all the hydrographic and other scholarly work of Litke, there is the mark of his great talent, strict accuracy and unusual patience. With the qualities of superb observer and calculator, he combined his broad education, great erudition, and his reliable opinion on the subject and its broad scientific horizon."[5]

Litke became the leader of the *Seniavin* expedition when he was an already mature (though quite young in age) scientist-hydrographer. The expedition's results surpassed all expectations. Nearly a thousand miles of coast were described, taking in the Pribilof, Bering and Karaginskii islands, along with the Chukotka and Kamchatka coast and the archipelagos of Bonin Sima and the Carolines which consist of twenty-six groups of islands, twelve of which were previously unknown. An atlas containing fifty-one charts was compiled. The magnetic observations made at fifty-two different sites, one of the earliest works in this field, were processed and published by Academician E. Kh. Lents in 1836. The meteorological observations, made without interruption during the entire time of this expedition, and in particular the observations made in the course of an entire year on the hourly changes of the barometer between the parallels of 30° north and south latitude allowed one of the first investigations of the daily air pressure on the oceans in the tropics and made it possible to suggest an increase in air pressure from the equator to the poles. Litke worked his observations on the currents into an article "The high tides in the North Pacific and Arctic oceans." These observations allowed him to discover an equatorial countercurrent in the western part of the Pacific Ocean.

As F. F. Wrangell correctly put it, the main "part of the scientific tasks, namely work on hydrography, cartography and physics, rested on Litke himself with the help of those officers who accompanied him and whose work he directed and encouraged by his example and zeal."[6] Litke's vast data collection found its way into several works, the chief ones of which are undoubtedly his specialized hydrographic works (description and atlas), and give us a clear view of the titanic work done by their author. These works served as useful guides for navigators for a long time to come. And it is impossible not to agree with the truthful characterization of Litke made by F. F. Veselago: "Because of his spiritual qualities and his character in general, [Litke] was a true sailor, while his intellect and abilities, which brought him into the scientific field, made him into a scientist-sailor-hydrographer."[7] It was not by accident that for these works he was honored in 1829 with the title of corresponding member of the Academy of Sciences, while in 1836, after the publication of his work on the *Seniavin* expedition, he received the full Demidov Prize.

Until the end of his days, Litke did not stop participating very closely in the hydrographic research taking place in Russian seas. He wrote up projects for such research and made various suggestions on improving the organization of hydrographic service. Thus, in particular, in a letter to Constantine from Revel (26 February 1853), Litke raised the question of unifying the [office for] Navigation of the gulfs of Riga and Finland with the [office for] Management of Lighthouses: "If the [office for] Navigation of the gulfs of Riga and Finland were assigned to the [office for] Management of Lighthouses, and the ships of both divisions formed a single lighthouse flotilla, then the affairs of both divisions would considerably benefit from it. In the spring, when it is necessary to set up all the spar-buoys again and use all the vessels for that enterprise, the job would be accomplished much more quickly. The same would be true when the lighthouses have to be supplied. During the navigation season it is not rare that spar-buoys are either carried off or damaged during storms in various places. Their inspection and repair throughout the gulf would be facilitated by a greater number of vessels. The Director of Lighthouses or one of his assistants, while going from lighthouse to lighthouse, could also check the buoys and other markers on the way. The vessels sent to check the buoys could also perform services dealing with the lighthouses. In a word, the centralization of everything having to do with navigational safety in the gulfs of Riga and Finland under the leadership of one experienced officer would make the running of this important matter much more efficient than the present scattering of these functions."[8]

It was precisely after this letter and several other steps taken by Litke that the Navigation Office and Management of Lighthouses were combined into one hydrographic subdivision, which concentrated in itself all responsibility for navigational safety in one or another region of the sea or in the basin of the whole sea. Later, surveys and hydrographic expeditions were organized to carry out new hydrographic research and to correct the charts.[9]

It is interesting to read Litke's response to a memo from Vice Admiral Melikhov, addressed to Constantine, which foresaw the unification of the Hydrographic Department with the Naval Scientific Committee and which was motivated by the fact that each allegedly performed the same functions. Litke emphasized that this was not the case. "Hydrography as a science," he wrote, "can of course be included among the activities of the Scientific Committee, but only as one of the many branches of an extensive nautical science which have nothing to do with the Hydrographic Department. It is also unjust that, with the exception of activities run by the Corps of Fleet Navigators, all other responsibilities of the department should be exclusively the domain of the scientific section. Besides navigational duties, it is also charged with administrative and home-office duties. Let us take as an example the duties concerning surveys and descriptions, which were mentioned by Vice Admiral Melikhov. Here the department is not limited to making scientific drawings; it must concern itself with the material means to that end: it must deal with the officers, people, ships, and money required for such matters. Then come engravings and publication of the charts and getting these charts distributed to all the military ships. This matter is tedious and complicated, but not at all scientific. Then there is the problem of typesetting. Finally, there is the Navigation Office, that is, everything dealing with navigational safety, which encompasses lighthouses, buoys, markers, etc. All of these activities take much trouble and correspondence, but it is not at all scientific work. All of these things must be concentrated under one central office, and it does not matter what it is called."[10]

An event unknown up to now is extremely interesting for Litke's biography. In 1858–1862 there was wide discussion of the question of establishing the post of hydrographer general, which had not been awarded to anyone after the death of G. A. Sarychev. On 8 August 1859, Constantine wrote Litke that he "thought that for hydrography to be successful in Russia, it would be very useful to put it under the supervision and guidance of someone who not only has the necessary knowledge, but also the moral influence in the navy based on his name and general scientific activities. In doing this, it would seem necessary to turn over to this person only the scientific and technical part, and leave the administrative part out of his jurisdiction, not so much so as not to burden him with minor work, but to avoid various conflicts with the home-office administration and inspection section in the Naval Department, misunderstandings and arguments."[11] For that purpose, Constantine suggested the reinstitution of the post of hydrographer general, who would be responsible only to the admiral general. "In conclusion, I have only to note," he wrote Litke, "that the post of Hydrographer General is a highly respected one and that I would with sincere pleasure nominate to that position the person I deeply respect and love."

Litke, who was then resting at Avandus, wrote to Constantine on 21 August that he agreed to all his suggestions on improving hydrographic service in Russia and the establishment of the post of hydrographer general, and thanked him for offering him such a high post. He wrote that even though he was not as strong as he once was, being in his sixties, he would "work as long as he had strength."

It is now hard to understand why Constantine's suggestion never reached the tsar. It is fully possible that it could have been due in no small part to Litke's appointment as president of the Academy of Sciences.

Litke was concerned with a whole series of organizational as well as special hydrographic questions. It was he who insisted on the appointment of M. F. Reineke to the post of director of the Hydrographic Department, which Reineke held until his death in 1859. In 1853 Litke worked out a program for hydrographic research in the Caspian Sea. The matter began on 29 May 1853, when Constantine forwarded to Litke M. S. Vorontsov's memorandum about the necessity of a new description of the Caspian Sea. In June, Litke answered that he approved such an idea since the only charts of the Caspian Sea available were those made in 1826 by A. E. Kolodkin. "Therefore," he wrote, "there is no doubt about the necessity of a new, or better to say, the first full survey of the Caspian Sea." He suggested that in order to speed up the receipt of a good chart, all materials from surveys of the last twenty-five to thirty years should be gathered. "Having selected and reworked all these materials, making a series of astronomical determinations on the basis of which we could connect all these materials into one entity, and after making the necessary soundings for navigational safety, and if necessary, surveys of the most important roadsteads, then we could have a chart which would to a certain extent fulfill navigation needs. This work, it seems to me, could be accomplished in two years. It should be assigned to a reliable sailor-astronomer of the school of Struve, Reineke, or Wrangell, and that person should be given the necessary instruments and brief instructions describing only his general goals; he should be given a steamship and the rest should be left to his skill and zeal." Litke ended this memo with the following words: "Such an expedition must be considered as preliminary to a larger, general survey, of which we must not lose sight."[12] With this note Litke proposed the beginning of a systematic hydrographic investigation of the Caspian Sea, which later led to the organization of a hydrographic expedition under the command of N. A. Ivashintsov.

On 10 April 1861, the American oceanographer M. F. Maury sent a letter "Concerning exploration of the southern polar regions" to the Russian envoy to the United States of America. In his letter he proposed the idea of organizing a series of simultaneous expeditions by several governments for the purpose of studying the Antarctic. Similar proposals were sent to the governments of other countries. The Naval Ministry printed several copies and sent them to many outstanding scholars and navigators for comment: A. A. Popov, B. V. Wrangell, I. I. Shants, P. F. Anzhu, F. P. Litke, F. P. Wrangell, G. I. Butakov, E. Kh. Lents, E. A. Berens, A. N. Savich, F. F. Matiushkin, K. I. Istomin, O. V. Struve, B. A. Glazenap, A. Ia. Kupfer, V. Ia. Struve, A. I. Zelenyi, K. N. Pos'et, G. I. Nevel'skoi, V. A. Rimskii-Korsakov, N. M. Chikhachev, N. A. Ivashinstov, A. I. Borisov, and many more scholars who were not mariners.

The majority of the Russian scientists and navigators responded negatively to this very interesting international venture, motivated by the fact that Russia still had its own unexplored regions of Siberia, its own Arctic, which had to be studied first. V. A. Rimskii-Korsakov expressed these thoughts most clearly: "...before dreaming about a southern polar expedition, we must remember Novaia Zemlia; or if we want to participate in the first without fail, then we must also take up the second. Otherwise we risk, for the sake of abstractness, sinning before our countrymen by preferring a great undertaking over what is useful."[13]

In his characteristic categorical manner, Litke wrote: "Nori's [Maury's] proposed expedition, which would consist of ships from various nations acting independently of one another in various regions, also seems useless to me because they will all end up in various areas of those limits (he had the ice barrier in mind, which, according to the view held at that time, completely surrounded Antarctica—A. A.) and by not being of any use, they will only increase the expense of the expedition."[14]

In connection with this, we would like to mention Litke's negative reaction to P. I. Kruzenshtern's voyage to the mouths of the Siberian rivers Pechora, Ob', and Yenisei on the schooner *Ermak*. The initiator of this question had been the famous Russian researcher and industrialist M. K. Sidorov, who had dreamed of connecting the Turukhan region by land and water transport to get to the deposits of coal, graphite, and other minerals there. Sidorov published a note on his activities in this direction. Litke, who had discussed this question with Sidorov, commented on the note in the following manner: "Opening an overland route between the Turukhan region and the Pechora through Obdorsk would be quite useful for the development of that region; such an enterprise seems very feasible and deserves even more attention and support because a water communication would be impossible. At a meeting with Mr. Sidorov in Petersburg I predicted the lack of success of Lieutenant Kruzenshtern's attempts. The events justified my predictions. It is a pity that a proposal by certain persons in England to send a vessel around Novaia Zemlia to the Yenisei to pick up a load of Sidorov's graphite was not implemented. In all probability their ship would not have reached the Yenisei either. But for science's sake, such an attempt would not have been useless. Such expeditions can be successfully equipped only in England, where generations of sailing specialists for icy seas have been educated in the last fifty years."[15]

Litke highly valued everything that was English—navy, sailors, and even their science. He insisted that the Russians not undertake voyages to the mouths of the Ob' and Yenisei out of Arkhangel'sk. Reflected in this, of course, was the negative influence of his own four years' experience in the region. In 1874, the English captain I. Wiggins, at M. K. Sidorov's expense, was the first to sail through the Kara Sea on the steamship *Diana*, despite the fact that Russian mariners had repeatedly declared their willingness to complete such a voyage. The famous mariner V. A. Rimskii-Korsakov, the elder brother of the famous composer, especially fought for this. As concerns Litke, he remained to the end an adherent to the school of Golovnin, a passionate follower of the English navy who had served several years in it. Besides that, the influence of his friends the academician-*ostzeitsy* played a great role in Litke's Anglomania. To many of them, the level of science abroad always seemed much higher than the level of science in Russia, although they all lived and worked in Russia.

Litke took a direct part in organizing magnetic observations in the [Russian] Far East. For this purpose he summoned to St. Petersburg K. S. Staritskii, who had been assigned to the Far East, trained him, and commissioned him to make the observations.

Litke wrote an interesting work "Discourse on High Tides and Waves at Sea" which is not identical to his "Tides in the North Pacific and Arctic Ocean." In "Discourse ..." he strictly presents the theory of tides according to Laplace and Newton. The work consists of an "Introduction" and the following sections or chapters: "The common occurrence of high tides," "Newton's theory of high tides or the theory of equilibrium," "Laplace's theory of high tides," "Theory of waves in channels," "Various means of observing high tides and calculations of these observations," "A comparison of previous theories on tides with observations," "About separate tides in certain confined seas," and so on. It is a pity that this book remained unpublished. The author was very strict with his own works and did not allow everything he did to be judged by society.

The same thing happened with his work on the history of the Russian navy. Despite the fact that Litke once turned down the opportunity to write such a history, he still wrote a significant part of it in two voluminous notebooks under the modest title "Materials for a History of the Russian Navy." The first part, a fair copy with corrections by Litke, presents a history of the navy from 1689 to 1711, which treats the Azov campaign of 1696; it also analyzes the shipbuilding program and its accomplishments and discusses the war with Sweden. The second part, from 1722 to the end of the reign of Peter I, tells the history of the Petrine yawls, the grandfathers of the Russian fleet. It tells in detail of the annexation of the Caspian Sea to Russia, and the expeditions of Bekovich, Urusov, Verden, Soimonov, and Kozhin. Litke devoted much attention in this work to hydrographic studies of the seas. Thus, while recounting the appearance of the Russian navy on the Baltic Sea, he wrote about investigation of the Gulf of Finland: "The description and sounding of the Gulf of Finland in 1724, which had been undertaken earlier (1715), were continued to a large extent. Naval officers Gens, Ekgof, Debrin'i,

Alaberdyev, Volkov, Mishukov, and Colonel Liuberas were employed in surveying the shores. Many of the decrees of the emperor show how important he considered these activities to be, but they were not completed during his reign. We cannot judge these works because we have neither journals nor charts from that expedition, but we can suppose that Admiral Nagaev used them more or less to compile his atlas of the Baltic Sea."[16]

Litke was a man of many talents, but he always considered hydrography to be his main scientific occupation. He is justly called the successor of F. I. Soimonov, A. I. Nagaev, and G. A. Sarychev, although (like Soimonov) he held no official, high post in hydrographic service.

We have attempted to show the long life and fruitful scientific activities of one of the greatest Russian scientists, the founder of the Russian Geographical Society and for many years the president of the Academy of Sciences, Fedor Petrovich Litke. In his convictions, Litke was a man of his century, loyal and true to the throne, who even took an active role under the leadership of Grand Duke Constantine in preparing the reforms of 1861. The scientific merits of this outstanding scholar, organizer of science, and famous mariner and hydrographer are extraordinarily important to us.

Fifteen geographical sites in the Far Eastern seas and the Arctic Ocean have been named after Litke. In 1921 the ice-cutter *Kanada*, built in 1909, was renamed the *Fedor Litke*. It was precisely this ship which, in 1934, was the first in history to navigate through the Arctic Ocean from east to west in a single navigation season, using the route which Litke considered impassable even for a comparatively small distance. Soviet people sailed on this ice-cutter. This veteran ship was taken apart for scrap metal in 1938. The equipment from its deckhouse is on display at the permanent exhibition "Navy" in Moscow. But a new and powerful ice-breaker *Fedor Litke* has been built at the Admiralty factory in Leningrad to replace the ice-cutter *Fedor Litke*. Equipped with the latest technology, it bears with honor the name of the glorious scientist-admiral, outstanding navigator, geographer, polar researcher, president of the Academy of Sciences, Fedor Litke.

Fedor Petrovich Litke's name has been inscribed in golden letters in the history of Russian and world science. It will remain forever in the memories of his grateful descendants.

CITATIONS AND NOTES

1. V. P. Bezobrazov, *F. P. Litke* (St. Petersburg, 1888), p. 107.

2. Ibid., p. 105.

3. Ibid., p. 143.

4. AVGO, r. 110, op. 1, d. 23, 1. 25.

5. V. P. Bezobrazov, *F. P. Litke*, p. 162.

6. AVGO, r. 110, op. 1, d. 23, 1. 14–15.

7. V. P. Bezobrazov, *F. P. Litke*, pp. 154–155.

8. TsGADA, f. Gosarkhiv, r. 30, d. 13, 1. 20–20 ob.

9. For example, the survey of the Baltic Sea, the hydrographic expedition of the Arctic Ocean, etc., were, in a manner of speaking, made into permanent hydrographic sub-departments.

10. TsGADA, f. Gosarkhiv, r. 30, d. 13, 1. 49–50.

11. TsGADA, f. Gosarkhiv, r. 30, d. 18, 1. 60–60 ob.

12. Ibid., d. 13, 1. 72 ob.–74 ob.

13. TsGAVMF, f. 402, op. 2, d. 2447, 1. 28 ob.–29.

14. Ibid., 1. 4–4 ob.

15. *Trudy Imp. vol'no-ekonom. ob-va*, vol. 2 (St. Petersburg, 1863), pp. 176–177.

16. TsGADA, f. Gosarkhiv, r. 30, d. 65, 1. 38 ob.–39.

* * *

a. The illustrations shown on pages 220, 221, and 222 are from *Opyty nad postoiannym maiatnikom, proizvedennye v puteshestvie vokrug sveta na voennom shliupe* Seniavine *v 1826, 1827, 1828, 1829 godakh flota kapitanom F. Litke* [Experiments with the fixed pendulum performed by Fleet Captain F. P. Litke during a voyage around the world on the sloop *Seniavin*, 1826–1829]. St. Petersburg, 1833.

APPENDIX
IMPORTANT DATES IN F. P. LITKE'S LIFE

1797, September 17/28. Born in St. Petersburg.

1813, April 27. Volunteered in the navy.

1813, September 26. Commissioned as an officer.

1817, August 26, to 1819, September 5. Completed round-the-world voyage on the sloop *Kamchatka* under the command of V. M. Golovnin.

1821, July 14 to September 11. First voyage to the Arctic Ocean on the brig *Novaia Zemlia*.

1822, June 17 to September 6. Second voyage to the Arctic Ocean on the *Novaia Zemlia*.

1823, June 11 to August 30. Third voyage to the Arctic Ocean on the *Novaia Zemlia*.

1824, June 17 to September 11. Fourth voyage to the Arctic Ocean on the *Novaia Zemlia*.

1826, August 20, to 1829, August 25. Round-the-world voyage on the sloop *Seniavin*.

1828. Publication of book *Chetyrekratnoe puteshestvie v Severnyi Ledovityi okean, sovershennoe po poveleniiu imperatora Aleksandra I na voennom briga* Novaia Zemlia *v 1821, 1822, 1823, i 1824 godakh* [Four voyages to the Arctic Ocean accomplished by order of Emperor Alexander I on the military brig *Novaia Zemlia* in 1821–1824].

1829, December 29. Selected as corresponding member of the Academy of Sciences.

1832. Assigned as tutor to Grand Duke Constantine, destined to become admiral general of the Russian Navy.

1832, July 1. Selected as honorary member of the Royal Geographical Society in London.

1834–1836. Three sections published of the book *Puteshestvie vokrug sveta, sovershennoe po poveleniiu gosudaria imperatora Nikolai I na voennom shliupe* Seniavine *v 1826, 1827, 1828, i 1829 godakh* [Voyage around the world accomplished by order of the Emperor Nicholas I on the military sloop *Seniavin* in 1826–1829] with atlas of charts and drawings.

1835, June 24. promoted to rear admiral.

1835, December 17. Marriage to Julia Browne.

1836. Awarded the full Demidov Prize for his book on the voyage of the *Seniavin*.

1843, December 6. Promoted to vice admiral.

1843–1845. Preparations for organization of Russian Geographical Society.

1845, October 7. Ceremonial opening of the Geographical Society by Litke.

1845–1850. Vice chairman of the Russian Geographical Society.

1850–1853. Commander-in-chief and governor of the city and port of Revel.

1853–1855. Commander-in-chief and military governor of the port of Kronstadt.

1855, March 27. Promoted to admiral and appointed as member of Government Council.

1855, December 28. Selected as honorary member of Academy of Sciences.

1857–1873. Vice chairman of the Russian Geographical Society.

1864, February 24, to 1882, April 25. President of the Academy of Sciences.

1882, August 8. Died in St. Petersburg.

APPENDIX
BASIC WORKS BY F. P. LITKE

1. "Proekt opisi Laplandskogo berega, predstavlennyi F. P. Litke" [Proposal for a survey of the Lapland coast, presented by F. P. Litke], *Zapiski Gosudarstvennogo Admiralteiskogo departamenta*, book 6. St. Petersburg, 1824, pp. lxxviii–lxxxii.

2. "Proekt F. P. Litke opisi Kol'skoi guby" [Proposal by F. P. Litke for a survey of Kol'skii Bay], *Zapiski Gosudarstvennogo Admiralteiskogo departamenta*, book 10. St. Petersburg, 1826, pp. x–xiv.

3. "Donesenie o plavanii F. P. Litke iz Novo-Arkhangel'ska ot 19 iiulia 1827 g." [Report on F. P. Litke's voyage from Novo-Arkhangel'sk, 19 July 1827], *Zapiski Uchenogo Kommiteta Morskogo Shtaba*, part 3. St. Petersburg, 1829, pp. 125–137.

4. "Donesenie o plavanii F. P. Litke iz Petropavlovska ot 17 oktiabria 1827g." [Report on F. P. Litke's voyage from Petropavlovsk, 17 October 1827], *Zapiski Uchenogo Kommiteta Morskogo Shtaba*, part 3. St. Petersburg, 1829, pp. 138–155.

5. "Donesenie o plavanii F. P. Litke iz Petropavlovska ot 18 iiulia 1828 g." [Report on F. P. Litke's voyage from Petropavlovsk, 18 July 1828], *Zapiski Uchenogo Kommiteta Morskogo Shtaba*, part 3, St. Petersburg, 1829, pp. 156–164; part 4, 1829, pp. 176–202.

6. *Chetyrekhkratnoe puteshestvie v Severnyi Ledovityi okean, sovershennoe po poveleniiu imperatora Aleksandra I na voennom brige* Novaia Zemlia *v 1821, 1822,1823 i 1824 godakh flota kapitan-leitenantom Fedorom Litke* [Four voyages to the Arctic Ocean ... aboard the brig *Novaia Zemlia* in 1821–1824], parts 1 and 2. St. Petersburg, 1828.

7. *Opyty nad postoiannym maiatnikom, proizvedennye v puteshestvie vokrug sveta na voennom shliupe* Seniavine *v 1826, 1827, 1828, 1829 godakh flota kapitanom F. Litke* [Experiments with the fixed pendulum performed by Fleet Captain F. P. Litke during a voyage around the world on the sloop *Seniavin*, 1826–1829]. St. Petersburg, 1833.

8. *Puteshestvie vokrug sveta, sovershennoe po poveleniiu gosudaria imperatora Nikolaia I na voennom shliupe* Seniavine *v 1826, 1827, 1828, i 1829 godakh*

flota kapitanom Fedorom Litke [Voyage around the world ... aboard the sloop *Seniavin* in 1826–1829], parts 1–3. St. Petersburg, 1834–1836 (part 1, 1834; part 2, 1835; part 3, 1836).

9. "O prilivakh v Severnom Velikom okeane i Ledovitom more" [On tides in the Arctic Ocean], *Zapiski Gidrograficheskogo departamenta Morskago ministerstva,* part 2. St. Petersburg, 1844, pp. 353–376.

10. "Otkrytie Russkogo geograficheskogo obshchestva" [Opening of the Russian Geographical Society], speech by F. P. Litke. St. Petersburg, 1845.

11. "Doklad ego imperatorskomu vysochestvu velikomu kniaziu Konstantinu Nikolaevichu ob ekspeditsii v Azovskom more" [Report to His Imperial Highness Grand Duke Constantine Nikolaevich on an expedition to the Sea of Azov], *Zapiski Imperatorskogo russkogo geograficheskogo obshchestva,* book 3, section "Deistviia obshchestva [Activities of the society]." St. Petersburg, 1862, pp. 8–11.

12. Excerpt from letter of honorary member and correspondent of the Academy of Sciences F. P. Litke to the permanent secretary, 12 January 1862. "Tridtsat' pervoe prisuzhdenie uchrezhdennykh P. N. Demidovym nagrad 25 maia 1862 goda" [Thirty-first award of the Demidov Prize, 25 May 1862], St. Petersburg, 1862, pp. 89–90.

13. F. P. Litke's opinion on M. K. Sidorov's memorandum. *Trudy Imperatorskogo vol'no-ekonomicheskogo obshchestva,* vol. 2. St. Petersburg, 1863, pp. 176–177.

14. *Viermalige Reise durch das nordische Eismeer Brigg* Nowaja Semlaja *in den Jahren 1821 bis 1824 ausgeführt vom Kapitain-Lieutenant Friedrich Litke.* Berlin, 1835.

15. *Voyage autour du monde, exécuté par ordre de S. Majesté l'Empereur Nicolas Ier, sur la corvette "le Séniavine" dans les années 1826, 1827, 1828 et 1829 par Frédéric Lütke, capitaine de vaisseau, aide-de-camp de s. m. l'Empereur, commandant de l'Expédition.* Paris. Tome I, II, 1835; Tome III, 1836.

16. *Voyage autour du monde, exécuté par ordre de S. M. l'Empereur Nicolas I sur la corvette "le Séniavine" dans les années 1826, 1827, 1828 et 1829 sous le commandement de Frédéric Lütke,* traduit du russe sous les yeux de l'auteur par le conseiller d'Etat J. Boyé, partie nautique, avec un atlas. St. Petersbourg, 1836.

17. *Observations du pendule invariable, exécutées dans un voyage autour du monde pendant les années 1826, 1827, 1828 et 1829 par M. le Contre-Admiral Lütke* traduit du russe par M. Laustaunau. St. Petersbourg, 1836.

APPENDIX
BASIC LITERATURE ON F. P. LITKE*

1. Alekseev, A. I. "Issledovaniia morei, omyvaiushchikh Rossiiu" [Explorations of the seas washing Russia]. In: V. A. Esakov, A. F. Plakhotnik, A. I. Alekseev, *Russkie okeanicheskie i morskie issledovaniia v XIX—nachale XX v.* [Russian explorations of the oceans and seas in the nineteenth to early twentieth century]. Moscow: Nauka, 1964, pp.116–119.

2. Alekseev, A. I. *Gavriil Andreevich Sarychev.* Moscow: Nauka, 1966, pp.143–145.

3. Antonov, A. E. *F. P. Litke*, edited by A. D. Dobrovol'skii. Moscow: Geografgiz, 1955.

4. Anuchin, D. N. *O liudiakh russkoi nauki i kul'tury* [On people of Russian science and culture]. Moscow: Geografgiz, 1950.

5. Bashmakov, P. I. *Pervye russkie issledovateli Novoi Zemli* [The first Russian explorers of Novaia Zemlia]. Petrograd, 1922.

6. Bezobrazov, V. P. *Graf Fedor Petrovich Litke (Ocherk zhizni grafa F. P. Litke—Avtobiografiia Fedora Petrovicha Litke—Prilozheniia)* [Count Fedor Petrovich Litke (Sketch of the life of Count F. P. Litke—Autobiography of Fedor Petrovich Litke—Appendices], vol. 1. St. Petersburg, 1888 (only the first volume was published).

7. Berg, L. S. *Vsesoiuznoe Geograficheskoe obshchestvo za sto let* [The All-Union Geographical Society after one hundred years]. Moscow, Leningrad: AN SSR, 1946, pp. 22–48.

---

* There is scarcely a single reference book on geography, an encyclopedia, or any work on the northern polar regions which does not mention Litke's name. It is obvious that we cannot possibly list all of them here. In addition, we must note that Litke's work on high tides is translated into French and published in the *Memoires* of the Academy of Sciences. Still, we are certain that we were far from successful in compiling a complete bibliography on this outstanding Russian scholar. It is probable that more works on Litke have been published and continue to be published here and abroad.

8. Berg, L. S. "Puteshestvie admirala F. P. Litke iz Petersburga v Konstantinopol' v 1845 g." [Admiral F. P. Litke's trip from Petersburg to Constantinople in 1845], *Trudy II Vsesoiuznogo Geograficheskogo s"ezda*, vol. 3, 1949, pp. 263–271.

9. Vengerov, S. A. *Istochniki slovaria russkikh pisatelei* [Sources for a dictionary of Russian writers], vols. 1–4. St. Petersburg, Petrograd, 1900–1917, see vol. 3.

10. Veselago, F. F. "Vospominaniia ob uchenykh zaslugakh chlena uchreditelia imperatorskogo Russkogo Geograficheskogo obshchestva grafa Fedor Petrovicha Litke" [Reminiscences of the scholarly services of founding member of the Imperial Russian Geographical Society Count Fedor Petrovich Litke], read at the annual meeting of the IRGO, 26 January 1883. St. Petersburg, 1883.

11. Vize, V. Iu. *Moria Sovetskoi Arktiki* [Seas of the Soviet Arctic]. Moscow, Leningrad: Glavsevmorputi, 1948, pp. 96–98, 143–144.

12. Vrangel', F. F. "Graf Fedor Petrovich Litke, 17 sentiabria 1797–8 avgusta 1882 g." [Count Fedor Petrovich Litke, 17 September 1797 to 8 August 1882], read at a ceremonial meeting of the Imperial Russian Geographical Society, 17 September 1897. St. Petersburg, 1897.

13. *Vydaiushchiesia russkie puteshestvenniki. Portrety s kratkimi biografiami* [Outstanding Russian travelers. Portraits with brief biographies], Series 1–3. Leningrad: Geograficheskoe obshchestvo SSSR, 1948. Series 1 is on Litke.

14. "Vysochaishaia gramota admiralu F. P. Litke na pozhalovanie grafskogo dostoinstva" [Imperial patent to Admiral Litke awarding him the rank of count], *Morskoi sbornik*, vol. 87, 1866, no. 12, pr. r., p. 4.

15. "Vysochaishii reskript admiralu F. P. Litke po sluchaiu piatidesiatiletnego sluzheniia ego v ofitserskikh chinakh" [Imperial rescript to Admiral F. P. Litke on the occasion of his fifty years of service in officer rank], *Morskoi sbornik*, vol. 69, 1863, no. 11, pr. r., p. 5.

16. "Vysochaishii reskript na imia admirala grafa F. P. Litke" [Imperial rescript in the name of Admiral Count F. P. Litke], *Morskoi sbornik*, vol. 106, 1870, no. 2, of., pp. 2–3.

17. Gel'strem, G. G. *Nabliudeniia barometricheskie, simpiezometricheskie i termometricheskie, proizvedennye v puteshestvie vokrug sveta kapitana Litke, vychislennye professorom Gel'singforskogo univeristeta G. G. Gel'stremom* [Barometric, sympiesometric, and thermometric observations made on Cap-

tain Litke's voyage around the world, calculated by G. G. Hällström, professor of Helsingfors University]. St. Petersburg, 1838.

18. Gekhtman, G. N. "Chetyre vydaiushchikhsia rukovoditelia Geograficheskogo obshchestva SSSR; F. P. Litke i drugie (K 100-letiiu Vsesoiuznogo geograf. ob-va.)" [Four outstanding leaders of the Geographical Society of the USSR; F. P. Litke and others (For the centenary of the All-Union Geographical Society)], *Izvestiia Geograficheskogo obshchestva GruzSSR*, 1946, no. 2, pp.11–20.

19. Dobrovol'skii, A. D. *Plavaniia F. P. Litke* [The voyages of F. P. Litke]. Moscow: Geografgiz, 1948.

20. "Dopolnenie k instruktsii, dannoi F. P. Litke, otpravliaiushchemusia v tretii raz dlia opisi Novoi Zemli" [Supplement to the instructions given to F. P. Litke, leaving a third time to survey Novaia Zemlia], *Zapiski Gosudarstvennogo Admiralteiskogo departamenta*, book 6. St. Petersburg, 1824, pp. xvii–xviii.

21. Esakov, V. A. "Morskie krugosvetnye plavaniia, ikh tseli, nauchnye zadachi i resul'taty" [Round-the-world Naval voyages, their goals, scientific questions, and results], In: V. A. Esakov, A. F. Plakhotnik, A. I. Alekseev, *Russkie okeanicheskie i morskie issledovaniia v XIX -nachale XX v.* [Russian explorations of the oceans and seas in the nineteenth to early twentieth century]. Moscow: Nauka, 1946, pp. 72–81.

22. Zubov, N. N. "Fedor Petrovich Litke." In: *Otechestvennye fiziko-geografy i puteshestvenniki* [Physical geographers and travelers of the Fatherland]. Moscow: Uchpedgiz, 1959, pp. 204–213.

23. Zubov, N. N. *Otechestvennye moreplavateli—issledovateli morei i okeanov* [Mariners of the Fatherland—explorers of the seas and oceans]. Moscow: Geografgiz, 1954, pp.198–202, 246–249, 255–257.

24. Ivanov, V. V. "K biografii F. P. Litke" [Toward a biography of F. P. Litke], *Morskoi sbornik*, vol. 55, no. 9, 1861, smes', pp. 59–62.

25. Ivashintsov, N. A. "Russkie krugosvetnye puteshestviia" [Russian round-the-world voyages], *Zapiski Gidrograficheskogo departamenta*, vol. 7. St. Petersburg, 1849, pp. 1–116; vol. 8, 1850, pp. 1–190.

26. Iversen, Iu. B. *Medali v chest' russkikh gosudarstvennykh deiatelei i chastnykh lits* [Medals in honor of Russian statesmen and private persons], vols. 1–3. St. Petersburg, 1880–1896. See vol. 1, A through L, St. Petersburg, 1880.

27. "Instruktsiia kapitan-leitenantu Litke, po povodu naznacheniia pod ego vedenie otpravliaemykh shturmanov Ivanova na Pechoru i drugogo dlia promera Belogo moria" [Instructions to Captain Lieutenant Litke on the assignment to his leadership of navigator Ivanov, leaving for the Pechora, and another navigator leaving to survey the White Sea], *Zapisksi Gosudarstvennogo Admiralteiskogo departamenta*, vol. 7. St. Petersburg, 1824, pp. xxi–xxiv.

28. "Instruktsiia leitenantu Litke I, naznachennomu dlia obozreniia Novoi Zemli sostavlennaia vitse-admiralom Sarychevym" [Instructions to Lieutenant Litke I, assigned to survey Novaia Zemlia, compiled by Vice Admiral Sarychev], *Zapiski Gosudarstvennogo Admiralteiskogo departamenta*, vol. 5. St. Petersburg, 1823, pp. xliii–xlix.

29. "Instruktsiia, sostavlennaia Shcheglovym, naturalistam, otpravliaiushchimsia na transportakh "Mollere" i "Seniavine," dlia opisaniia severo-zapadnykh beregov Ameriki i severo-vostochnykh Azii, pod komandoiu kapitan-leit. Staniukovicha i Litke" [Instructions compiled by Shcheglov for the naturalists leaving aboard the transports *Moller* and *Seniavin* for a survey of the northwest shores of America and the northeast shores of Asia, under the command of captain lieutenants Staniukovich and Litke], *Zapiski Gosudarstvennogo Admiralteiskogo departamenta*, vol. 13. St. Petersburg, 1827, pp. xxxv–xl.

30. "Instruktsiia flota kapitan-leitenantu Litke, komanduiushchemu shliupom "Seniavin," otpravlennomu dlia opisi beregov severo-vostochnoi Azii. Sostavlena kontr-admiralom Kruzenshternom" [Instructions to Fleet Captain Lieutenant Litke, commanding the sloop *Seniavin*, dispatched to survey the shores of Northeast Asia. Compiled by Rear Admiral Kruzenshtern], *Zapiski Gosudarstvennogo Admiralteiskogo departamenta,* vol. 11. St. Petersburg, 1826, pp. xlix–liv.

31. Komissarov, B. N. "Dnevnik puteshestvii F. P. Litke na shliupe "Kamchatka" v 1817–1819 gg." [Diary of F. P. Litke's voyage aboard the sloop *Kamchatka* in 1817–1819], *Izvestiia Vsesoiuznogo Geograficheskogo obshchestva*, 1964, vol. 96, vyp. 5, pp. 414–419.

32. Kudriavtsev-Skaif, S. "Fedor Petrovich Litke." In: *Russkie moreplavateli* [Russian mariners]. Moscow: Voenizdat, 1953, pp. 250–266.

33. Lents, E. Kh. *Nabliudeniia nad nakloneniem i stepen'iu sily magnitnoi strelki proizvedennye v puteshestvie vokrug sveta na shliupe "Seniavin" v 1826, 1827, 1828 i 1829 godakh flota kapitanom F. Litke, obrabotannye i vychislennye E. Lentsom* [Observations on the inclination and degree of force of the magnetic needle made during a voyage around the world aboard the

sloop *Seniavin* in 1826–1829 by Fleet Captain F. Litke, processed and computed by E. Lents]. Translated from German by Fleet Lieutenant B. Glazenap. St. Petersburg, 1836.

34. Litke, N. F. *Rol' admirala F. P. Litke v razvitii geograficheskoi nauki* [The role of F. P. Litke in the development of geographical science]. Synopsis of dissertation. Leningrad, 1952.

35. Marich, M. D. *Zhizn' i plavaniia flota kapitan-lieutenanta Fedora Litke* [Life and voyages of Fleet Captain Lieutenant Fedor Litke]. Moscow, Leningrad: Glavsevmorputi, 1949.

36. Medunin, A. E. *Razvitie gravimetrii v Rossii* [Development of gravimetry in Russia]. Moscow: Nauka, 1967.

37. "Mnenie deist. st. sovetnika Shuberta ob astronomicheskikh i meteorologicheskikh nabliudeniiakh F. P. Litke v ekspeditsii 1823 g. k Novoi Zemle" [Opinion of Active State Councilor Shubert on the astronomical and meteorological observations of F. P. Litke on the expedition of 1823 to Novaia Zemlia], *Zapiski Gosudarstvennogo Admiralteiskogo departamenta,* vol. 7. St. Petersburg, 1824, pp. ii–v and ix–xi.

38. "Mnenie deist. st. sovetnika Shuberta ob opredelenii dolgoty mest po lunnym rasstoianiiam (po povodu rassmotreniia opredeleniia dolgoty g. Arkhangel'ska F. P. Litke)" [Opinion of Active State Councilor Shubert of the determination of the longitude of places by lunar distances (apropos of an examination of a determination of the longitude of the town of Arkhangel'sk by F. P. Litke], *Zapiski Gosudarstvennogo Admiralteiskogo departamenta,* vol. 6. St. Petersburg, 1824, pp. xi–xvii.

39. Nevskii, V. V. *Russkie puteshestvenniki-issledovateli* [Russian traveler-explorers]. Leningrad: Lenfotokhudozhnik, 1950.

40. Nozikov, N. N. *Russkie krugosvetnye moreplavateli* [Russian circumnavigators]. Moscow: Voenizdat, 1947.

41. Nozikov, N. N. *Krugosvetnoe puteshestvie Litke na voennom shliupe "Seniavin" v 1826–1829 gg.* [Round-the-world voyage of Litke aboard the sloop *Seniavin* in 1826–1829]. Moscow: Mosk. tov-vo pisatelei, 1938.

42. Orlov, B. P. *Fedor Petrovich Litke, zamechatel'nyi russkii puteshestvennik i uchenyi. (K 150-letiiu so dnia rozhdeniia)* [Fedor Petrovich Litke, remarkable Russian traveler and scholar. (For the 150th anniversary of his birth)]. Moscow: Pravda, 1948 (Vsesoiuznoe obshchestva po rasprostraneniiu politicheskikh i nauchnykh znanii).

43. Pasetskii, V. "Vydaiushchiisia issledovatel' Severa" [Outstanding explorer of the North], *Morskoi flot*, 1962, no. 9, pp. 39–40.

44. "Plavaniie voennykh sudov iz Arkhangel'ska v Kronshtadt v 1844 g." [Voyage of military vessels from Arkhangel'sk to Kronstadt in 1844], *Zapiski Gidrograficheskogo departamenta*, part 3. St. Petersburg, 1845, pp. 377–387.

45. *Portretnaia galereia russkikh deiatelei* [Portrait gallery of Russian public figures], vols. 1–2. St. Petersburg, 1865–1868. See vol. 1.

46. Postel's, A. F., and F. Ruprekht. *Izobrazheniia i opisaniia morskikh rastenii, sobrannykh v Severnom Tikhom okeane u beregov rossiiskikh vladenii v Azii i Amerike v puteshestvie vokrug sveta, sovershennoe po poveleniiu gosudaria imperatora Nikolaia I na voennom shliupe "Seniavin" v 1826, 1827, 1828 i 1829 godakh pod komadoiu flota kapitana Fedora Litke, izdannye Aleksandrom Postel'som i Frantsem Ruprekhtom* [Drawings and descriptions of marine flora collected in the North Pacific near the shores of the Russian possessions in Asia and America during a voyage around the world ... aboard the sloop *Seniavin* in 1826–1829 under the command of Fleet Captain Fedor Litke, by Aleksandr Postels and Frantz Ruprekht]. St. Petersburg, 1840.

47. "Prilivomery A. Liudzhera" [Tidal measurements of A. Liudzher], *Zapiski Gidrograficheskogo departamenta*, part 2, St. Petersburg, 1844, pp. 337–352.

48. Rovipskii, D. A. *Podrobnyi slovar' russkikh gravirovannykh portretov* [Detailed dictionary of Russian engraved portraits]. St. Petersburg, 1889. See vol. 1, A–O, 1202 stb.

49. Rusakov, V. *Znamenitye issledovateli russkoi zemli. Biograficheskie ocherki i rasskazy* [Famous explorers of Russia. Biographical sketches and stories]. Petrograd, Moscow, 1916.

50. *Russkie geografy i puteshestvenniki* [Russian geographers and explorers], vyp. 1. Moscow, Leningrad: Iskusstvo, 1948.

51. *Russkii biograficheskii slovar'* [Russian biographical dictionary], vol. 10, Labzina-Liashchenko. St. Petersburg, 1914.

52. Semenov-Tian-Shanskii, P. P. *Istoriia poluvekovoi deiatel'nosti Imp. Russkogo Geograficheskogo obshchestva, 1845–1895 gg.* [History of a half century of activities of the Imperial Russian Geographical Society, 1845–1895], parts 1–3. St. Petersburg, 1896.

53. Solntsev, N. A. "Fedor Petrovich Litke (1797–1882). Geograf i moreplavatel'. Biogr. ocherk" [Fedor Petrovich Litke (1797–1882). Geographer and mariner. Biographical sketch], *Nasha strana*, 1940, no. 12, pp.34–38.

54. Struve, O. V. "Ob uchenykh zaslugakh grafa F. P. Litke" [On the scholarly services of Count F. P. Litke]. Speech of Academician O. V. Struve, read at a ceremonial meeting of the Academy of Sciences, 29 December 1882. St. Petersburg, 1883.

55. "Trista puteshestvennikov i issledovatelei" [Three hundred travelers and explorers]. In *Biograficheskii slovar'* [Biographical dictionary]. Moscow: Mysl', 1966, pp.136–137.

56. Iazykov, D. D. *Obzor zhizni i trudov pokoinykh russkikh pisatelei* [Review of the life and works of deceased Russian writers], vyp.1–13. St. Petersburg, Petrograd, 1885–1916. See vyp.2.

APPENDIX
LIST OF ABBREVIATIONS

AVGO	Archive of the All-Union Geographical Society
GIAE	State Historical Archive of the Estonian SSR
TsGAVMF	Central State Archive of the Navy
TsGADA	Central State Archive of Ancient Documents
AAN	Archive of the Academy of Sciences SSSR
TsGAOR	Central State Archive of the October Revolution
IVGO	the periodical *Izvestiia Vsesoiuznogo Geograficheskogo obshchestva*

APPENDIX
RUSSIAN WEIGHTS AND MEASURES

arshin	28 inches or 71.1 cm
sazhen	2.3 yards or 2.1 m
verst	0.66 miles or 1.07 km
pud	36.11 pounds or 16.38 kg

INDEX